Advances in Japanese Business and Economics

Volume 33

Advances in Japanese Business and Economics (AJBE) showcases the work of Japanese and non-Japanese scholars researching the Japanese economy and Japanese businesses. Published in English, the series highlights for a global readership the unique perspectives of Japan's most distinguished and emerging scholars of business and economics. It covers research of either theoretical or empirical nature, in both authored and edited volumes, regardless of the sub-discipline or geographical coverage, including, but not limited to, such topics as macroeconomics, microeconomics, industrial relations, innovation, regional development, entrepreneurship, international trade, globalization, financial markets, technology management, and business strategy. At the same time, as a series of volumes written by Japanese and non-Japanese scholars studying Japan, it includes research on the issues of the Japanese economy, industry, management practice, and policy, such as the economic policies and business innovations before and after the Japanese "bubble" burst in the 1990s.

AJBE endeavors to overcome a historical deficit in the dissemination of Japanese economic theory, research methodology, and analysis. The volumes in the series contribute not only to a deeper understanding of Japanese business and economics but to revealing underlying universal principles.

Overseen by a panel of renowned scholars led by Editor-in-Chief Professor Ryuzo Sato, AJBE employs a single-blind review process in which the Editor-in-Chief, together with the Managing Editors and specialized scholars designated by the Editor-in-Chief or Managing Editors, rigorously reviews each proposal and manuscript to ensure that every submission is a valuable contribution to the global scholarly readership.

All books and chapters in AJBE are indexed in Scopus.

Toshiaki Hiromitsu

Resolving Intergenerational Conflicts

An Approach from Philosophy, Economics, and Experiments

Springer

Toshiaki Hiromitsu
Policy Research Institute, Ministry
of Finance
Government of Japan
Tokyo, Japan

ISSN 2197-8859 ISSN 2197-8867 (electronic)
Advances in Japanese Business and Economics
ISBN 978-981-97-0613-6 ISBN 978-981-97-0614-3 (eBook)
https://doi.org/10.1007/978-981-97-0614-3

Translation from the Japanese language edition: "Tetsugaku to keizaigaku kara toku sedaikan mondai - keizai jikken ni motozuku kosatsu" by Toshiaki Hiromitsu, © Toshiaki Hiromitsu 2022. Published by Nihon Hyoronsha. All Rights Reserved.

This Springer imprint is published by the registered company Springer Nature Singapore Pte Ltd.
The registered company address is: 152 Beach Road, #21-01/04 Gateway East, Singapore 189721, Singapore

Paper in this product is recyclable.

Preface

This book is a cohesive work that examines the moral relationships that should exist between different generations, including those yet to be born. Intergenerational relations seem to be one-sided and one-time, flowing from the past to the future. In addition, the unborn have neither form nor shape in the present, and their existence depends on the actions of people in the present. This book addresses a highly general and fundamental consideration of the relationship; we should have with this particular entity, the future generation, and moves the discussion toward proposals for workable institutions and policies. It is not possible to avoid the problem of reconciling the interests of different generations, as seen in the issues of climate change and the accumulation of public debt. This book will show the moral relationship that should exist between the different generations, and present methodologies to make that relationship a reality.

To solve this problem, three features of the approach taken in this book are considered. The first is that this book approaches the problem by combining the methods and findings of two disciplines: philosophy and economics. Philosophy is interested in proposing a new interpretation of the moral obligations and values we owe while referring to a certain theoretical framework. Economics, however, takes certain obligations and values as given and reveals the consequences of the interactions of people acting on them. This book, through philosophical thinking, presents an ideal conception of intergenerational ethics, while also constructing an economics model in order to reveal its economic and social consequences. The second characteristic of the approach is the introduction of an economic experiment, to maintain the generality of the argument and extend the scope of the discussion beyond theoretical possibilities, to what could occur in reality. An environment that simulates intergenerational relationships is created in a laboratory, and the behavior of the subjects is observed. These observations indicate what might actually happen between generations, and the suggestions derived can then be used in institutional and policy proposals. The third characteristic of the approach is that each generation's preferences are not necessarily fixed. In economics, the preference is usually considered to be stable. For example, if the order of preference between apples and oranges varies without any context, it is impossible to have a serious discussion. This book will consider situations in which preferences are endogenously determined under a certain context (logic) and show that the logic is in fact likely, through the results of economic experiments. The purpose of this book is to help scholars and policymakers from a wide range of disciplines deepen their understanding of the distinctive set of intergenerational challenges and to provide clues for addressing these issues. The passage of the Social Security and Tax Reform Act in the summer of 2012, which called for a shift away from deferring burdens on children, has been accompanied by a renewed interest in intergenerational issues in Japan. Furthermore, the January 2021 inauguration of the Biden administration in the USA has been accompanied by an increased global focus on decarbonization, and Japan is no exception. In this context, the whole picture of intergenerational issues needs to be presented in an easy-to-understand manner, based on academic methods and without compromising standards, to researchers, policymakers, the general public, and students from various disciplines, including philosophy and economics. Even if the current enthusiasm is transitory, both climate change and fiscal sustainability are inevitable problems that must eventually be faced. I believe that basic research, such as that presented in this book, will have lasting value, and will constantly be referred to in the future.

I am engaged in academic research, while also holding a position in the Ministry of Finance, Government of Japan. I am grateful to all my professors who have given me the opportunity to conduct a full-fledged study. In particular, I would like to thank Prof. Reiko Gotoh (Hitotsubashi University), Prof. Shinji Yamashige (Hitotsubashi University), Prof. Tatsuyoshi Saijo (Institute for Global Environmental Studies), and Prof. Satoshi Kodama (Kyoto University) for their guidance, without which this book could not have taken the coherent form that it has. To repay the academic debt owed to them, I have no choice but to continue to produce high-quality research.

In addition to these professors, many others contributed to the writing of this book. The following is an incomplete list (titles omitted, in alphabetical order). Riaru Arai (Aichi University), Tyler Cowen (George Mason University), Stephen Gardiner (University of Washington), Keishiro Hara (Osaka University), Midori Hirokawa (Hosei University), Iwao Hirose (McGill University), Tatsuya Kameda (University of Tokyo), Yasuko Kamikawa (Toyama University), Kunio Kamiyama (Josai University), Akihiro Kawase (Toyo University), Yoko Kitakaji (Hiroshima University), Keiichiro Kobayashi (Keio University), Mitsuteru Nakayama (Ministry of Finance), Seki Obata (Keio University), Kazumasa Oguro (Hosei University), Takashi Oshio (Hitotsubashi University), Henry S. Richardson (Georgetown University), Samuel Scheffler (New York University), Tatsuhiro Shichijo (Osaka Prefecture University), Kotaro Suzumura (Hitotsubashi University, Waseda University, deceased), Eiji Tajika (Hitotsubashi University), Kan Takeuchi (Hitotsubashi University), Kimiko Terai (Keio University), Makoto Usami (Kyoto University), Tomoyuki Watanabe (Hitotsubashi University), Naoki Yoshihara (University of Massachusetts Amherst), Akira Yokoyama (Chuo University), I thank them for their suggestions. I am responsible for all possible errors in this book.

Among those who helped me, it is my privilege to receive the late Dr. Koutaro Suzumura's opinion on the discussion that forms Chap. 4 of this book, during a workshop at Hitotsubashi University on June 23, 2017. On July 27 of the same year,

I was invited to a celebration to commemorate Dr. Suzumura's national award. The title of his commemorative lecture was "Toward the normative economics of intergenerational equity." I remember having the courage to give him my opinion. To me, Dr. Suzumura's point that the values of future generations are agnostic seemed to be inconsistent with his other argument that the present generation owes the responsibility of choosing historical pathways to future generations. During the standing buffet that followed, Dr. Suzumura shared his memories of Oxford (where he stayed at the same time as me), and at the end of the meeting, he said, "Let's discuss the issue again." However, the opportunity for discussion never arose. This book is a continuation of the discussion with him, in my own way.

I appreciate Prof. Samuel Scheffler for discussing the outline of this book and providing valuable comments, and for the opportunity to discuss his books *Death and Afterlife* and *Why Worry About Future Generations?* Prof. Scheffler's argument that people are concerned about the continuation of humanity after their personal death holds a crucial place in this book. His idea is the beginning of the introduction of direct intergenerational reciprocity in this book. The concern for the life after death is broader than our moral obligations and interests. We humans are born surrounded by people from the beginning, we learn many things from them, and when we die, we leave things to those who come after us. His point sheds light on an important aspect of human nature that has been missed by the narrow, individualistic view of mankind.

The Japanese edition of this book has the good fortune to win the Nikkei Book and Culture Award (Economics) in November 2023. I would like to thank the members of the Screening Committee, including Chairman Hiroshi Yoshikawa, Professor Emeritus of the University of Tokyo, NIKKEI, and the Japan Center for Economic Research.

Finally, on a personal note, I would like to report the completion of this book to my father, Nobuyoshi, and my mother, Kyoko, and express my gratitude to them. Without their love, I would not have been able to work in government, much less complete this book. This book is dedicated to my father and mother.

Tokyo, Japan Toshiaki Hiromitsu

Contents

List of Figures

List of Tables

Chapter 1
Introduction

Abstract Conflicts of interests and their coordination among multiple generations are called intergenerational issues. These are new problems that have emerged with the increase in human power. Four challenges in the context of intergenerational issues are raised: (i) the temporal location of future people, (ii) ignorance about future generations, (iii) contingency of future people, and (iv) difficulties in realizing intergenerational ethics. Of these, this book focuses primarily on the fourth issue, that is, the difficulties in realizing intergenerational ethics. Three characteristics of the approach of this book are raised: (i) the joint work of two disciplines, philosophy and economics, (ii) use of economic experiments, and (iii) variable preferences of generations. An overview of each chapter and the overall flow of this book are presented.

God, when He gave the world in common to all mankind, commanded man also to labour, and the penury of his condition required it of him. God and his reason commanded him to subdue the earth—i.e., improve it for the benefit of life and therein lay out something upon it that was his own, his labor. He that, in obedience to this command of God, subdued, tilled, and sowed any part of it, thereby annexed to it something that was his property, which another had no title to, nor could without injury take from him.

> 32. Nor was this appropriation of any parcel of land, by improving it, any prejudice to any other man, *since there was still enough and as good left*, and more than the yet unprovided could use. So that, in effect, there was never the less left for others because of his enclosure for himself. For he that leaves as much as another can make use of does as good as take nothing at all. Nobody could think himself injured by the drinking of another man, though he took a good draught, who had a whole river of the same water left him to quench his thirst. And the case of land and water, where there is enough of both, is perfectly the same. (Locke, 1689, p. 118; *italic* by quoter)

T. Hiromitsu, *Resolving Intergenerational Conflicts*, Advances in Japanese Business and Economics 33, https://doi.org/10.1007/978-981-97-0614-3_1

1.1 Intergenerational Issues

Global issues, such as climate change, that span generations, are rapidly becoming increasingly important. The Intergovernmental Panel on Climate Change (IPCC) notes that human impact has undoubtedly contributed to global warming, and that unless emissions of carbon dioxide and other greenhouse gases are significantly reduced over the next several decades, global temperatures will increase by 1.5 °C to over 2 °C in the twenty-first century (Intergovernmental Panel on Climate Change [IPCC], 2021).[1] This is expected to have widespread and irreversible impacts, which include extreme weather events, rising sea levels, adverse effects on ecosystems, and impacts on crop yields. A study on biodiversity commissioned by the UK Treasury to Professor Partha Dasgupta at the University of Cambridge and his colleagues (Independent Review on the Economics of Biodiversity, 2021a, 2021b) finds that[2]: in the aggregate, humanity is not using nature in a sustainable manner; humanity's demand for nature far exceeds the latter's ability to provide goods and services; and current ways of interacting with nature are both unsustainable and dangerous to people's livelihoods now, as well as in the future.[3]

Turning from the natural environment to the human world, unprecedented demographic changes have sharpened the problem of intergenerational resource allocation. Particularly in Japan and Europe, public debt has ballooned, as social security-related costs have increased due to rapid population aging. As a result, proper management of the debt and the continuing added expense of the aging of societies have become necessary over the long term in order to avoid the divergence of the debt (fiscal collapse). According to the "Long-term projection for Japan's public finances (revised version)" (Fiscal System Subcommittee Drafting and Review Committee, Fiscal System Council, 2018), the permanent improvement in the primary fiscal balance needed to stabilize the debt-to-gross domestic product (GDP) ratio after FY2060 would be 8.0–9.2% of GDP (expenditure cut or revenue increase).[4] This estimate is conditional on the improvement all at once in 2020. If the improvement is postponed, the necessary improvement will be larger.

In these important public issues, not just the present generation but multiple, including future generations yet to be born, have come to appear as stakeholders.

---

[1] IPCC (2021, pp. 4–14). The Intergovernmental Panel on Climate Change is an intergovernmental organization of international experts that collects and organizes scientific research on climate change.

[2] This study is called the Dasgupta Review after Professor Dasgupta of the University of Cambridge, who led the study. It is based on the UK government's desire to raise international public opinion on biodiversity issues as the chair of the G7 in 2021.

[3] Independent Review on the Economics of Biodiversity (2021a, p. 1).

[4] The necessary balance improvement, when mechanically converted to the consumption tax rate (without the reduced tax rate), would result in a tax increase of slightly less than 20%. This estimate assumes high economic growth (economic revitalization case), and if growth is not as strong as expected, even greater improvement will be required. In Chap. 4, an experimental study based on the 2015 version of these estimates is discussed, however there are no major differences between the 2015 and 2018 versions.

In this book, we term the problems related to the conflicts of interest and their coordination among multiple generations "intergenerational issues."

> I suppose that the received opinion, that the public debts of one generation devolve on the next, has been suggested by our seeing habitually in private life that he who succeeds to lands is required to pay the debts of his ancestor or testator: without considering that this requisition is municipal only, not moral; flowing from the will of the society, which has found it convenient to appropriate lands, become vacant by the death of their occupant, on the condition of a payment of his debts: but that between society and society, or generation and generation, there is no municipal obligation, no umpire but the law of nature. We seem not to have perceived that, by the law of nature, one generation is to another as one independent nation to another. (Jefferson, 1789, p. 3)

Thomas Jefferson, one of the founding fathers of the United States, viewed different generations as different nations. This view of each generation as distinct is not unique to Jefferson, but is widespread on both sides of the argument. For example, Eric Posner of the University of Chicago, known for his market-based arguments, states that government agencies should ignore distant future generations (Posner, 2007). However, Rawls's (1971a) *Theory of Justice*, the foremost liberal work, adopts the interpretation that people know they are living in the same era, but do not know which era they will be born in as the setting of original position, when discussing intergenerational savings (the present time of entry interpretation). He does not adopt the assumption of a general assembly that includes, at one moment, everyone who will live at some time, and generations remain isolated. Rawls states that, according to the general assembly, "the conception would cease to be a natural guide to intuition and would lack a clear sense" (p. 120). According to Reiko Gotoh, well known for her work on Rawls and Amartya Sen, the idea behind the present time of entry interpretation is to understand generations as one autonomous political entity (Gotoh, 2006, pp. 339–341). Each generation is under the system of divided political representation. Generational differences translate into national differences, and it is not surprising that Posner is opposed to governments that are not directly elected to adopt policies for future generations on their own.

However, that the dramatic increase in human power is at the root of the problematic relationship with future generations cannot be overlooked. Indeed, for a long time, when we were forced to live lives full of dangers, intergenerational issues for humans were, at best, about what we would bequeath to our children. Human power was limited and had no intergenerational impact. Generations could live untroubled by each other, as if they were different species living on different planets. However, human power has now increased to the point where it is capable of exhausting the earth's resources. We have learned to invest, to leave our fortunes to the distant future, and to exhaust the legacy of previous generations in a single generation. John Locke, in the passage quoted at the beginning of this chapter, while arguing that all those taken out from the nature becomes his property, did not forget to make the reservation that there must be "still enough and as good left" for those who come later (Locke, 1689). Now that the days when nature's bounty was conceived as inexhaustible are past, and this reservation (Locke's proviso) has become a real constraint, it is necessary to seriously consider the intergenerational issues involved.

> The last (quoter's note, the enjoyment of such possessions as we have acquired by our industry and good fortune) only are both expos'd to the violence of others, and may be transferr'd without suffering any loss or alteration; while at the same time, there is not a sufficient quantity of them to supply every one's desires and necessities. As the improvement, therefore, of these goods is the chief advantage of society, so the instability of their possession, along with their scarcity, is the chief impediment. (omitted) After this convention, concerning abstinence from the possessions of others, is enter'd into, and everyone has acquir'd a stability in his possessions, there immediately arise the ideas of justice and injustice; as also those of property, right, and obligation. (Hume, 1739–40, pp. 254–255)

David Hume argues that justice is an artificial virtue. He means, first and foremost, that justice is the establishment of ownership. Because of the nature of possessions that are "both expos'd to the violence of others, and may be transferr'd without suffering any loss or alteration," a convention that it is in the interest of all concerned to fix the possession is formed; ownership is established from this convention. In the quoted passage, Hume does not discuss intergenerational issues. However, reading Hume, and taking account of the dramatic increase in human power, it is now recognized that possessions are "expos'd to the violence of others" between distant generations, while resource "is not a sufficient quantity of them to supply every one's desires and necessities" including those of all generations. Understandably, there is now a growing need to forge a convention on new ethics, what Hume calls justice, among generations. Intergenerational ethics is the branch of ethics that examines the moral relationships that should exist between different generations, including the past and future generations that are not in existence. Intergenerational ethics is a new field of ethics that emerges through the progress of the history of humanity.

1.2 Positioning in Research History

In the introduction of their co-edited book of intergenerational equity and sustainability, John Roemer and Koutaro Suzumura, who are known for their work on distributive justice, review the history of research in the intergenerational issues (Roemer & Suzumura, 2007). They begin their review with the economists active in Cambridge, England, in the 19th and early twentieth centuries, including Sidgwick (1907, p. 414), Pigou (1920, pp. 24–25), and Ramsey (1928, p. 543), who denied discounting future utility streams from the perspective of intergenerational equity. Their studies emphasize that the utilities of present and future generations should be treated equally, pointing out that there is no reason to treat the utility of future generations less favorably. Roemer and Suzumura also point out that Koopmans' (1960) study shows that intergenerational equity, in the sense of treating each generation's utility equally, is no longer logically feasible only by imposing the most aggregable axioms (conditions) of rationality, continuity, and stationarity to evaluate resource allocation over an infinite future. Rather, Koopman means that if we want to maintain an evaluation rule for allocation that satisfies the three axioms, we have no choice but to discount future utility. Roemer and Suzumura also refer to a study by Diamond (1965), in which he proved the impossibility theorem that the three axioms of Pareto efficiency, intergenerational equity (equal treatment of the utilities of present and future generations), and continuity in social valuation between utility streams, cannot be satisfied simultaneously. Since Diamond's proof, there has been a flurry of research examining escape routes from this impossibility theorem. A lineage of research along this line has resulted in contributions leading to a deeper understanding of the implications of seemingly innocuous axioms.[5]

However, Roemer and Suzumura also emphasize that research along the lines of Diamond's genealogy is limited in that it only addresses the order of social valuations for sets of infinite utility streams, and neither assumes pathways for different generations to interact, nor places explicit resource constraints. They point out that while Koopman's and Diamond's frameworks provide a convenient beginning for considering intergenerational issues, they miss other important intergenerational issues, and therefore, other kinds of research in this context are necessary.[6] As one of many such key issues, Roemer and Suzumura raise the question of how the path of human progress to the present is determined by the choices of past generations, and moreover, how the path of future generations depends on the choices of the present one. They note that the non-identity problem of Oxford philosopher Parfit (1984), according to which the choices of the present generation change the attributes of future generations themselves, further complicates the issue.[7]

As discussed in Sect. 1.1, the basic understanding of this book is that intergenerational issues became problematic because of the strong influence that grew between generations according to increase of human power. Therefore, the discussion in this book naturally follows the genealogy of the studies focusing on intergenerational interrelationships pointed out in the latter part of Roemer and Suzumura's introduction.[8] In this book, the discussion moves in the direction of closer ties between different generations by clarifying the basis, if any, on which a moral relationship between generations exists, i.e., by examining the foundations of intergenerational ethics. In particular, this book not only proposes to consider intergenerational ethics as unilateral duties of the present generation to future generations, but also to find reciprocal relationships between different generations and view intergenerational relations as a joint activity. Reciprocity here is the relationship established between people who mutually recognize each other as human beings with similar capabilities and interests. This book emphasizes, based on Rawls' (1971b) argument, that recognizing future generations as human beings is the premise for discussion.[9]

---

[5] For example, Geir Asheim and his colleagues (Asheim et al., 2007), abandoning continuity, argue that egalitarianism based on classical utilitarianism or the leximin principle survives as evaluation function that satisfies intergenerational equity.

[6] Roemer and Suzumura (2007, p. xv).

[7] Roemer and Suzumura (2007, pp. xv–xvii).

[8] The issues involved in the evaluation of future utility streams in the first part are dealt with in Chap. 5 in the discussion of time discounting. Chapter 5 finally arrives at the discounting associated with the loss of controllability of future events, which focuses on the intergenerational relationship by way of the responsibility of the preceding generation to the succeeding one.

[9] Chapters 2 (2.5) and 6 (6.3).

As the framework for such discussion, this study assumes the existence of a social planner in a society and considers the choices and actions taken by the planner. The planner controls the state of society (s_t) at each point in time, from the present ($t = 0$). The evaluation function is as follows.

$$W_0 = W(s_0, s_1, s_2, \ldots, s_t, s_{t+1}, \ldots) \tag{1.1}$$

Here, the social planner shall select a stream of social states that maximizes W_0. The evaluation by the planner is considered because we are interested in the way of thinking that chooses the best of all possible social states (the nature of the evaluation function W). Intergenerational ethics exactly corresponds to this way of thinking.

If we look for an entity similar to a social planner in the real world, this would be a policy official or government. However, this does not mean that the considerations in this book are unrelated to individuals considering intergenerational issues. In democratic societies, sovereignty resides with the people. When individuals look back on themselves as citizens, they can think of themselves as social planners and evaluate the streams of social states from the present to the future. Although there is no world government equivalent to national governments for global issues such as climate change, it is still possible for individuals, as members of the world's citizenry, to think of themselves as global social planners. Hirohide Takigawa, a philosopher of law at the University of Tokyo, views the state as a means to fulfill the natural duties that individuals assume, such as, not harming others, and helping those in crisis (Takigawa, 2017). The state possesses certain human and physical resources and has the capacity to adequately fulfill those duties that cannot be fulfilled by individuals.[10] In this view, individuals directly bear the responsibility of considering how they should behave if they are social planners.

1.3 Challenges in Intergenerational Issues and the Approach of This Book

When considering intergenerational issues specifically, several challenges require special examination. The emergence of future generations may have challenges that cannot be simply considered in the same way as the emergence of new spatially separated neighbors of the same generation. Philosopher Gregory Kavka has pointed out that these challenges require special attention because of (1) the temporal location of future people, (2) our ignorance of future people, and (3) the contingency of future people (Kavka, 1996).[11] In addition to these, I believe it is necessary to address (4) the problems associated with the implementation of intergenerational ethics, i.e., the difficulties in making intergenerational ethics a reality.

[10] Takigawa (2017, p. 303).

[11] Kavka (1996, p. 187).

In addressing these challenges, it is important to understand the points unique to intergenerational issues, as distinguished from issues that also arise in contemporaneous (synchronic) situations. Unlike contemporaneous situations, an intergenerational relationship is characterized by sequentiality, in which the preceding generation appears first, followed by the succeeding one. While sequentiality can also exist in contemporaneous situations, intergenerational sequentiality is characterized as being unidirectional and one-time only, from the preceding to the following generation, since it involves an extremely long period of time. This unidirectionality not only means that the subsequent generation has no choice but to unilaterally receive the actions of the preceding generation, but also implies that the preceding generation (by passing away) cannot know how the subsequent generation will actually act. Thus, generations are under the characteristic relationship of sequentiality, which presents unique challenges between generations.

Note that a one-way, one-time sequential relationship need not necessarily be limited to literal generational relationships. For example, national and municipal governments and corporate executives, which are successively replaced (assuming that there is no return to government or management), are also characterized by sequential relationship. In the case of individuals, when today's self and tomorrow's self are considered as different personalities, an analogous relationship to that between generations can be established even between an individual's personalities at different points in time. The application of findings from the intergenerational issues to contemporaneous issues will be taken up in Chap. 3 (Sect. 3.5.4) and Chap. 5. Chapter 3 (Sect. 3.4) also attempts to gain insight into the intergenerational issues by replicating the sequential relationship in the laboratory.

Below, four challenges in intergenerational issues are examined, with an attention to the points unique to intergenerational relationship.

1.3.1 The Temporal Location of Future People

The first challenge is whether and how temporal location affects the evaluation of what will happen to future generations. Although future generations are yet unborn, the present generation can take the necessary actions now to influence the former's levels of satisfaction or dissatisfaction. As pointed out by Sidgwick and others, it does not seem appropriate to treat the interests of future generations lightly based solely on the difference in their positions on the time axis. However, Koopman and Diamond pointed out that if the present and future generations' interests were weighted impartially, even the least objectionable axiom would not be satisfied at this time. Kenneth Arrow, a notable Harvard economist, pointed out that treating generations equally could require the present generation to make enormous sacrifices for future ones. Since the present generation is only one generation while future generations will continue indefinitely, any act that seeks the well-being of the present generation at the expense of saving for the future ones may be considered immoral. However, since the present generation then becomes like an instrument to promote the happiness of future generations, Arrow (1999, p. 16) calls this dilemma a conflict of basic principles of morality.

In the real world, there is a practice of discounting events in the distant future. The rationale behind this practice must be questioned. In recent years, the reasons for discounting have been elucidated from a variety of fields, including philosophy, economics, and psychology. Parfit, mentioned earlier, has identified several candidates in his reasoning for discounting, and is working to elucidate the nature of each (Parfit, 1984, pp. 480–486). Through experiments, behavioral economists and psychologists have accumulated reports that humans and animals discount, not by exponential discounting as assumed by economics, but by hyperbolic discounting[12], which discounts heavily in the near future and slowly in the far future. Additionally, there is an active debate on how to ground the hyperbolic discounting (Myerson & Green, 1995; Frederick et al., 2002).

Discounting events separated in time is called time discounting, and the focus of interest in it is in terms of whether or not it is possible to find discounts inherent in the temporal separation as distinguished from spatial separation. This book ultimately presents the idea of time discounting on the rationale of the loss of controllability over events, which reduces the responsibility for future events. The rationale is derived from the nature of time, that is the sequential nature of events.[13]

1.3.2 Ignorance About Future Generations

The second challenge is our ignorance of future generations. We are agnostic about what future generations will want, and we have no way of figuring out how to advance their interests. Kotaro Suzumura touches on this point in his warning against the easy application of the Golden Rule to intergenerational issues (Suzumura, 2018). "So, whatever you wish that others would do to you, do also to them, for this is the Law and the Prophets" (Matthew 7.12). The Golden Rule is a maxim that requires us to do to others what we would want them to do to us. When this golden rule is applied between generations, it means that we should do to future generations what we would be happy to have done to our present generation. Suzumura referred to a maxim of the Irish playwright Bernard Shaw, "Do not do unto others as you would that they should do unto you. Their tastes may not be the same" (Shaw, 1903, p.1), warning that the values of future generations may not be the same as those of the present.[14]

However, overemphasizing this point risks providing an excuse to neglect future generations. Chapter 4 shows through an experiment that this concern is not unwarranted. We can be as ignorant about spatially distant people of our own time (as we are about future generations). Yet, we know that spatially distant people also

---

[12] In exponential discounting, the discount rate is constant over time. A comparison of exponential and hyperbolic discounting is discussed in detail in Chap. 5 (Sect. 5.4.1).

[13] Chapter 5 (Sect. 5.2).

[14] Suzumura (2018, pp. 117–118).

need clean air, safe water, food, and good companionship. These basic needs should remain constant, even if the generations differ.

1.3.3 The Contingency of Future People

The third of the challenges is that the very existence of future generations is contingent on the actions of the present generation. The entirety of this challenge is an intrinsic issue between generations. Depending on the choices of the present generation, future persons may or may not be conceived. It would then appear that those who come into existence in the future will not be able to blame the present generation for its choices, whatever they may be. This is the non-identity problem raised by Parfit, as has been touched upon in Sect. 1.2. If the entire human race voluntarily chooses not to procreate, and to perish instead, the question of whether such a choice is permissible arises.[15] In the non-identity problem, the inherent structure of intergenerational relations of sequential appearances in history is clearly manifested in the form of the existence or non-existence of subsequent generations.

The non-identity problem is a deeply rooted question of ethics. Morally evil acts are said to be those that harm someone in particular. This view is termed the "person-affecting theory," and intuitively appears to be a perfect argument. However, the non-identity problem points out that beneath the person-affecting theory, there is no other way but to derive the absence of responsibility to future generations. To examine the non-identity problem is to consider the fundamentals of ethics. This book addresses the foundations of intergenerational ethics through the search for a solution to the non-identity problem.[16]

1.3.4 Difficulties in Realizing Intergenerational Ethics

The fourth and final challenge is the difficulties in making intergenerational ethics a reality. Even if the three challenges mentioned so far are resolved and the foundations of intergenerational ethics are laid, they are meaningless if the ethical demands are not implemented.

The British philosopher Brian Barry points out that there are no circumstances of justice between generations, and justice cannot function in intergenerational relationships (Barry, 1996). Time moves in only one way, and just as the relationship between humans and animals is one-sided, subsequent generations have no choice

[15] Kavka (1996, pp. 194–195).

[16] Chapter 2.

but to accept the consequences of the preceding generation's actions.[17] The one-way, one-time, sequential relationship that we have identified as a characteristic of intergenerational relationships, prevents the realization of intergenerational ethics.

Even if the present generation has duties toward future ones, there is no guarantee that it will carry out its duties, as human beings do not always seek to realize their own moral ideals. This problem is known as *akrasia* (weakness of will).[18] From an economic perspective, incentive problems also hinder the implementation of duties. Even if people take their duties required by intergenerational ethics seriously, there are incentives among individuals in the present generation to free-ride the fulfillment of duties by others.

The discussion of intergenerational ethics is not complete without presenting methodologies for making intergenerational ethics a reality. As long as intergenerational ethics are understood as problems of the externality that the activities of the present generation bring to future generations, it is possible to make intergenerational ethics a reality, for example, through the introduction of Pigovian tax on greenhouse gas emissions. However, the difficulty of this realization, which is the concern here, relates to the prospect that the present generation is not willing to voluntarily adopt Pigovian tax. When making intergenerationally appropriate policy choices, it is necessary for the present generation, which dominates decision-making, to somehow internalize the harm incurred to future generations. Methodologies for internalization could include encouraging people to implement their duties through such measures as deliberation. However, this book will devote particular attention to finding reciprocal relationships between different generations and thereby rebuilding intergenerational ethics. Rawls notes the reciprocal relationships that emerge between people with similar capabilities and interests through sharing rules.[19] In this book, it will be shown that reciprocity, in the sense of Rawls, is possible between different generations and the function of this reciprocity will also be examined.[20]

1.3.5 Approach of This Book

By addressing these intergenerational challenges, this book lays the groundwork for an intergenerational ethics and examines ways to make it a reality. The four challenges encourage us to view each generation as a separate country,[21] but how, if at all, can we speak of moral relationship that should exist between the different generations? Furthermore, are these moral relations realizable?

---

17 Barry (1996, pp. 220–223).

18 Aristotle (fourth century B.C., Book 7).

19 Rawls (1971b, pp. 208–212).

20 A discussion focusing on deliberation is presented in Chap. 4. A discussion of the origins and functions of reciprocity is presented in Chaps. 2 and 3.

21 The contingency of future people (the third challenge) also works to separate the generations in the sense that future generations are not able to make any moral claims on the present generation.

The first approach to solve this problem is to conceptualize the issue properly through philosophy and to develop the concepts using economics. The interest of philosophy is to present new interpretations of the moral obligations and values we have, with reference to certain theoretical frameworks. Economics is good at identifying the outcomes of the interaction of people acting on the basis of certain obligations and values, while taking them as given. This book, through philosophical contemplations, presents ideal conceptions of intergenerational ethics, and constructs economic models to reveal their economic and social consequences. The major direction is to derive a philosophical interpretation that links isolated generations, and to elucidate how this intergenerational linkage works. This work is the primary mission of Chaps. 2 and 3. Chapter 5 will arrive at a deeper understanding of time discounting by combining the philosophical and conceptual arrangements with the economic models.

The second approach is the use of economic experiments. By introducing experiments, this book maintains the generality of the arguments and extends the scopes of the discussions beyond mere theoretical possibilities, to what could occur in reality. Laboratory experiments replicate intergenerational relationships and provide opportunities to observe the behaviors of subjects. These observations suggest what could actually happen between generations, which are useful to propose institutions and policies. Specifically, Chap. 3 conducts an experiment with rewards that mimics intergenerational reciprocity. In Chap. 4, subjects are presented with options of long-term fiscal policy and are encouraged to deliberate the policy that is desirable. The experiment is used to discover what should be considered in policy decisions to promote intergenerational cooperation. Appendix 4.1 in Chap. 4 presents an experiment that reveals what people say when deliberating intergenerational issues.

A third approach of this book is that it does not necessarily assume that the preferences of each generation are fixed. In economics, preferences are usually assumed to be stable. If we begin to allow preferences to vary for convenience, then ad hoc explanations become possible. This book allows limited situations in which preferences are endogenously determined under certain logics. Specifically, Chap. 3 examines situations in which the preferences of subsequent generations are influenced by the behavior of the preceding one. Chapter 4 discusses the influence of deliberation on the preceding generation's preferences. In presenting these endogenous determinations of preferences, a key point of this book is to present them not merely as possibilities, but also with empirical support from economic experiments.

In his discussion of the methodologies of normative economics, Kotaro Suzumura stated that while fact-finding economics, which examines the state of existing institutions, treats institutions as exogenous variables, "normative economics considers institutions as selectable variables and pursues the possibility of their design, evaluation, selection, and implementation" (Suzumura, 2016, p. 97). In Suzumura's version of normative economics, the preferences of individuals living within institutions were still exogenous. Going one step further, this book aims to consider endogenous determination of preferences under certain logics. Tatsuyoshi Saijo, one of the pioneers of experimental economics in Japan, pointed out that mechanism design takes "social mechanisms" as variables, but not "human thinking;" this point is also valid for

Suzumura's normative economics. Saijo, in his own research on future design for social sustainability (Saijo), "aims to design 'social mechanisms' that change 'the way people think' itself in order to realize a sustainable society" (Saijo, 2018, p. 32). Chapter 4 of this book is a discussion based on an experiment inspired by Saijo.

1.4 Organization of Chapters

The remaining chapters of this book are organized as follows.

Chapter 2: **Duty and Reciprocity in Intergenerational Ethics**. Based on a survey of previous studies, Chap. 2 will examine the foundation of intergenerational ethics within the framework of duty and reciprocity. The first step is to lay the groundwork for intergenerational ethics through the non-identity problem. Through this examination, the possibility of grounding the present generation's duties to future generations, on the basis of common understandings within the present generation, will be shown. However, the problem that arises is that simply considering intergenerational ethics as duties does not guarantee the actualization of those ethics. There is the problem of *akrasia* (weakness of will), which means that even if people have moral ideals, they do not necessarily seek to realize them.

While there are several methodologies to address this difficulty, this chapter examines the manner in which the foundation of intergenerational ethics can be rebuilt by finding reciprocity among generations. First, it is pointed out that a chain of cooperation between overlapping generations (indirect reciprocity) is widely observed among generations. The parents nurture their children, and the children take care of the grandchildren (descending reciprocity). Alternatively, the parents provide care to the elderly, and are eventually nurtured by their children (ascending reciprocity). However, these reciprocities are fragile because they rely on chains of cooperation between overlapping generations. For this reason, this chapter proposes an alternative approach that finds direct reciprocity between generations. According to philosopher Scheffler (2013, 2018), humans are concerned with the survival of humanity after their own personal death. Considering this as a starting point, it is understood that the survival of humanity after one's own death is a value that can be shared among different generations. This chapter refers to the notion of public reciprocity developed by Reiko Gotoh, based on Rawls' concept of reciprocity, and shows that reciprocal relationships can be established between generations, based on a shared rule of caring for the survival of humanity and others. Starting from the recognition of future generations as human beings like ourselves, a joint venture is established between generations through the sharing of the rule of caring for the survival of humankind.

Chapter 3: **Developing of Intergenerational Cooperation based on Public Reciprocity: Intergenerational Cooperation through the Kantian Categorical Imperative**. This chapter develops a model consisting of generations in public reciprocity to understand the mechanisms that lead to cooperation and non-cooperation between generations. Cooperation occurs under public reciprocity, but is not always sufficient due to incentives. Beginning with insufficiency of cooperation, methodologies to promote cooperation between generations are examined. Specifically, the idea of funds establishment (constitutionalization) as a method to elicit cooperation from the preceding generation through direct binding on the actions of the subsequent generation.

I then conduct an economic experiment that mimics the model developed in this chapter. The experiment confirms that incentive problems impede intergenerational cooperation. Interestingly, it finds that the behavior of the subjects in the preceding generation role influences the subjects in the succeeding generation role (moral inspiration of the subsequent generation by the preceding generation). The preferences of the subsequent generation are not fixed, but are now endogenously determined.

The remainder of this chapter incorporates this influential relationship into the model. It will be shown that when the preceding generation takes into account the influence on the subsequent generation, it will increase the degree of cooperation. Furthermore, when the preceding generation desires cooperation from the subsequent one, its initiative to cooperate on its own will elicit cooperation from the subsequent generation. If the preceding generation wants the subsequent generation to cooperate, it should cooperate itself, and then the preceding generation actually cooperates. That cooperation follows this path is interpreted in this chapter through reference to previous studies in economics on the Kantian categorical imperative[22].

Appendix 3.1 presents a new methodology of the negotiation between generations to solve intergenerational conflicts, and clarify its significance and challenges. Appendix 3.2 discusses the relationship between personality and intergenerational issues based on the experimental results in this chapter.

Chapter 4: **Considerations for Policy Decisions Involving Multiple Generations: An Examination through Economic Experiments on Fiscal Policy**. This chapter takes long-term fiscal policy as an example, and discusses the economic experiments conducted, in order to discover the considerations in policy decisions to promote intergenerational cooperation.

In the experiment, participants are asked whether they would prefer to postpone the burden to 30 years or later (Fiscal Policy 1 [FP1]), or share the burden between now and the future (Fiscal Policy 2 [FP2]), after which they are asked to decide which policy to adopt through deliberations in groups of three. Additionally, the idea of intergenerational negotiations presented in Appendix 3.1 in Chap. 3 is expanded. One of three subjects is asked to participate in the deliberation as an "imaginary future generation" (IFG; Saijo, 2020a, 2020b) as if they were a person living 30 years in the future.

The results of the experiment reveal that as age increases, the number of subjects who support Fiscal Policy 2 decreases. However, we find that this decrease is slower than when the choice is based on personal interests. The hypothesis that people prefer policies based on their interests for the rest of their limited life expectancy

[22] Roemer (2010, p. 2) formulates the Kantian categorical imperative as "one should take those actions and only those actions that one would advocate all others take as well.".

(the silver democracy hypothesis) is overemphasized. As people age, they make decisions that are distinct from their personal interests (considerations of the interests of society as a whole and of their immediate descendants). It became clear that deliberations solely by the present generation do not necessarily promote decisions that take future generations into account. However, the introduction of IFGs into deliberations encourages decisions that take future generations into consideration. Through deliberations with IFGs, preferences of subjects change to take the future generation into consideration. Here, a way for the present generation's preferences to be endogenously determined is found as well. Imaginary future generations increase the chances of obtaining balanced decisions by adding more pro-future perspectives as the inputs in the deliberative process. In light of these findings, the final section of this chapter presents some considerations to solve long-term fiscal problems, and then generalizes these points to broad policy decisions involving multiple generations.

Appendix 4.1, through another experiment with IFGs, examines what people will say when they are instructed to become future people. imaginary future generations are invited to deliberations among residents of a town. It is seen that the deliberations among IFGs raise interest in issues that are related to common fundamental needs across generations. Imaginary future generations are positioned within the broad context of general rules for good decision-making, in light of philosophical arguments such as Rawls's veil of ignorance. Appendix 4.2 examines the structure of fiscal policy as an intergenerational issue.

Chapter 5: **The Meaning of Equal Treatment of Present and Future Events—Time Discounting**. Up to Chap. 4, the discussions have been based on the premise that it is desirable to give consideration to future events. However, in Chap. 5, we will again ask whether it is really possible and desirable to treat present and future events equally. The specific problem is the conflict of basic principles of morality raised by Arrow in Sect. 1.3.1, namely, that if we try to treat present and future events equally, any act of pursing for happiness in the present may be regarded immoral. One way to resolve this conflict is to introduce time discounting. However, it is necessary to find discounts that satisfy the following two conditions: it must be time-specific and consistent with morality in the sense of treating the present and the future equally. Through the discussion in this chapter, it will be shown that time discounting based on the sequential succession of events reducing responsibility for future events due to the loss of controllability over them satisfies both conditions.

There are two types of discounting associated with loss of controllability: one is due to the intervention of subsequent decision-makers, and the other is due to the succession of natural hazards. According to the former, discounting is caused by strategic relationships between sequentially ordered decision-makers. Time discounting from natural hazards is the idea that the longer the gain is delayed, the more uncertain it becomes, and this uncertainty then becomes the rationale for time discounting. This chapter explains how these two types discount future events, and discusses their policy implications.

Only on resolving the conflict presented by Arrow through the introduction of time discounting, will the equal treatment of present and future events be feasible and worthy of support.

Chapter 6 **Conclusion**. This chapter summarizes the discussion thus far and concludes with a view toward solving the intergenerational issues. This chapter also provide prospects for further research. Finally, it is argued that, as a minimum, we must not use future generations as tools for our own interests.

Figure 1.1 is a flowchart illustrating the major flow of discussion in each of the chapters. Chapter 2 shows that, in laying the foundation for intergenerational ethics, there is one argument that emphasizes the duties from the preceding generation to the succeeding generation, and another that provides reciprocity among generations important roles. From the necessity of making intergenerational ethics a reality, this book focuses on arguments concerning reciprocity, especially direct reciprocity, which is interpreted as "public reciprocity". Chapters 3 and 4 are devoted to deepening our understanding of this public reciprocity. After pointing out that intergenerational cooperation remains inadequate even under public reciprocity, Chap. 3 emphasizes the need to find methodologies to encourage further cooperation and make intergenerational ethics a reality. The specific methodologies discussed in this book are: funds establishment (constitutionalization), Kantian categorical imperative, intergenerational negotiation (Chap. 3), and deliberation (Chap. 4), including deliberation with IFGs. Chapters 3 and 4 will examine these issues through experiments. The experiments reveal that the behavior of the preceding generation morally inspires the subsequent one (Chap. 3). Further, deliberation with IFGs changes the policy preferences of the present generation (the preceding generation) (Chap. 4), and thereby both the preferences of the subsequent and preceding generations are endogenized under certain logics. Chapter 5 addresses the fundamental quest for the deeper understanding of intergenerational relations. Specifically, it questions whether the equal treatment of present and future events, which is assumed in the other chapters, is truly feasible and supportable. We show that this question can be answered affirmatively by introducing time discounts associated with the loss of controllability over events. Chapter 6 concludes the discussions and provides directions of further research.

Table 1.1 lists the various ways in which the challenges in intergenerational issues are addressed throughout this book. While paying attention to the various challenges, discussions have been carried over to the methodological issue of overcoming the difficulties involved in making intergenerational ethics a reality.

As a final part of this chapter, definitions are given for the key terms used in this book. The definitions here are not in general terms, but from the perspective of this book, which deals with intergenerational issues.

Duty:

A unilateral obligation of the present generation to future generations to act in such a way as to avoid harm to future generations or to alleviate the predicament of future generations.

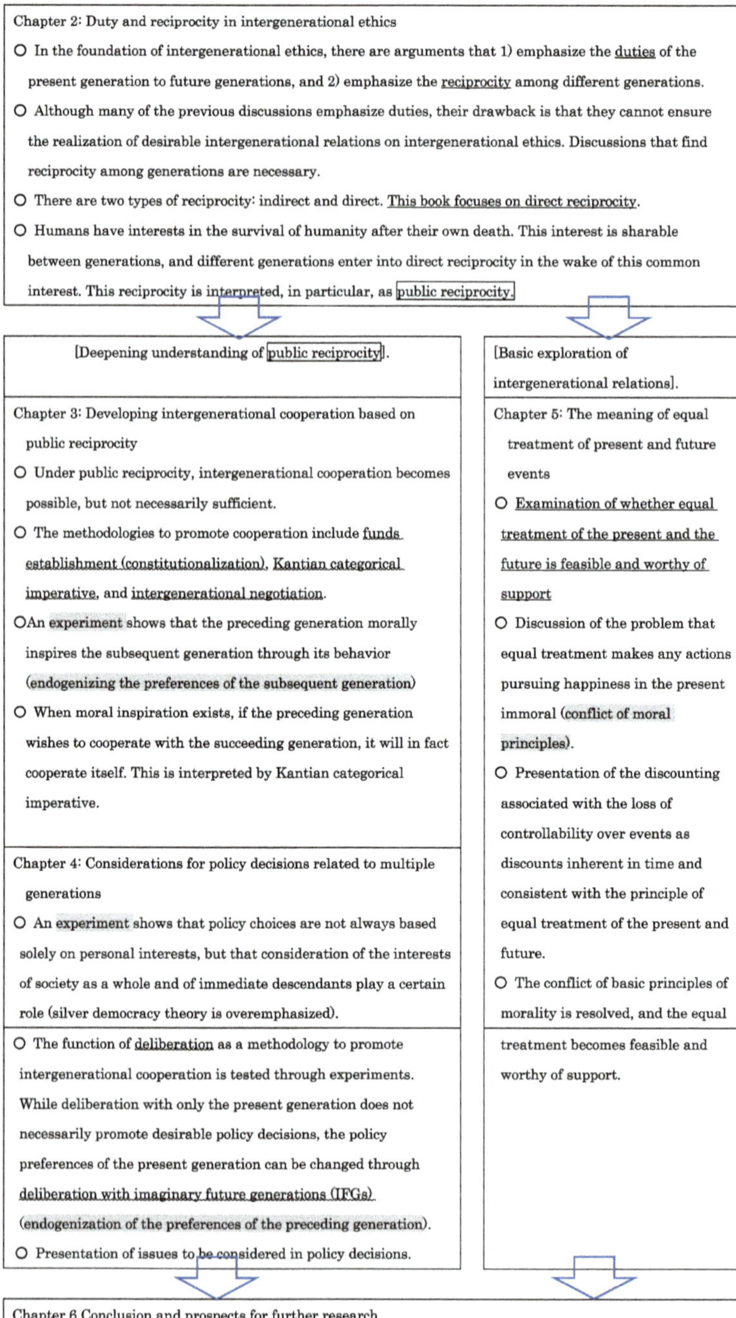

Fig. 1.1 Flowchart

Table 1.1 Issues discussed in each chapter and challenges in intergenerational issues

Challenges chapters	The temporal location of future people	Ignorance about future generations	The contingency of future people	Difficulties in realizing intergenerational ethics
Chapter 2: Duty and reciprocity in intergenerational ethics			• Examination of non-identity problem • Foundations of intergenera-tional ethics	• Problems of intergenerational ethics as a duty • Intergenerational ethics based on reciprocity - Descending and ascending reciprocity (indirect reciprocity) - Direct reciprocity based on sharing the rule of caring for the survival of humanity (public reciprocity)
Chapter 3: Developing intergenerational cooperation based on public reciprocity				• Effectiveness and limitations of funds establishment (constitutionaliza-tion) • Laboratory verification • Interpretation by Kantian categorical imperative

(continued)

Table 1.1 (continued)

Challenges chapters	The temporal location of future people	Ignorance about future generations	The contingency of future people	Difficulties in realizing intergenerational ethics
Chapter 4: Considerations for policy decisions related to multiple generations		• Influence of the ignorance about future generations on policy choices.		• Validation of the Silver democracy hypothesis • Validation of deliberative democracy hypothesis, and testing of deliberation with IFGs • Presentation of consideration for solving long-term fiscal problems and their generalization
Chapter 5: The meaning of equal treatment of present and future events	• Discounts by losing controllability over events — Intervention of subsequent decision-makers — Succession of natural hazards			• Concern that lack of knowledge about the stable structures inherent in societies leads to short-sighted policy decisions. • Concern that society is not flexible enough to apply appropriate discount rates

Reciprocity:

A two-way relationship based on mutual benefits between different generations. It includes indirect reciprocity, i.e., the type in which generation $t - 1$ gives favors to generation t and from generation t to generation $t + 1$ (descending reciprocity), and the type in which generation t receives favors from generation $t + 1$ in return for favors from generation t to generation $t - 1$ (ascending reciprocity). This book focuses on the relationships based on direct reciprocity between different generations.

Funds establishment (Constitutionalization):

A method of making it easier for preceding generations to act in accordance with their own interests in the future through direct binding, by the preceding generation, of the actions of the succeeding generations. For example, the preceding generations directly bind the behavior of subsequent generations by leaving savings or other resources to subsequent generations, which are irreversible, or by constitutional measures that are difficult to amend.

The Kantian categorical imperative:

It is a maxim that one should take only those actions that one would advocate (all) others to also take. In this book, it is used to indicate that the preceding generation initiates actions that it would like subsequent generations to take.

References

Arrow, K. J. (1999). Discounting, morality, and gaming. In P. R. Portney & J. P. Weyant (Eds.), *Discounting and intergenerational equity, resources for the future* (pp. 13–21).

Asheim, G. B., Mitra, T., & Tungodden, B. (2007). A new equity condition for infinite utility streams and the possibility of being Paretian. In J. Roemer & K. Suzumura (Eds.), *Intergenerational equity and sustainability* (pp. 55–68). Palgrave MacMillan.

Barry, B. (1996). Circumstances of justice and future generations. In R.I. Sikora & B. Barry (Eds.), *Obligations to future generations* (pp. 204–248). White Horse Press.

Diamond, P. A. (1965). The evaluation of infinite utility streams. *Econometrica, 33*(1), 170–177.

Fiscal System Subcommittee Drafting and Review Committee, Fiscal System Council. (2018). *Long-term projection for Japan's public finances* (Revised Version), April 6, 2018. Document 2. (in Japanese)

Frederick, S., Loewenstein, G., & O'Donoghue, T. (2002). Time discounting and time preference: A critical review. *Journal of Economic Literature, 40*(2), 351–401.

Gotoh, R. (2006). Principle of intergenerational justice and its enactment procedure: Rawls's theory of social contract revisited. In K. Suzumura (Ed.), *Logic and ethics of intergenerational equity* (pp. 337–358). Toyo-Keizai. (in Japanese)

Hume, D. (1739–40). *A treatise of human nature.* Center for Security Studies, https://ethz.ch/content/specialinterest/gess/cis/center-for-securities-studies/en/services/digital-library/publications/publication.html/125487. Last accessed July 19, 2020.

Independent Review on the Economics of Biodiversity. (2021a). *Final report—The economics of biodiversity: The Dasgupta review, headline messages.* HM Treasury.

Independent Review on the Economics of Biodiversity. (2021b). *Final report—The economics of biodiversity: The Dasgupta review.* HM Treasury.

Intergovernmental Panel on Climate Change (IPCC). (2021). *Climate change 2021: The physical science basis, summary for policymakers, working group I contribution to the sixth assessment report of the intergovernmental panel on climate change.*

Jefferson, T. (1789). Thomas Jefferson to James Madison (Paris September 6. 1789). In *Papers of Thomas Jefferson.* https://jeffersonpapers.princeton.edu/selected-documents/thomas-jefferson-james-madison. Last accessed October 22, 2019.

Kavka. (1996). The futurity problem. In R.I. Sikora & B. Barry (Eds.), *Obligations to future generations* (pp. 180–203). White Horse Press.

Koopmans, T. C. (1960). Stationary ordinal utility and impatience. *Econometrica, 28*(2), 287–309.

Locke, J. (1689). *Two treatises of government, archive for the history of economic thought.* McMaster University. https://historyofeconomicthought.mcmaster.ca/locke/government.pdf. Last accessed on August 8, 2020.

Myerson, J., & Green, L. (1995). Discounting of delayed rewards: Models of individual choice. *Journal of the Experimental Analysis of Behavior, 64*(3), 263–276.

Parfit, D. (1984). *Reasons and people.* Oxford University Press.

Pigou, A. C. (1920). *The economics of welfare* (4th ed., 1932). Macmillan.

Posner, E. (2007). Agencies should ignore distant-future generations. *University of Chicago Law Review, 74*(1), 139–143.

Ramsey, F. P. (1928). A mathematical theory of saving. *Economic Journal, 38*(152), 543–559.

Rawls, J. (1971a, 1999). *A theory of justice* (Revised). Harvard University Press.
Rawls, J. (1971b, 1999). Justice as reciprocity. In S. Freeman (Ed.), *Collected papers: John Rawls* (pp. 190–224). Harvard University Press.
Roemer, J. (2010). Kantian Equilibrium. *Scandinavian Journal of Economics, 112*(1), 1–24.
Roemer, & Suzumura, K. (2007). Introduction. In J. Roemer & K. Suzumura (Eds.), *Intergenerational equity and sustainability* (pp. xiv–xxii). Palgrave MacMillan.
Saijo. T. (2018). Futrue design. *Kankyo Keizai, Saisaku Kenkya, 11*(2), 29–42. (in Jabanese)
Saijo, T. (2020a). Future design: An introduction. In *Future design: Incorporating preferences of future generations for sustainability*. Springer.
Sajjo, T. (2020b). Future design: Bequeathing sustainable natural environments and sustainable societies to future generations. *Sustainability, 12*(16), 1–21.
Scheffler, S. (2013). *Death and the afterlife*. Oxford University Press.
Scheffler, S. (2018). *Why worry about future generations?* Oxford University Press.
Shaw, B. (1903). Maxims for revolutionists. eBookTakeAway. https://www.ebooktakeaway.com/ebta/titles/maxims_for_revolutionists/maxims_for_revolutionists_pdf.pdf. Last accessed January 11, 2021.
Sidgwick, H. (1907). *The methods of ethics* (7th ed.). Macmillan.
Suzumura, K. (2016). Scope, methods, and informational bases of normative economics. *The Economic Review, 67*(2), 97–106. (in Japanese)
Suzumura, K. (2018). Intergenerational equity and responsibility for future generations. In S. Rangan (Ed.), *Capitalism beyond mutuality? Perspectives integrating philosophy and social science* (pp. 107–127). Oxford University Press.
Takigawa, H. (2017). *Philosophy of the state: From political responsibility to the global republic*. University of Tokyo Press. (in Japanese)

Chapter 2
Duty and Reciprocity in Intergenerational Ethics

Abstract In laying the foundation for intergenerational ethics, arguments emphasize: the duty of the present generation and; reciprocity among different generations. The conventional argument emphasizes duty. However, the drawback of this argument is that it cannot ensure the realization of desirable intergenerational relations based on intergenerational ethics. It is necessary to develop the argument that finds reciprocity among generations. The two types of reciprocity are: indirect and direct. This book focuses on direct reciprocity. People are interested in the continuation of human beings after their personal death. This interest can be shared among different generations and triggers them to enter into a relationship of direct reciprocity. The function of this reciprocity is developed in an economic model and interpreted as public reciprocity.

2.1 Introduction

As discussed in Chap. 1, intergenerational social decisions are becoming increasingly important. However, future generations are not only those that are yet to been born, but also those that may or may not come into existence, depending on the actions of the present generation. The main purpose of this chapter is to lay the foundation for ethics between the future and present generations, that is, intergenerational ethics. In the first place, is it possible for the present generation to owe obligations to the future ones? This is the first issue addressed in this chapter. The second issue is the feasibility of the obligation, assuming that some obligation is owed. This is the question of whether intergenerational ethics can be actualized. There are some prior works on these issues, primarily in the field of philosophy. This chapter examines these issues from the perspective of economics, paying attention to the revelations of philosophy, and develops their implications. Through such an examination, this chapter presents a framework for the foundation of intergenerational ethics, namely, duty and reciprocity, and in particular, reciprocity, which had not been fully developed in the past. Particularly, it develops an idea of direct reciprocity through the sharing of rules between different generations (public reciprocity), in order to gain perspective

T. Hiromitsu, *Resolving Intergenerational Conflicts*, Advances in Japanese Business and Economics 33, https://doi.org/10.1007/978-981-97-0614-3_2

for the foundation and realization of an intergenerational ethics. The interest of philosophy is to offer a new interpretation of the moral obligations and values we owe, with reference to a certain theoretical framework. Economics, however, is adept at identifying the consequences of the interaction of people acting on certain obligations and values. Reciprocity through the sharing of rules between different generations, as this chapter reveals, is a new philosophical interpretation. Economists can then construct a model to specifically reveal what intergenerational relations look like when people act on this interpretation.

Amartya Sen, an economist with major influence on philosophy and political science, outlined three sources of a reasoned sense of obligation to future generations in his article entitled "Our Obligation to Future Generations" (Sen, 2018).[1] The first source is cooperation, the obligation to make our bit in pursuit of some social goal with others. Second is responsibility for having caused harm, the obligation to seek to eliminate the suffering of others when our actions are the cause of their suffering. Third is the obligation of power, which is the obligation to help those who suffer when we have the power to improve their situation. The obligation of cooperation, which as mentioned above is the first source, is based on common interests between different parties. An important feature of cooperation is that the parties involved are mutually obligated. Focusing on this bilateral relationship, this source is called reciprocity in this chapter. The second and third sources involve unilateral obligations from one party to the other. The line of demarcation between the second and third sources is faint, since it is possible to view not helping someone despite having the power to ameliorate their suffering as harming them. Conversely, it is possible to view making efforts to avoid being the cause of their suffering as helping them. In this chapter, the second and third sources are combined, and the unilateral obligation to help others is called duty.[2]

Regarding reciprocity, the particular difficulties when working between generations are noted. Within a generation, mutual benefit encourages cooperation between individuals. However, time only flows in one direction. Subsequent generations have no choice but to accept the consequences of the actions of the preceding one, and

[1] Sen (2018, pp. 133–134).

[2] There is not necessarily a sharp difference in English between the meanings of obligation and duty. In an article by the American philosopher Brandt (1964), after a detailed examination of the meanings of obligation and duty, Brandt states that the two terms are generally interchangeable (p. 392). However, he recognizes a subtle difference between the two, stating that obligation is concerned with the idea of binding that derives from some prior act or event, such as an agreement (p. 390), whereas duty functions in an organizational role (p. 392). For the general use of the term, see Oxford Leaner's Dictionaries (2019), which defines obligation as "the state of being forced to do something because of a duty or law, etc.", and duty as "something you feel you have to do because it is your moral or legal responsibility." Obligation focuses on objective state of being forced to do some duty or law. As Brandt points out, some prior act or event is involved in generating the objective state. Duty focuses on the subjective state of the mind of the person assuming the duty, which, as Brandt points out, often derives from some role. This chapter (Sect. **2**.2) argues that the duty in intergenerational ethics is established through common understandings within the present generation. Such a duty is appropriately represented as duty in the sense that it does not force the present generation to carry it out from the outside, but is within the mind of the present generation.

reciprocity is difficult to establish. This situation has been described by Brian Barry (1996) as a lack of circumstances of justice between generations.[3]

In considering the obligation to future generations, the first step is to find a way to ground it as duty. In Sect. 2.2, the philosophical and economic discussions of Parfit's (1984) non-identity problem are traced. Relying in particular on Meyer (2003) and Gotoh (2018), it is shown that intergenerational ethics can be established as duty to future generations through common understandings within the present generation. However, it is necessary to point out that there are difficulties in realizing intergenerational ethics as duty. In Sect. 2.3, as a problem of duty that is only unilaterally established within the present generation, there are difficulties, including the weakness of human beings not trying to realize their own moral ideals, known as *akrasia*. A possible countermeasure to this problem is to rebuild the foundation of intergenerational ethics as bilateral cooperative relationship by finding new reciprocity between generations.[4] In Sect. 2.4 and beyond, this chapter engages in a discussion focusing on intergenerational reciprocity. Based on studies by Kolm (2006a, 2006b, 2008) that have comprehensively examined reciprocity, it is pointed out that a chain of cooperation between overlapping generations can be found among generations. Parents provide for their children, the children provide for the grandchildren, and so on. Or, the parent generation takes care of their elderly parents, and then eventually receives care from their children's generation. In these cases, there is indirect realization of the relationship between giving and receiving (indirect reciprocity). However, at the same time, it is argued that these cases have the disadvantage of relying on a chain of cooperation among overlapping generations. In Sect. 2.5, this chapter examines another approach to finding reciprocity between generations. According to Scheffler (2013, 2018), one is concerned with the survival of humanity after personal death. Taking this suggestion as a starting point, this chapter arrives at the understanding that the survival of humanity and others after one's own death is a value that can be shared among different generations. This chapter, referring to the notion of public reciprocity developed by Reiko Gotoh through the concept of reciprocity of Rawls (1971a, 1971b, 1993),[5] shows that reciprocal relationships are established between generations based on sharing the rule of caring for the survival of humankind and others between different generations. Section 2.6 summarizes the conclusions and remaining issues.

Throughout this chapter, the collective existence of generations will be discussed as the decision-making unit. Generations are entities that may or may not cooperate with each other, depending on the choices made by their social planners.[6]

---

[3] Barry (1996, pp. 220–223).

[4] There is a way to resolve the issue within the framework of intergenerational ethics as a duty, which will be discussed in subsequent chapters.

[5] Gotoh (2009, 2013, 2018).

[6] For the definition of a social planner, see Chap. 1 (Sect. 1.2).

2.2 Intergenerational Ethics as Duty

2.2.1 Non-identity Problem

Philosophers have long argued that the intergenerational use of utilitarianism creates the disadvantage of making it a moral imperative to have happy children. As long as one takes the position that increasing the total amount of happiness is good, adding one happier child to society is considered doing good. Philosopher Narveson (1967, p. 63) avoids this inconvenience by reformulating utilitarianism to mean "if a person exists, he should be as happy a possible". Moral good and evil are always good and evil for specific persons.

However, a paradox arises when this view, which is intuitively perfect, is used intergenerationally, as pointed out in Parfit's (1984) *Reasons and Persons*. Future generations depend on the actions of the present one for their very existence. Parfit terms Naveson's view the person-affecting theory,[7] pointing out that according to this theory, morally evil acts are those that harm someone in particular, and therefore, future generations, whose existence depends on the acts of the present one, cannot be harmed by the acts of the present generation. He calls this paradox the non-identity problem.[8]

> In a society in which slavery is legal, a couple that is planning to have no children is offered $50,000 by a slaveholder to produce a child to be a slave to him. They want the money to buy a yacht. (Kavka, 1982, p. 100)

This is a well-known example of the" slave child," a case study of the non-identity problem given by the philosopher Gregory Kavka. Kanka assumes that the life of a slave is worth living and is not so terrible that it would be better if he had never been born. In the case of the child, it would appear that no harm was done to them because they would never have been conceived and born had they not been born a slave. According to the person-affecting theory, there is no ethical wrongdoing in any of the couple's actions. The absence of obligation to future generations is derived from this theory. The philosopher Sikora (1996) has argued that what people owe to future generations is not obligation, but only "supererogation" that is commendable if fulfilled.[9]

Although the slave child example is styled as a private decision by a couple, the same problem appears in the public decision to continue slavery for trivial commercial gain. Economic research on cases involving public policy has also been conducted. One study by economists that examines the non-identity problem is that of Suzumura and Tadenuma (2007). Policies affect subsequent historical paths. Even if the changes are slight at the beginning, they are cumulative and ultimately produce large changes. People raised in automobile-intensive societies will produce a generation

---

[7] Parfit (1984, p. 394).

[8] Parfit (1984, pp. 351–379).

[9] Sikora (1996, p. 153).

that will prefer the use of automobiles in the future. Suzumura and Tadenuma are not concerned with personality (biological) identity—which is the concern of philosophers—but with the plasticity of social existence, including the preferences of the people of the time.[10] The economist Gotoh's (2018) study focuses again on personal identity. Using fetal Minamata disease as an example, Gotoh addresses the paradox of the non-identity problem that arises when the victims hold those who caused Minamata disease responsible for their causal acts. The paradox is that while the victims do exist, they are people who would not have been born if anti-pollution measures were adopted.[11] The issue of plasticity as a social being raised by Suzumura and Tadenuma is an interesting one in itself, but to lay the foundation for intergenerational ethics, which is this chapter's task, it is necessary to address the more fundamental issue of personal non-identity.

2.2.2 *Acceptance, Impersonal Ethics*

The following examines proposed solutions to the non-identity problem.[12] Since the non-identity problem makes it difficult to establish intergenerational ethics, it is hoped that solving it will allow the same to be established. The first solution is simply to accept what the non-identity problem states. The second is to abandon personal theories, such as the person-affecting theory, and construct ethics on impersonal values. The third is to reinterpret the concept of harm.

The simple acceptance of the non-identity problem is that the slave child is not harmed in any way and that nothing ethically evil has happened to them. If one speaks for them, those arguments are no longer regarded as ethical ones. This idea is coherent; however, it takes an extremely narrow conception of morality. Our moral intuition suggests that some evil is done to the slave child, and ignoring this intuition and narrowing the moral scope does not solve the paradox.

The second direction, the construction of impersonal ethics, provides a slightly more promising argument. According to this idea, even if the individual slave child is not harmed, the actions of the parents in giving this child life might still be blamed as impersonal evil. The best example of impersonal ethics is classical utilitarianism. Giving birth to a slave child reduces the sum total of society's well-being compared to giving birth to a free child, even if the parents must forego the trivial enjoyment they derive from the yacht. If climate change will bring ruin, the prescription for utilitarianism is to endure the inconvenience now. The argument for the construction of an impersonal ethic is also considered by Parfit as a promising line of inquiry.

---

[10] Suzumura & Tadenuma (2007, pp. 324–326).

[11] In the case of fetal Minamata disease, if the case is regarded as an assault on the personality of the fetus, it is possible to interpret that there is no room for the non-identity problem. Whether it is appropriate to consider fetal Minamata disease within the framework of the non-identity problem is related to the point of whether the fetus has a personality; this chapter does not go into this point in depth.

[12] A survey of the relevant literature by Roberts (2019) is useful.

Reason and Persons, as a whole, argues against the individuality of personality, and it is natural to consider the framework of impersonal ethics in solving the non-identity problem. However, Parfit raises the repugnant conclusion as a drawback of classical utilitarianism,[13] and leaves the final treatment of the non-identity problem undecided. In other words, if the sum of happiness is to be maximized, it justifies abandoning a hundred lives filled with happiness and choosing a hundred thousand lives that are better than death, but miserable. Additionally, there is also the problem of returning to the idea of the duty to have happy children, which was avoided by the introduction of the person-affecting theory. When the increase in the number of happy people is taken as good in itself (rather than as a side good, such as the happiness felt by their parents), it is inevitable to assume that it is good for an entity apart from the individual, such as society or God. It is desirable to avoid the assumption of such an entity.

2.2.3 Reinterpretation of the Concept of Harm: Intergenerational Ethics as Common Understandings Within the Present Generation

The third direction is to reinterpret the concept of harm and try to interpret the slave child as being harmed. It can also be interpreted that something wrong is being done to the child. The advantage of this argument is that it tries to retain the intuitively perfect idea of person-affecting theory as much as possible.[14]

The idea of the threshold notion of harm is proposed by Meyer (2003). Meyer proposes stopping identifying the presence or absence of harm, based on comparison with previous states, and instead, using a certain threshold as a standard. If a person is below the threshold as a result of an act, then it is recognized that harm has been done to that person. According to this threshold notion, it would seem that slave child and future generations suffering from climate change could be interpreted as having been harmed. A similar argument brings up rights in a nutshell (Woodward,

[13] Parfit (1984, pp. 381–390).

[14] A study by Roberts (2003) adheres to the person-affecting theory and at the same time tries to maintain the moral scope. According to Roberts, as long as there is a logical possibility that the succession of events leading to (the child's) conception would be realized even if a contract had not been made with the slave owner, no differently than if it had been, then being born into the world as a slave is not essential but harmful to the child. This forces an impossible argument when it comes to climate change; but it is not incomprehensible. Indeed, the logical possibility of the conception of every single future sufferer of climate change would seem to be based on nothing more than the succession of actual events as the world moves toward the disaster of climate change. However, to push the argument, it is not impossible to imagine a situation in which the extraction and conception (by unknown artificial means) of gametes from which all individuals are derived occurs without delay, even as the world moves toward climate change prevention, and thus the logical possibility of Roberts is maintained. It is not impossible to say that this is the case. However, what is really important, in my view, is not so much to point out that slavery is not essential to the individual as to acknowledge that slavery is, quite simply, harmful to the individual.

1986).[15] Some rights of the slave child have been violated, and the child has thus been harmed. The thesis of philosopher Kumar (2009) uses a broader concept of wrong than harm. When a person is not given the due consideration that they should have received in a certain type of situation, they are considered to have suffered wrong. The threshold notion or argument by right is the idea of determining the existence of harm through comparison with some absolute standard. Also, in the argument in favor of wrong, "due consideration" is objectively determined according to the type of situation in which the person is placed. In understanding the idea of reinterpreting the concept of harm, it is easier to comprehend the idea that there is a kind of soul of people who will be born in the future, and that the level experienced by that soul is below a certain threshold. Reiko Gotoh terms the existence corresponding to the souls of people who will be born in the future "integrated personality," stating that the integrated personality is in a pivotal position to select appropriate policies.[16] The integrated personality has the social role of advocating for the need to prevent harm before it occurs and for the provision of compensation after harm has occurred.[17]

It may be conceded that these reinterpretations of the concept of harm have a certain persuasiveness. However, it is my opinion that going back to the source of the persuasiveness, there is a socially accepted notion of what is to be recognized as a threshold, a right, or due consideration. Underpinning the persuasiveness of this reinterpretation are the common understandings *within* present generation of what constitutes moral harm. Through this reinterpretation of the concept of harm it is understood that the present generation can have a duty to future generations, but it is the common understandings of one's own duty within the present generation that supports the duty. It is the present generation that places the integrated personality in the key position of advocating the need for harm prevention. The criteria by which the integrated personality advocates policies are ideally in line with the interests of the unborn, but ultimately, they must be based on common understandings *within* the present generation. Here, despite the non-identity problem, through common understandings *within* the present generation, a path to establish the duty of the present generation to the future generation has been barely secured.

---

[15] Makoto Usami argues that the view that future generations have the right to request consideration at the present time is not valid, since there is no future generation—the right holder—due to the non-identity problem (Usami, 2006). As long as one takes the position that those who do not exist do not hold rights, it would be difficult to recognize the rights of future generations. However, it may be possible to consider the act of predestination to be a slave from the moment of birth as the beginning of the violation of the rights of those who will be born.

[16] Gotoh (2018, pp. 4–5).

[17] The idea of an integrated personality advocating the need to prevent harm to those yet to be born is commonly associated with the idea of "imaginary future generations" proposed by Saijo (2020a, 2020b), according to which imaginary future persons represent the interests of future generations. See Chap. 4 (Sect. 4.2.3) for details.

2.3 The Problem of Intergenerational Ethics as Duty

2.3.1 *Akrasia*

As discussed so far, candidates for duty to future generations, established through a path of common understandings within the present generation, include the following[18]:

(1) One should achieve the greatest happiness of the greatest number of people through generations (utilitarianism).
(2) If one has the power to improve the plight of future generations, one should exercise it (Sen, 2018).
(3) One should treat each generation equally (egalitarianism).

There are many more. The present generation understands that it has these duties and is committed to fulfilling them.

However, even if intergenerational ethics is established in this way, in my view, it cannot be satisfied that the established ethics will solve the intergenerational issues Even if the duties of the present generation are established, there is still no guarantee that these duties will be carried out, that is, there is no guarantee that intergenerational ethics will become a reality.

Although philosophers have charged many debates about the candidates on the above list, there is also a long tradition among philosophers of debates focusing on the implementation of duties. Aristotle's *Nicomachean Ethics* (in the context of discussing ethics in general) uses the Greek word *akrasia* to describe how people are drawn to their desire, even when they know that they should not eat sweet.[19] Drawing on the Greek word *akrasia*, the philosopher Richard Mervyn Hare also contends with the term moral weakness, stating that our morality is made up of high ideals that we cannot successfully persuade ourselves to carry out (Hare, 1963). Wataru Kuroda states that *akrasia* is the situation, in which "one who accepts a certain norm and should know it as a practical principle, is tempted by pleasure to act against that principle" (Kuroda, 1992, p. 96). In order for a norm to be truly binding, it must not only have "normative necessity," which means that "one who accepts a certain practical principle should always act in accordance with that principle in appropriate circumstances" (p. 95), but also "causal necessity," that is, "knowledge of a principle has a power in a person's mind, and if it is encountered within certain circumstances,

[18] This securing of the path toward the establishment of duties was made to preserve the person-affecting theory as much as possible. However, now it is not necessary to limit the duties to be established to those that are personality-based. For example, one can establish utilitarianism among generations by following the person-affecting theory and understanding that not having a happy child is harming that child, or one can establish utilitarianism by taking the impersonal principle of the greatest happiness of the greatest number as the common understandings. David Heyd also points out that personal and impersonal theories can reach the same content of intergenerational ethics, although on different grounds (Heyd, 2009a).

[19] Aristotle (fourth century B.C., Book 7).

that power activates proper conducts." In *akrasia*, the problem is the lack of causal necessity.

Economics generally assumes that people have consistent preferences. It has been noted earlier (Sect. 1.3.5) that no serious discussion is possible if the order of preferences between apples and oranges fluctuates without context. Therefore, problematizing a situation like *akrasia* is an exceptional consideration. However, by introducing John Harsanyi's distinction between the ethical and subjective preferences of individuals, economics is equipped with a structure sufficient to consider a problem equivalent to *akrasia* (Harsanyi, 1955). Harsanyi's ethical preferences "express what this individual prefers (or, rather, would prefer) on the basis of impersonal social considerations alone" (p. 315), while subjective preferences "express what he actually prefers, whether on the basis of his personal interests or on any other basis" (p. 315). Amartya Sen goes beyond Harsanyi and proposes a framework that can handle more complex structures than the dualistic structure of ethical and subjective preferences (Sen, 1977). Sen's framework involves a situation in which there is a set X of actions that can be chosen, with three or more rankings on this set of actions (one of these rankings may be the most moral ranking M). Sen's main contribution is to consider how to further rank these various rankings.[20]

In the context of intergenerational ethics, Heyd's (2009b) paper examines this issue of *akrasia*. Heyd termed the world which consists of people who comply with their duties as an "ideal situation." Conversely, called the world which does not always consist of people who comply with their duties a non-ideal situation. Heyd points out that the real world is in a non-ideal situation and that the question of how to ensure that duties are carried out in a non-ideal situation is also an ethical challenge.[21] Compared to intragenerational states where mutual monitoring and sanctions are effective, intergenerational ethics is particularly vulnerable to *akrasia*. Barry's (1996) article, which has been referred to frequently, states that the circumstance of justice is lacking in intergenerational settings. Time moves only in one direction, and subsequent generations have no choice but to accept the consequences of the actions of preceding generations.[22] Intergenerational ethics as duty has the difficulty that it relies on the state of mind of the people of the present generation who establish it, and lacks the logic to make it a reality. In Kuroda's words, it lacks the support of "causal necessity."

Taking utilitarianism—the first item in the list of candidates for duties—as an example, it is useful to look at some of the weaknesses in the implementation of the duty. Even if the present generation accepts utilitarianism as duty, it is doubtful whether the present generation will actually sacrifice its own interests in favor of the greatest happiness over the course of generations. Indeed, according to Jeremy Bentham, the pleasures that are the concern of utilitarianism include "the pleasures and pains of benevolence and of malevolence presuppose and have regard to, a pleasure or pain of some other person" (Bentham, 1789, p. 28). In other words,

---

[20] Sen (1977, pp. 335–341).

[21] Heyd (2009b, p. 181).

[22] Barry (1996, pp. 220–223).

one empathizes with the pleasures or pains of others. Thus, it does not follow that the present generation does not sympathize with future generations and wishes to increase (decrease) their pleasures (pains). However, as the psychologist Paul Slovic points out, empathy is demonstrated for a small number of visible needy people but is not active for a large number of invisible needy people (Slovic, 2010). He illustrates this argument by referring to words of Mother Teresa, "if I look at the mass in need of help, I will never act. If I look at the one, I will." The future generation is one that does not yet exist. Empathy has limited power to fulfill the duty to future generations, which utilitarianism demands.

2.3.2 Incentives

The problem of intergenerational ethics as duty is not confined to *akrasia*. A difficulty that standard economics sees as problematic is the incentive problem. When the present generation consists of multiple individuals, the same incentive problem as with the supply of public goods arises: who among these individuals will be the bearer of duty? It is generally pointed out that there is an incentive to free-ride by entrusting the supply of public goods to others, and as a result, public goods are underprovided. Even if individuals in the present generation understand that their generation, as a whole, is responsible for reducing greenhouse gas emissions, they still want others to carry out the emission reductions.[23]

Interestingly, the situation worsens when the incentive problem is combined with *akrasia*. It is ineffective and futile to live frugally when one is aware that their peers are unable to fulfill their duty of curbing greenhouse gases because of *akrasia*.

2.3.3 Countermeasures

These problems can be addressed within the framework of intergenerational ethics as duty. For example, a possible solution to *akrasia* would be to hold deliberations among people, in order to educate and encourage each other to take their duty seriously. The hope is that deliberation will increase the ranking of ethical preferences. For incentive issues among individuals within the present generation, enforcement

[23] There is a second type of incentive problem that arises between generations that is different from the intra-generational one. Each generation successively appears in history and makes decisions in a decentralized manner. In such a situation, for example, even if the present generation reduces greenhouse gas emissions but future generations emit large amounts of gases, then the present generation loses its incentive to reduce emissions. This second type of incentive problem stems from independence of the subsequent generations and strategic relationships between different generations. Strategic relationships between generations are introduced in Sect. 2.5.3, and Chap. 3 (Sect. 3.3.3) discusses the manner in which the relationships lead to inadequate intergenerational cooperation.

through legislation based on political consensus could also be considered, in order to ensure the implementation of duty.

However, I believe what is necessary here is to return to the path along which intergenerational ethics as duty was established (Sect. 2.2.3), to understand the inherent problems in intergenerational ethics as duty, and to devise measures overcoming the problems based on this understanding. The present generation's duty to future generations is unilateral, and is established by common understandings within the present generation itself. It remains as a boon to the future generations, from a distant present generation. Whether or not to implement this unilateral duty is left to the state of mind of the present generation, and it lacks the power to bring about the proper action from causal necessity. If intergenerational ethics is based not on duty but on reciprocity (which has been considered difficult) and exists bilaterally between different generations, then unilateral intergenerational relations can be transformed into cooperative relations. Reciprocal cooperation can make handling of intergenerational issues stable and free from the whims of the present generation.[24]

In order to find reciprocity between generations, it is necessary to identify bilateral relationships between giving and receiving in the one-way flow of time. The remainder of this chapter examines how to rebuild the foundation of intergenerational ethics by introducing reciprocity between generations.

2.4 Reciprocity Among Generations

2.4.1 Reciprocity

Serge-Christophe Kolm, a French economist known for his work on the economics of norms, compiled a handbook of basic economic research on gifts, altruism, and reciprocity. He defines reciprocity as "a gift or favor motivated by another gift, for instance the return gift of an initial gift" (Kolm, 2006a, p. 25). To better understand reciprocity as an important social relationship, Kolm (2006b), identifies coercion, exchange, and pure gift-giving as social relations that should be contrasted with reciprocity, and organizes the differences among them (Table 2.1).

Unlike coercion, exchange, reciprocity, and pure gift-giving are not coerced. However, each individual exchange must be carried out with certainty. In that sense, exchange is individually coercive. Exchange and reciprocity are interrelated, two-way transfers, as opposed to pure gift-giving, which is an independent one-way transfer. Exchange is beneficial and is based on self-centered motives. Reciprocity,

[24] The incentive problem between individuals in the present generation appears repeatedly in the form of who in that generation will bear the burden of duty, even under the assumption that reciprocity will work between generations. The interindividual incentive problem is not unique to the intergenerational issue. Even when reciprocity is found between generations, it may be necessary to take steps, such as legislative enforcement based on political consensus, to resolve the intragenerational incentive problem.

Table. 2.1 Difference between reciprocity and other social relations

Coercion	Exchange	Reciprocity	Pure gift-giving
Forced	Globally voluntary		
Individually forced transfers		Independently voluntary transfers	
Independent one-way transfers	Interrelated two-way transfers		Independent one-way transfers
Self-centered motivation		Other-oriented	

Source Kolm (2006b, p. 451)

however, is based on an other-oriented motive, since it is left to the recipient's own initiative to return the gift. Reciprocity is positioned between exchange and pure gift-giving. This intermediate positioning is also manifested in the social relation described by French anthropologist Mauss (1925) as *gift*. Drawing on ethnography from Polynesia and elsewhere, Mauss discusses the mechanisms of gift-giving and the ways in which gifts can activate social institutions. Unlike Kolm's pure gift-giving, the gift that Mauss refers to is accompanied by a mechanism that compels the recipient to give back for the gift received. "Giving back" is, by construction, left to voluntariness and is not individually enforced; in that sense, it differs from exchange. The discussion in this chapter has proceeded under the framework of duty and reciprocity, beginning with Sen's (2018) argument cited in Sect. 2.1. A unilateral duty from the present to future generations corresponds to gift-giving in Kolm's classification presented in Table 2.1. The present generation reaches out to future generations when it feels pity for the latter. Reciprocity has already been discussed; however, it is important to note that adjacent to reciprocity is the relationship of exchange, which is individually forced transfers. It is more difficult to find an exchange relationship between generations than reciprocity, but exchange, along with reciprocity, is one of the logics of cooperation.[25]

In a typical reciprocal relationship, there is direct giving and receiving between the pair. However, Kolm (2006a) lists generalized reciprocity, reverse reciprocity, and chain reciprocity as extended reciprocity that lacks directness.[26] Generalized reciprocity is a relationship in which A's giving to B entails B's giving to C. Reverse reciprocity is a relationship in which B's giving to A entails C's giving to B. Chain reciprocity is a relationship in which A gives to B, B–C, and C–D, in a chain of relationships. General reciprocity is reciprocity between an entity and society in general.

[25] In the discussion of "intergenerational negotiation", Appendix 3.1 of Chap. 3 touches on the exchange that takes place between generations.

[26] Kolm (2006a, p. 25).

2.4.2 Descending and Ascending Reciprocity

It seems difficult to establish direct reciprocity between pairs in the intergenerational context. What about extended reciprocity? The first aspect to consider is chain reciprocity. When chain reciprocity is used between generations, Generation 1 gives to Generation 2, Generation 2 gives to Generation 3, and so on. Kolm's reverse reciprocity, discussed in Sect. 2.4.1, does not assume that C receives from someone else, but when we add a chain where C receives from D and D receives from F, it can be applied to intergenerational use. These two types of reciprocity share the form of a *chain*; the difference between them is the direction of transfer of goods, which descends from the present to the future in chain reciprocity, but ascends from the future to the present in reverse reciprocity. Axel Gosseries, a philosopher who has published extensively on intergenerational issues, refers to each type of reciprocity as descending reciprocity and ascending reciprocity based on this difference (Gosseries, 2009); this book follows this terminology henceforth.

A classic example of descending reciprocity is the chain of parents educating their children, who in turn educate their children. It is true that education of children can be motivated by altruism toward them. However, altruism and reciprocity have different logics. Relationships based on altruism are the equivalent of pure gift-giving, as described by Kolm (2006b), whereas education based on altruism is unconditional giving. Unlike altruism, education based on reciprocity provides education to one's own children in return for the education they received in their own childhood.

Compared to the descending type of reciprocity—in which goods descend along the flow of time to the younger generation—ascending reciprocity is not as intuitively understandable. For this reason, it is useful to first look at the following case by Hume.

> Your corn is ripe to-day; mine will be so to-morrow. 'Tis profitable for us both, that I shou'd labour with you to-day, and that you shou'd aid me to-morrow. I have no kindness for you, and know you have as little for me. I will not, therefore, take any pains upon your account; and should I labour with you upon my own account, in expectation of a return, I know I shou'd be disappointed, and that I shou'd in vain depend upon your gratitude. Here then I leave you to labour alone: You treat me in the same manner. The seasons change; and both of us lose our harvests for want of mutual confidence and security. (Hume, 1739–40, pp. 266–267)

Farmer 1's (you) harvest day is today and Farmer 2's (me) is tomorrow. Farmer 2 thinks that even if they help Farmer 1 today, Farmer 1 will not help them tomorrow. Farmer 2 has no choice but to refrain from helping Farmer 1 today. This is a prisoner's dilemma game expanded into sequential moves. The desirable situation for both players is a cooperative relationship in which Farmer 2 helps Farmer 1 today and Farmer 1 helps Farmer 2 tomorrow.

The key to deriving cooperation is repetition of the game. Harvests come in cycles. If the farmers begin the game with cooperation and adopt a strategy according to which they continue to cooperate until their opponent betrays them (trigger strategy), then cooperation may continue. Interestingly, the players need not be limited to Farmers 1 and 2; the next player to appear after Farmer 2 could be Farmer 3. Farmer 3 would help Farmer 2 if there was a chance that Farmer 4 would help in Farmer

3's own harvest, provided that Farmer 3 helped in Farmer 2's harvest. Farmer t has overlapping periods with Farmer t − 1 and Farmer t + 1, and will help Farmer t − 1 first, and then be helped by Farmer t + 1.

It is not difficult nowadays to read cooperation between overlapping farmers into cooperation between overlapping generations. The philosopher David Gauthier (1986, pp. 351–352) is credited with spearheading this conception, and taking over from him, Heath (1997, 2013) has been using game theory to advance his studies.[27] However, in economics, Paul Samuelson already pointed out the possibility of ascending cooperation between overlapping generations in his paper in 1958 (Samuelson, 1958), following which other studies have been carried out (e.g., Hammond, 1975; Cigno, 1993, 2006). The model used in these studies is called the overlapping generations model. In Samuelson's paper, individuals survive three periods. In the third period (old age), there is no productive capacity.

$$C_1 + C_2 R_t + C_3 R_t R_{t+1} = 1 + 1R_t + 0R_t R_{t+1}. \tag{2.1}$$

where, C_1 is the consumption in young age, C_2 is that in the prime age, and C_3 is that in old age. R_t (= $1/(1 + i_t)$; i_t is the interest rate in period t) is the discount rate between the good in period t and the good in period t + 1, for instance when $R_t = 1.5$, 1.5 units of today's consumption must be sacrificed in order to obtain 1 unit of consumption in the next period. The productive capacity of the young and the prime age is 1, respectively, and the product of the old is zero. Equation 2.1 means that the present value of a person's lifetime consumption (left-hand side) is equal to the present value of their lifetime production (right-hand side).

Now, following Samuelson, it is useful to assume that Robinson Crusoe is isolated on a desert island, increasing or decreasing his goods against nature. If the goods are reproducible goods, such as rabbits, R_t is less than 1. However, in the case of perishable goods, R_t is greater than 1. When it is an icy good, it cannot be passed on to the next period, R_t becomes infinite. In other words, no matter how much Crusoe sacrifices today's consumption, he cannot increase his consumption in the next period. At this time, $C_1 = 1$, $C_2 = 1$, $C_3 = 0$, and Crusoe has no choice but to starve in old age.

Samuelson's proposal is to relocate Crusoe to a society in which people of various age groups live in overlapping groups, and then introduce a social compact (contract) in which people can be provided for by the younger generation when they grow old, provided that they took care of the elderly when they were young. Assuming that people desire equal consumption in each period, the young and prime-age contribute one-third of the goods and give two-thirds to the old. If this transfer continues as the generations progress, each generation can achieve two-thirds consumption in each period during its lifetime. Samuelson points out that the introduction of money can facilitate the chain of cooperation. The elderly are given money, which they exchange with the young generation to receive goods. When the young generation

[27] The explanation for replacing the farmer's harvest story in this section with an intergenerational issue is taken from Heath (2013).

grows old, they are taken care of by the younger generation, in exchange for the money. This model has been socially implemented as a "pay-as-you-go" pension system. The pension premiums paid by the prime and young generations are not used to fund their own pensions, but those of the old generation. Although there is no direct reciprocity between the generations here, there is the reciprocity that ascends through the generations, whereby the young generation, in return for supporting the old generation, is provided for by the younger generation.

2.4.3 Disadvantages of Descending and Ascending Reciprocity

However, the use of indirect reciprocity between generations, either descending or ascending, has drawbacks that cannot be ignored.

First, intergenerational issues are not always overlapping generational ones. For example, what if the consumption of Generation 1 benefits itself and provides moderate benefits to Generations 2–5, but causes serious harm to Generation 6? This is an example of an action that does no immediate harm, such as the placement of a time bomb, but causes harm in the distant future. Philosopher Gardiner (2009) refers to such cases as pure intergenerational problems.[28] In this example, there is no reciprocity between Generation 1 and Generation 6. Important parts of intergenerational problems, such as climate change, are included in this pure type.

The second drawback is that cooperation through descending or ascending reciprocity is fragile, because once such cooperation is broken, subsequent cooperation will also break off. In descending reciprocity, once a parental generation abandons the education of their children, the subsequent generations stop educating their children as well.[29] As an example of ascending reciprocity, in the case of Samuelson's money, cooperation is also interrupted when subsequent generations refuse to accept the money, for whatever reason. In ascending reciprocity, complex rules to prevent the interruption of cooperation have been suggested. The Italian economist Alessandro Cigno, in a three-generation overlapping model with productive capacity only in the prime age, proposed the rule that if the prime age generation (Generation t) does not support the old generation (Generation $t-1$), then the (post-adult) young generation (Generation $t+1$) will not support the (unfilial) prime age generation (Generation t); however, the grandchild generation (Generation $t+2$) will not punish Generation $t+1$, who punished Generation t (Cigno, 1993). A similar rule has also been proposed by Hammond (1975) as well.

The more complex the rules, the more difficult their social implementation. The behavioral economist Theo Offerman tested Samuelson-like intergenerational cooperation in a laboratory and reported that cooperation was generally sluggish due to

[28] Gardiner (2009, p. 90).

[29] If abandonment of education is regarded as child abuse, then an intergenerational chain of abuse will emerge.

the presence of subjects who always chose non-cooperation (Offerman et al., 2001). In terms of individual gains, the constant non-cooperators had higher gains than those who took the trigger strategy (baseline). Offerman also conducted an experiment in which subjects were recommended various strategies by the experimenter. He found that when the recommended strategy was the trigger strategy, overall cooperation was rather weak compared to the baseline without the recommended strategy. When the recommended strategy was to "punish the traitors," that is, a strategy that punishes only unfilial piety as suggested by Cigno and Hammond, the overall degree of cooperation exceeded the baseline. However, the percentage of subjects who chose to cooperate remained just under 20%. Furthermore, in terms of personal gains, the constant non-cooperators had higher gains than those who adopted the "punish the traitors" strategy. This result suggests that rules that encourage cooperation are not implemented by default.[30]

The third drawback is specific to ascending reciprocity. Cooperation based on ascending reciprocity is structured such that *present* cooperation depends on the inheritance of rules through intergenerational chains. Therefore, when the inheritance of rules is expected to be interrupted somewhere in the future, cooperation cannot begin in the first place. Therefore, ascending reciprocity is vulnerable to future changes of social conditions, such as population decline or changes in values. When a sharp population decline is expected at the time of Generation t, Generation $t - 1$ will not be able to receive support from Generation t. Generation $t - 1$ will not receive anything in return for providing for Generation $t - 2$, and then, Generation $t - 1$ will not provide for Generation $t - 2$. This logic eventually reaches the point where Generation 2 will not provide for Generation 1. This backward approach is called "backward induction," which causes the entire chain of cooperation to collapse. Assume that the virgin forest is not developed, but is held in trust and transferred through generations. When the future Generation t does not see any value in a virgin forest and does not purchase the trust from Generation $t - 1$, and instead proceeds to develop the forest, then cooperation cannot begin, even if both Generations 1 and 2 have the same opinion about the value of the forest. In cooperation through ascending reciprocity, if the society lacks stability and the rules will eventually be broken, even the current cooperation will be threatened by backward induction.

Thus, descending and ascending reciprocity have weaknesses that stem from their being based on overlapping intergenerational chain relationships. These indirect reciprocities are ineffective on important issues like climate change and are vulnerable to the breakdown of the chain of cooperation.

[30] Offerman et al. suggest a solution in the direction of encouraging cooperation through direct communication between generations. As an example of such a solution, he mentions the proposal by Kotlikoff et al. (1988) to establish rules as a social contract and pass them on as a kind of asset between generations.

2.5 Direct Intergenerational Reciprocity

2.5.1 The Value of Human Survival After Personal Death

The focus now is to find greater direct reciprocity between generations, to complement, or even replace, intergenerational ethics as duty.

What I take up here as the logic of direct reciprocity between generations is a focus on the value of humanity's continued existence after personal death.

Samuel Scheffler, a philosopher at New York University, points out that people value the continuation of humanity after their personal death (Scheffler, 2013, 2018). He says that the continuation of humanity after one's own death (afterlife) is rather more important than the continuation of an individual's life, because only then does the individual's activities during their lifetime have value. Scheffler illustrates this through a scenario of infertility in which no one dies prematurely, but no children will be born on earth in the future.[31] While this scenario causes problems such as the dysfunction in pay-as-you-go pensions, Schaeffler states that the real problem is the apathy that pervades society.[32] According to Scheffler, the businesses one is involved in have long-term goals that extend beyond one's individual lifetime, and one is interested in what happens to their businesses after their own death.[33] For example, a medical researcher knows that a cure for cancer will not be realized during their lifetime, but continues research in the hope that it will eventually bear fruit.[34] Through artistic activities, one not only finds personal enjoyment, but is also expanding the boundaries of human potential, with the hope that these activities will be carried on after one's death and help to explore the possibilities of humanity.[35] People lose their motivation to engage in these activities when they know that humanity's existence will be cut off.[36,37] According to Scheffler, this concern for life after death is widespread among humans. This interest stems from a fundamental feature of the self-understanding of humans, that they are surrounded by people from the beginning when they are born and learn a lot, and that they leave things to those who come

---

[31] Scheffler (2013, pp. 38–49).

[32] Using the backward-looking induction method, the pension system would collapse immediately upon the revelation of infertility.

[33] Scheffler (2018, p. 44).

[34] Scheffler (2018, p. 49).

[35] Scheffler (2018, p. 51).

[36] Even in research histories away from Scheffler (2013, 2018), concern about afterlife can be found. One example is developmental psychologist Erikson's (1950) concept of generativity. Erikson named the developmental task of midlife as generativity, and stated that the act of teaching and passing on the evidence of one's life to the next generation leads to acceptance of death that comes in the future.

[37] To concern with afterlife is to devote resources to the afterlife, which does not directly serve the survival of the individual. Explaining why one might have such concern must be left for future study. One possible explanation is based on group selection (e.g., Henrich 2004, 2016), which argues that greater concern about afterlife would improve the prospects of survivals of the group in the competition among societies.

after them when they die, thus their activity of passing on the script is a universal activity.[38]

Scheffler points out that through this concern about life after death, reciprocity is established between the present and future generations.[39] For the present generation to the future one, a causal relationship is established in which the behavior of the present generation affects the standard of living of the future generation. For the future generation to the present one, although there is no causal relationship that goes back in time, an evaluative relationship exists, according to which the value of the present generation's life depends on the existence of the future generation.[40]

I believe that Scheffler's view can be modified in two ways to better ground intergenerational ethics. First, as an applicable scope of concern for life after death, Scheffler emphasizes the value of the survival of humanity; but what survives can be projects generally, including communities, businesses, and research and artistic activities. When the value of these projects surviving after death is considered, Scheffler's idea can be used for a broader range of issues. The second is to consider the issue not within the framework of pairs of present and future generation, but within the framework of the relationship between the present generation and multiple future generations, as well as with posthumous values in general. If the concern for life after personal death is universal to human beings, then this concern can be shared among different generations as well, and through this common value, there will be direct reciprocity between generations. Unlike Scheffler, who believes that future generations reward the present generation simply by existing, a particular future generation will reward the present one only by fulfilling its share of the value of the survival of humanity and other projects.

2.5.2 Public Reciprocity—Sharing of Rules Between Different Generations

In Sect. 2.5.1, it was argued that that reciprocity could be found in between generations through the sharing of values that persist even after personal death. However,

---

[38] Based on an interview with Schaeffler by the author (September 13, 2021).

[39] Scheffler (2018, pp. 71–75).

[40] Samuel Scheffler is a well-known philosopher whose theory is akin to deontology. In Scheffler (1985), he discusses the case in which harming one person minimizes similar harm to many others, arguing that consequentialism is inappropriate, because it makes moral evaluations based solely on outcomes and necessitates harm to that one person. The relationship between Scheffler's Kantian orientation toward universal obligations and his concern for life after death, which is the subject of this chapter, is an interesting aspect. Scheffler states that what he raises as concern for life after death is related to the attitudes among people (Scheffler, 2013, p. 16). These attitudes are something people perceive, and he does not attempt to present them strictly as universal claims (p. 17). Thus, while leaving the position of concern for life after death in his own philosophical framework unresolved, Scheffler seems to propose his own novel intergenerational ethics by starting from the point where such attitudes seem reasonable to many including himself. This is a proposal for intergenerational ethics that differs from the conventional one.

in this intergenerational relationship, there is no reciprocal relationship in the sense of transferring goods and other benefits between the present and future generations. Therefore, it is necessary to clarify the logic that this relationship is based on, in order to be considered in the category of reciprocity.

The point that reciprocal behavior can be observed even in situations where there is no expectation of reward has been made widely by economists. Fehr et al. (2002) and Bowles (2004) term reciprocal behavior that is observed in one-time situations where there is no expectation of direct or indirect rewards as "strong reciprocity. It is well known that, in economic experiments, subjects treat cooperative others favorably and punish uncooperative others, even in one-time situations that do not benefit the subjects but rather hurt them.[41] Such behaviors are not based on occasional personal gains, but on general ethics that favor cooperation and discourage non-cooperation. Actions taken due to concern for the general welfare, dignity for people, and justice are also included in the category of reciprocity in Kolm's (2008).[42]

As research that develops the concept of reciprocity in relationships where the rewarding relationship is not directly seen, I focus on a series of studies by Rawls (1971a, 1971b, 1993), and Gotoh's (2009, 2013, 2018) development of these studies, which propose the concept of public reciprocity. The difference principle of *A Theory of Justice* (Rawls, 1971a), which favors the interests of the least advantaged, Rawls notes, expresses one of the concepts of reciprocity.[43] However, since the difference principle favors the least advantaged, it can be problematic that there is no reciprocal relationship between people, as those who receive only receive, and those who give only give. In this regard, Rawls makes the following point.

> Now it is true that given a just system of cooperation as a framework of public rules, and the expectations set up by it, those who, with the prospect of improving their condition, have done what the system announces it will reward are entitled to have their expectations met. In this sense the more fortunate have title to their better situation; their claims are legitimate expectations established by social institutions and the community is obligated to fulfill them. But this sense of desert is that of entitlement. It presupposes the existence of an ongoing cooperative scheme and is irrelevant to the question whether this scheme itself is to be designed in accordance with the difference principle or some other criterion. (Rawls, 1971a, pp. 88–89)

According to Rawls, the more fortunate do not receive goods or other returns from the least advantaged. Nevertheless, the difference principle is shared among the members of society as a reasonable framework for voluntary cooperation. Among

[41] The case of the ultimatum game, first experimentally examined by Werner Güth and his colleagues, is well-known (Güth et al., 1982). In this game, after the first player (the first mover) proposes a way to distribute the gains, the next player (the second mover) has no room to propose again, but can only decide whether to accept or reject the first player's proposal. If the second player rejects, both the first and second players' shares shall be assumed to be zero. It is observed that the lower the amount proposed by the first player, the more the second player rejects the proposal, even though accepting the proposal is the optimal response for the second player who is offered a positive allocation.

[42] Kolm (2008, p. 43).

[43] Rawls (1971a, p. 88).

those who share this principle, being innately fortunate is a reason to relocate goods to those who are less fortunate, as the fortunate have already received compensation.

Based on this reciprocity of Rawls, Gotoh presents the concept of public reciprocity. Gotoh (2009) cites the following sentence Rawls's work as a key statement guiding the concept of public reciprocity.

> Persons are reasonable in one basic aspect when, among equals say, they are ready to propose principles and standards as fair terms of cooperation and to abide by them willingly, give the assurance that others will likewise do so. (Rawls, 1993, p. 49)

Rawls lists "the assurance that others will likewise do so" as a necessary condition for "(being) ready to propose principles and standards as fair terms of cooperation and to abide by them willingly." According to Gotoh's interpretation of Rawls, such an assurance is necessary because even if one is convinced of the rightness of an act, if one cannot expect others to do likewise, then it will be difficult for one to act as well. Only when there is assurance that others will also accept the principle as a common rule, will they voluntarily comply with the principle as a fair condition for collaboration. This mutual relationship based on shared rules is Gotoh's interpretation of public reciprocity. If all individuals accept and respect a certain rule, and reciprocity is realized under that rule, then the rule is considered reciprocal when it is enacted under procedural reciprocity and represents reciprocity in itself.[44]

When the rule of the difference principle is shared among all members of a society, reciprocity is realized under this principle, and the rule is said to represent reciprocity. While the difference principle represents reciprocity, it is also established under the procedural reciprocity of compliance "given the assurance that others will likewise do so." Based on the shared rule of the difference principle and with the veil of ignorance lifted, each member recognizes the transfer of goods to the least advantaged, as reciprocal, even after learning that they are now in a more advantageous position.[45]

The relevance of reading the reciprocity of Rawls as public reciprocity is supported by his article "Justice as Reciprocity", in which he discusses his notion of reciprocity (Rawls 1971b). In this paper, Rawls emphasizes that reciprocity is between people who mutually recognize each other as having similar abilities and interests[46] and that it consists of establishing common rules among them and participating in joint activities.[47] Examining the notion of reciprocity, Christie Hartley distinguishes between reciprocity through mutual benefit and reciprocity through mutual respect for the purpose of social cooperation, placing Rawls' reciprocity within the latter (Hartley, 2014). Hartley argues that in reciprocity by mutual respect, equal people enter into a joint relationship with the shared goal of social cooperation.[48]

---

[44] Gotoh (2009, p. 154).

[45] The question may be whether the condition "give the assurance that others will likewise do so" is satisfied after the lift of veil of ignorance. This book discusses this point as Theorem 3.1 in Chap. 3 (Sect. 3.3.3), where the anticipation of betrayal by subsequent generations prevents intergenerational cooperation.

[46] Rawls (1971b, pp. 212–213).

[47] Rawls (1971b, p. 208).

[48] Hartley (2014, pp. 423–426).

It is reciprocity in this sense of public reciprocity, which is at work in the intergenerational relationship of shared concern for life after death, as presented in this chapter, in light of Scheffler's argument. The rule of fulfilling one's duty for the survival of humankind and other projects is only meaningful when it is shared among generations, and not when it is a one-sided duty taken on by a generation in isolation. In Sect. 2.2.3, it is pointed out that the duty of the present generation to the future ones are established though the common understandings within present generation. However, the duty established through this line of reasoning is established by the isolated present generation, and its implementation is left to the state of mind of this present generation, which is unreliable. The intergenerational ethics reestablished here under public reciprocity has a firmer foundation, based on shared rules among different generations. If a rule to fulfill their share of duties for values that survive after their personal death exists, and all generations accept and respect the rule, then this is good for all generations. Each generation will be willing to do its part only when it can expect all other generations to also do their part for the values that will endure after their death. In other words, by sharing the rule of caring for the survival of humanity and other projects among different generations, beginning from the recognition of future generations as free and equal persons like themselves, a joint project is established between generations. The joint project that emerges here is a joint activity that is passed on from generation to generation, in which the projects of humanity, companies, academia and others, live, work, and carve out history. Here, a kind of community is established through the sharing of objectives among generations.

How can rules be shared with future generations yet to be born? This rule-sharing becomes possible through mutual respect (in the term of Hartley), which means treating those yet to be born as persons like ourselves. As discussed in Sect. 2.2.3, in order to solve the non-identity problem, Gotoh (2018) introduces the concept of the soul/integrated personality that is established by the present generation. The assumption that this soul/integrated personality will do its share for the survival of humanity and other projects is supported by the assumption that the present generation regards people in the future as people like themselves. Where this assumption works, intergenerational cooperation through public reciprocity is set in motion.

2.5.3 Developing a Multi-generation Model Based on Public Reciprocity—An Example of the Exhaustible Natural Resources Model

Through Sect. 2.5.2, I have proposed a new philosophical interpretation: that reciprocity is possible through the sharing of rules between different generations. In this section, I clarify specifically what intergenerational relations look like when people act on the basis of this interpretation. To this end, I present the intergenerational relationship based on public reciprocity as an economic multi-generational model.

By formulating it as a mathematical model, it is possible to develop its implications, which are not apparent in Scheffler's and Rawls's philosophical considerations. Specifically, it will clarify the strategic relationship between generations that reciprocity brings about.

First, consider the case of two generations. The decision for each generation is left to the social planner. Generation 1 consumes an exhaustible natural resource and leaves the remaining resource to Generation 2, which divides this resource into two parts: one part is consumed, and the other is left untouched. The lower the level of the resource stock, the more threatened the survival of humankind is assumed to be. An example of such a natural resource is the greenhouse gas emission allowance. As the allowance declines, the threat of human extinction increases. What is important is that Generations 1 and 2 share the value of human survival and are prepared to do their share for the sake of survival, based on their respective historical positions.

The works of John Hartwick and Robert Solow—positioned as the classic studies of intergenerational allocation of exhaustible natural resources—examine the conditions that lead to the maximization of the discounted sum of the consumption stream of generations, in settings where resources are used as production goods (Hartwick, 1977; Solow, 1986). According to Solow's research, the condition is that the capital stock, which is the combination of natural resources and man-made capital, maintains a constant level throughout the generations. Consumption is the level corresponding to the interest on the capital stock, which is regarded as inherited property. The primary difference between these previous studies and the exhaustible natural resource model described in this section is that while the social welfare function of total consumption is given in the previous studies, no such function is given in the model, and the intergenerational allocation of consumption is realized through the decentralized maximization of each generation. In light of the social planner's framework as seen in Eq. 1.1 in Chap. 1 (Sect. 1.2), in the exhaustible natural resources model, the social planner considers their own consumption and the probability of human survival, leaving Generation 2's utility out of consideration.[49] In the following, $c_t, \omega_t R_t$ are consumption by Generation t, the probability of human survival from the perspective of Generation t, and the stock of exhaustible natural resources at the end of Generation t.

$$u_1 = u_1(c_1, \omega_1) = (1-\alpha)\log c_1 + \alpha \log \omega_1, \quad 0 \leq \alpha \leq 1. \tag{2.2}$$

$$u_2 = u_2(c_2, \omega_2) = (1-\alpha)\log c_2 + \alpha \log \omega_2. \tag{2.3}$$

$$\omega_1 = P_1 P_2, \quad \omega_2 = P_2. \tag{2.4}$$

$$R_1 = R_0 - c_1, \quad R_2 = R_1 - c_2, \quad R_2 \geq 0. \tag{2.5}$$

[49] The reason why Generation 1 shall leave the utility of Generation 2 out of consideration is that to consider the utility of Generation 2 is to introduce an altruistic motive, and to introduce altruism would mean a reversion to intergenerational ethics as duty, whose difficulties have been discussed.

$$P_1 = pR_1, \quad P_2 = pR_2, \quad 0 < p < 1/R_0. \tag{2.6}$$

where Eqs. 2.2 and 2.3 are the utility functions for Generations 1 and 2, and each generation maximizes its utility under the constraint Eq. 2.5. The true value of the second term on the right side of Eqs. 2.2 and 2.3 (ω_t) is the probability of human survival determined by the resource stock at the end of each generation.[50] From the perspective of Generation 1, there are two opportunities to test whether humans can survive: at the end of Generation 1 and; at the end of Generation 2. The multiplication of the two probabilities ($P_1 P_2 = \omega_1$) is assumed to be a true value. α is the degree of preference for human survival in Generations 1 and 2, that is, the degree of interest in the future. The magnitude of α is an interesting question how this is determined, but in this section α is taken as a given. That is, each generation appears in history with a certain degree of interest in the future, and the degree of interest is constant. For the sake of simplicity, this section also takes into account that the preference for the survival of humanity is a foundational one, and α is assumed to be the same throughout the generations.[51] Equation 2.5 is the resource constraint. The endowment given to Generation t (R_{t-1}; R_0 is the initial endowment) minus the consumption of Generation t is R_t. Equation 2.6 gives P_t the probability of human survival at the end of Generation t, which is a linear increasing function of R_t. p is a constant that gives the probability of human survival at R_t. Because of the Eq. 2.6, $p < 1/R_0$, $pR_0 < 1$, that is, even if Generation 1 does not consume at all, the probability of human survival is less than 1. In this sense, people are in a harsh situation. The extinction of the human race is assumed to occur immediately after the death of Generation t, although Generation t itself does not experience extinction.[52]

---

[50] Equations (2.2) and (2.3) assume that utility decreases as a logarithmic function with decreasing probability of human survival. A straightforward interpretation of this assumption is to interpret the marginal rate of substitution of probability (for consumption) as increasing as the probability of human survival decreases, as if probability were a good. However, under the expected utility framework, (expected utility from human survival) = (survival probability) * (utility of survival), and if the utility of survival is a constant, expected utility is a linear function of the survival probability. In this setting, it is possible to construct a model in which the marginal cost of consumption (in terms of expected utility of human survival) increases as the probability of human survival decreases, if Eq. 2.6, a liner function between natural resources and the probability of human survival, is revised to be $P_t = P(R_t)$, $P\prime > 0$, $P'' < 0$. Here, the probability of human extinction increases at an accelerating rate as natural resources. In this revised model, each generation behaves in the same way as in Eqs. 2.2–2.6.

[51] In Chap. 3, a setting in which the degree of interest in the future differs from generation to generation is discussed. While the degree of interest in the future of the subsequent generation is endogenized by the influence from the behavior of the preceding generation, that of the preceding generation is left as an exogenous variable. In Chap. 4, the relationship between the degree of interest in the future of the preceding generation and the subjects' age and other attributes are examined. The possibility that the degree of interest in the future of the subjects is determined endogenously through deliberations among the subjects is discussed.

[52] In this setting, each generation makes its decision in a decentralized manner. As noted in Note 24 in this chapter, an incentive problem arises between Generations 1 and 2. Here, the incentive problem arises between generations, rather than individuals within the same generation as noted

From Eqs. 2.2–2.6, the subgame perfect equilibrium is obtained. By the time the final amount of natural resources is realized by Generation 2, Generation 1 has already passed away. However, according to the choice c_1 by Generation 1, it can calculate which consumption Generation 2 will choose in c_2. Generation 1 needs to guess the utility function of Generation 2, but since it has the belief that the utility function is the same as its own, the solution can be obtained in the same way as for the complete information. Here, Generation 1 shares the rule of caring for the future with Generation 2, which has not yet been born.

Deriving the best response of Generation 2, assuming c_1 of Generation 1 is given.

$$R_2 = \alpha(R_0 - c_1) = \alpha R_1. \tag{2.7}$$

Generation 1 remains R_1 as the resource for Generation 2, which Generation 2 uses and leaves αR_1 as R_2.

Consumption of Generations 1 and 2 in equilibrium (c_1^*, c_2^*) and the last remaining natural resource (R_2^*) are as follows.

$$c_1^* = \left(\frac{1-\alpha}{\alpha+1}\right) R_0. \tag{2.8}$$

$$c_2^* = \left[\frac{2\alpha(1-\alpha)}{\alpha+1}\right] R_0. \tag{2.9}$$

$$R_2^* = \left(\frac{2\alpha^2}{\alpha+1}\right) R_0. \tag{2.10}$$

From Eqs. 2.8 and 2.9, when $0 \le \alpha < \frac{1}{2}$, $c_1^* > c_2^*$.[53] When $\alpha = \frac{1}{2}$, $c_1^* = c_2^*$. When $\frac{1}{2} < \alpha < 1$, $c_1^* < c_2^*$, When $\alpha = 1$, $c_1^* = c_2^* = 0$. Even if Generations 1 and 2 have the same level of concern for life after death (α), depending on the order in which they appear in history, the preceding generation may consume more, or vice versa. When there is little concern for human survival, Generation 1 consumes more than Generation 2; conversely, when there is a high concern for human survival, Generation 2 consumes more than Generation 1.

The two-generation model can be extended to an n-generation model. In this case, the utility functions of Generations 1, 2, and t are represented by Eqs. 2.11, 2.12, and 2.13. The consumption of Generations 1, 2, and t in equilibrium are given by Eqs. 2.14, 2.15, and 2.16.

$$u_1 = (1-\alpha)\log c_1 + \alpha \log \omega_1, \quad \omega_1 = pR_1 \ldots pR_n = p^n \prod_{i=1}^{n} R_i. \tag{2.11}$$

---

in Sect. 2.3.2. Chapter 3 (Sect. 3.3.3) argues that this intergenerational incentive problem makes intergenerational cooperation inadequate, which is discussed in detail.

[53] When $\alpha = 0$, generation 1 consumes all of R_0 and humanity perishes after Generation 1.

$$u_2 = (1-\alpha)\log c_2 + \alpha \log \omega_2, \quad \omega_2 = pR_2 \ldots pR_n = p^{n-1}\prod_{i=2}^{n} R_i. \tag{2.12}$$

$$u_t = (1-\alpha)\log c_t + \alpha \log \omega_t, \quad \omega_t = pR_t \ldots pR_n = p^{n-t+1}\prod_{i=t}^{n} R_i. \tag{2.13}$$

$$c_1^{**} = \left[\frac{1-\alpha}{\alpha(n-1)+1}\right] R_0. \tag{2.14}$$

$$c_2^{**} = \left[\frac{\alpha(1-\alpha)n}{\{\alpha(n-2)+1\}\{\alpha(n-1)+1\}}\right] R_0. \tag{2.15}$$

$$c_t^{**} = \left[\frac{\alpha^{t-1}(1-\alpha)\prod_{i=2}^{t}(n-i+2)}{\prod_{i=1}^{t}\{\alpha(n-i)+1\}}\right] R_0, \quad 2 \le \mathrm{t} \le \mathrm{n}. \tag{2.16}$$

From Eqs. 2.14 and 2.15, as in the case of the two-generation model, when $0 \le \alpha < \frac{1}{2}$, $c_1^{**} > c_2^{**}$, When $\alpha = \frac{1}{2}$, $c_1^{**} = c_2^{**}$. When $\frac{1}{2} < \alpha < 1$, $c_1^{**} < c_2^{**}$. When $\alpha = 1$, $c_1^* = c_2^* = 0$. A similar relationship exists between c_{t-1}^{**} and $c_t^{**}(2 \le t \le n)$.[54] Interestingly, from Eq. 2.16, consumption is a decreasing function of the number of Generations n. When n $\rightarrow \infty$, the consumption of Generation 1 asymptotically approaches zero. The probability of human extinction increases as the chain of generations grows. Since $\omega_1 = p^n\prod_{i=1}^{n} R_i$, Generation 1 is concerned about whether the human race will become extinct by the end of Generation n, and so, Generation 1 cuts back its own consumption. As in Solow's study, the solution approaches a consumption path that keeps the capital stock constant (in the sense of not touching natural resources).

Importantly, the exhaustible natural resource model is spared the drawbacks of descending and ascending reciprocity noted in Sect. 2.4.2. First, each generation, even if far apart, is related by their common interest in the survival of humanity. This works even in a pure intergenerational problem. That is, from Eq. 2.11, Generation 1 makes the current consumption decision even taking into account the choices of R_n by the distant generation n. The second advantage is that it does not depend on a chain of cooperation from the past. The value of natural resources increases when the prospects for the community's survival shift from optimism to pessimism. Equation 2.6 assumed a harsh situation in which the probability of human survival is less than 1. If the probability of human survival is 1, then regardless of the level of R_n, Generation 1 will put all of its resources into consumption. When it is recognized that no matter the level of greenhouse gas emissions, they do not pose a threat to human survival (even if $R_n = 0$, $\omega_1 = 1$), Generation 1 will increase consumption to the limit. By the same token, from the flip side, Generation 1 will conserve natural resources when it turns from optimism to pessimism. From the moment humanity

[54] Between the consumption of Generation t − 1 and that of Generation t, $\frac{\alpha(n-t+2)}{\alpha(n-t)+1} c_{t-1}^{**} = c_t^{**}$. When $0 \le \alpha < \frac{1}{2}$, $c_{t-1}^{**} > c_t^{**}$. When $\alpha = \frac{1}{2}$, $c_{t-1}^{**} = c_t^{**}$. When $\frac{1}{2} < \alpha < 1$, $c_{t-1}^{**} < c_t^{**}$. When $\alpha = 1$, $c_{t-1}^{*} = c_t^{*} = 0$.

learns the harsh truth that the warming effect exists, it sees the value in reducing gas emissions, and whether the previous generations were reducing emissions or not does not matter.

Ascending reciprocity has a third disadvantage: the dependence of current cooperation on future chains of cooperation. In the exhaustible natural resource model, current cooperation is not necessarily dependent on future chains of cooperation and is resilient to changes in the given conditions (unless one expects that some future Generation t will certainly try to erase human existence) even if one expects future Generation t to consume excessively for some reason, the entire chain cooperation will not collapse. In other words, regardless of Generation t's behavior, the viability of humanity from Generation 1 to the end of the t − 1, ($\prod_{i=1}^{t-1} P_i = p^{t-1}\prod_{i=1}^{t-1} R_i$), determined by the behavior of Generation 1 to t − 1, remains the concern of Generation 1.

While descending and ascending reciprocity remain significant as the logic behind education for children, and in pay-as-you-go pensions, it is worth emphasizing the significance of the fact that the possibility of intergenerational cooperation based on public reciprocity has been opened here. Intergenerational cooperation based on public reciprocity can work on important intergenerational issues such as climate change, and is more robust as a logic to encourage cooperation, because it does not rely on a chain of cooperation. More importantly, through intergenerational sharing of rules, intergenerational cooperation by public reciprocity overcomes the implementation weaknesses of intergenerational ethics by unilateral duty. By grounding intergenerational ethics as bilateral between different generations on the basis of reciprocity, intergenerational relations are now transformed into cooperative relationships. Reciprocal cooperation, rather than unilateral duty, can ensure that dealing with intergenerational problems is more stable and freer from the whims of the present generation.

2.5.4 Comparison with Barro (1974)

It is useful to clarify the position of the model that has been developed as a result of intergenerational cooperation through public reciprocity by contrasting it with Barro's (1974), whose examination of intergenerational issues through altruistic bequest motives.

To begin, we consider Table 2.1 by Kolm regarding the comparison between reciprocity and altruism (pure gift-giving). Both share the characteristics of voluntariness and other-oriented motivation. However, there is difference in that reciprocity is a two-way transfer, whereas altruism is an independent and one-way transfer. In intergenerational relationships based on public reciprocity, each generation enters into a cooperative relationship on the condition of sharing rules. Altruism, however, is unconditional. When motivated by altruism, the bequest is handed over regardless of what the next generation does.

Thus, there is a clear difference between cooperation through public reciprocity and the bequest motive. Interestingly, Barro's multi-generational model has a different setting than pure altruism, and as a result, commonalities between cooperation through public reciprocity and Barro (1974) are apparent.

In Barro's study, the following equation is the utility function for Generation 1

$$U_1 = U_1\left(c_1^y, c_1^o, U_2^*\right). \quad (2.17)$$

Here, the utility of Generation 1 is defined as the consumption at young and old ages (c_1^y, c_1^o) and the utility of Generation 2 (U_2^*). The utility of Generation 2 is formulated as follows

$$U_2^* = f_2^*\left[(1-r)A_1^o - B, w, r\right]. \quad (2.18)$$

where, A_1^o is the asset that Generation 1 has in its old age, and B is the bond issued by the government, w is the marginal productivity of labor, and r is the marginal productivity of capital. $(1-r)A_1^o - B$ is the net bequest of Generation 1 and the initial endowment to Generation 2.

From Eqs. 2.17 and 2.18, the utility function for Generation 1 can be rewritten as

$$U_1 = f_1\left[(1-r)A_1^o - B; c_1^y, A_1^y + A_0^o, w, r\right]. \quad (2.19)$$

where A_1^y is asset of Generation 1 when it is young. Generation 1 has a bequest motive (it has motivation of leaving net positive bequest). When c_1^y, $A_1^y + A_0^o$, w, r is given, the question for Generation 1 is how to adjust the amount of net bequest, under the constraint of non-negative A_1^o. From this point on, Barro develops the well-known consideration (neutrality proposition) that marginal change of B change resalts in the change of A_1^o, keeping $(1-r)A_1^o - B$ constant, when the nonnegativity constraint of A_1^o is not in effect (nonbinding).

It is important to note that in the utility of Generation 2, Barro incorporates the utility of Generation 3 and beyond as an explanatory variable. Generations 1 and 2 share an interest in the utility of Generation 3 and beyond. That is, based on Eq. 2.17, the utility function for Generation t is, $U_t = V_t + \gamma U_{t+1}$; then, the utility function of Generation 1 can be written as

$$U_1 = \sum_{j=1}^{T-1} \gamma^{j-1} V_j + \gamma^{T-1} U_T. \quad (2.20)$$

where, V_j is Generation j's utility from its own consumption, and γ is the degree of altruism of Generation j toward its children. When $\lim_{T\to\infty} \gamma^{T-1} U_T = 0$ holds, the utility of Generation 1 is an infinitely weighted sum of the utilities of the present and future generations' consumption.

$$U_1 = \sum_{j=1}^{+\infty} \gamma^{j-1} V_j = V_1 + \gamma V_2 + \sum_{j=3}^{+\infty} \gamma^{j-1} V_j. \qquad (2.21)$$

The utility of Generation 2 is written as $U_2 = V_2 + \sum_{j=3}^{+\infty} \gamma^{j-2} V_j$. Therefore, the increase or decrease of the infinite weighted sum of utilities due to consumption in Generation 3 and beyond is a common concern of Generations 1 and 2. This means that there is a shared interest among the generations in the weighted sum of the utilities of the generations after them. This is similar to the shared concern for the survival of the human race among the different generations in the exhaustible natural resources model. It is thus possible to conclude that the generations in Barro's study have a reciprocal relationship.

It should be noted, however, that this similarity stems from the fact that Barro's model incorporates a different setting than that of a pure gift-giving (altruism). It can be said that Barro's model incorporates a structure similar to that of public reciprocity in the design of the bequest motive. In Barro's model, the utility of Generation 2 includes that of Generation 3, and the utility of Generation 3 includes that of Generation 4. This structure implies that Generation 1 knows that Generation 2 has an altruistic motive toward Generation 3 at the same time that Generation 1 has an altruistic motive toward Generation 2. The different generations *share the rule of altruistic concern for the next generation*. The similarities between the exhaustible natural resources model and Barro's model are now clear. However, this does not, of course, undermine the significance of what was revealed in the exhaustible natural resources model. Rather, it highlights the fact that Barro's model deviates from pure altruism. According to Kolm (2006b), altruism is unconditional. Altruists deliver bequests regardless of what the next generation does. However, Barro's model does not meet this definition of altruism.

Thus, while Barro's model contains public reciprocity implicitly, it is important to point out that the exhaustible natural resource model differs from Barro's in important ways. First, Barro does not explicitly address intergenerational reciprocity (the common interest that Generations 1 and 2 have in the utility of Generations 3 and beyond). The interrelationship between generations through reciprocity is not the focus of consideration and does not have sufficient structure to elucidate intergenerational cooperation. Contrastingly, the exhaustible natural resource model has a framework to explicitly consider intergenerational reciprocity. For example, Eqs. 2.8 and 2.9 show that when interest in the future is weak, preceding generations consume more and subsequent generations are forced to curtail consumption. The second difference is that Barro's bequest motive takes into account the *utility* of the child (i.e., the subjectivity of others from the perspective of the preceding generation), whereas the concern for the survival of the human race, consider the certainty of survival. Third, the bequest motive is directed to the well-being of the blood children, whereas the interest in life after death is directed to the continuation of the project of humanity. The interest in life after death is an open interest that can be extended to the general public who can inherit the projects even in the absence of children.

2.6 Conclusions and Remaining Issues

Building on previous research, this chapter discusses the foundation of intergenerational ethics within the framework of duty and reciprocity. The philosophical interpretations were examined from an economic perspective and their implications were developed. The first task was to lay the groundwork for intergenerational ethics through the non-identity problem. Through this examination, it has been shown that it is a common understanding within the present generation that supports the duties required by intergenerational ethics. However, intergenerational ethics as unilateral duty from the present to future generations has the problem of not guaranteeing its realization. Humans do not necessarily seek to realize their own moral ideals (*akrasia*). Several methodologies address this difficulty, and this chapter discusses how to rebuild the foundation of intergenerational ethics by finding reciprocity between generations. Although it is noted that chains of cooperation between overlapping generations (indirect reciprocity) can be widely found among generations, particular attention is paid to an approach that finds direct reciprocity between generations. According to Scheffler, humans have an interest in the survival of the human race after their personal death. Taking this suggestion as a starting point, it is understood that the survival of humanity, after one's own death is a value that can be shared among different generations. In this chapter, the concept of public reciprocity is developed, and it is shown that a reciprocal relationship can be established between different generations, based on the shared rule of caring for the survival of humankind. By recognizing future generations as human beings similar to oneself, and by sharing the rule of taking the survival of humankind into consideration, a joint project can be established between generations. Here, this is a joint activity that is passed down from generation to generation, in which human beings, companies, academic institutions, and other businesses engage in activities and carve out history. Intergenerational ethics is usually constructed as the unilateral duty of the present generation because it concerns future generations that do not yet exist. However, under public reciprocity, the present and future generations enter into a bidirectional relationship, in which they behave in accordance with common rules.

Two issues remain to be addressed. First, this chapter focuses on a broad discussion of the duty and reciprocity that underlie intergenerational ethics, and does not delve into the appropriateness of the various duties that can be agreed upon among the present generation, as exemplified in Sect. 2.3.1. The organization and evaluation of the various duties needs to be addressed separately. Second, this chapter has developed the implications of the philosophical interpretation of the concern for life after death using economic methods, but so far has only demonstrated its superior significance in comparison with indirect reciprocity. Through its further development, it is necessary to consider, in detail, the difficulties and their solutions in making intergenerational ethics a reality. This second issue will be dealt with intensively in Chap. 3.

References

Barro, R. J. (1974). Are government bonds net wealth? *Journal of Political Economy, 82*(6), 1095–1117.

Barry, B. (1996). Circumstances of justice and future generations. In R.I. Sikora & B. Barry (Eds.), *Obligations to future generations* (pp. 204–248). White Horse Press

Bentham, J. (1789). *An introduction to the principles of morals and legislation.* In J. Bennett (Ed.), https://www.earlymoderntexts.com/assets/pdfs/bentham1780.pdf. Last accessed, January 24, 2021.

Bowles, S. (2004). *Microeconomics.* Russell Sage Foundation.

Brandt, R. B. (1964). The concepts of obligation and duty. *Mind, New Series, 73*(291), 374–393.

Cigno, A. (1993). Intergenerational transfer without altruism. *European Journal of Political Economy, 9*(4), 505–518.

Cigno, A. (2006). *The political economy of intergenerational cooperation.* CESifo Working Paper No. 1632.

Erikson, E. H. (1950). *Childhood and society.* Norton.

Fehr, E., Fischbacher, U., & Gächter, S. (2002). Strong reciprocity, human cooperation, and the enforcement of social norms. *Human Nature, 13*(1), 1–25.

Gardiner, S. (2009). A contract on future generations? In A. Gosseries & L. H. Meyer (Eds.), *Intergenerational justice* (pp. 77–118). Oxford University Press.

Gauthier, D. (1986). *Morals by agreement.* Oxford University Press.

Gosseries, A. (2009). Three models of intergenerational reciprocity. In A. Gosseries & L. H. Meyer (Eds.), *Intergenerational justice* (pp. 119–146). Oxford University Press.

Gotoh, R. (2009). Justice and public reciprocity. In R. Gotoh & P. Doumonchel (Eds.), *Against injustice, the new economics of Amartya Sen* (pp. 140–160). Cambridge University Press.

Gotoh, R. (2013). 'Justice as reciprocity' reexamined in the context of catastrophe. *Ritsumeikan Journal of Language and Culture, 24*(4), 33–42.

Gotoh, R. (2018). The non-identity problem and the philosophical foundation of intergenerational equity. In *The 14th social choice and welfare conference.*

Güth, W., Schmittberger, R., & Schwarze, B. (1982). An experimental analysis of ultimatum bargaining. *Journal of Economic Behavior and Organization, 3*(4), 367–388.

Hammond, P. J. (1975). Charity: Altruism or cooperative egoism? In E. S. Phelps (Ed.), *Altruism, morality, and economic theory* (Part 2, pp. 115–131). Russell Sage Foundation.

Hare, R. M. (1963). *Freedom and reason.* Oxford Scholarship Online. https://oxford.universitypress scholarship.com/view/10.1093/019881092X.001.0001/acprof-9780198810926. Last accessed January 11, 2021.

Harsanyi, J. (1955). Cardinal welfare, individualistic ethics, and interpersonal comparisons of utility. *Journal of Political Economy, 63*(4), 309–321.

Hartley, C. (2014). Two conceptions of justice as reciprocity. *Social Theory and Practice, 40*(3), 409–432.

Hartwick, J. (1977). Intergenerational equity and the investing of rents from exhaustible resources. *American Economic Review, 67*(5), 972–974.

Heath, J. (1997). Intergenerational cooperation and distributive justice. *Canadian Journal of Philosophy, 27*(3), 361–376.

Heath, J. (2013). The structure of intergenerational cooperation. *Philosophy and Public Affairs, 41*(1), 31–66.

Henrich, J. (2004). Cultural group selection, coevolutionary processes and large-scale cooperation. *Journal of Economic Behavior and Organization, 53*(1), 3–35.

Henrich, J. (2016). *The secret of our success: How culture is driving human evolution, domesticating our species, and making us smarter.* Princeton University Press.

Heyd, D. (2009a). The intractability of the nonidentity problem. In M. A. Roberts & D. T. Wasserman (Eds.), *Harming future people, ethics, genetics and the nonidentity problem* (pp. 3–25). Springer.

Heyd, D. (2009b). A value or an obligation? Rawls on justice to future generations. In A. Gosseries & L. H. Meyer (Eds.), *Intergenerational justice* (pp. 167–188). Oxford University Press.
Hume, D. (1739–40). *A treatise of human nature*. Center for Security Studies. https://ethz.ch/content/specialinterest/gess/cis/center-for-securities-studies/en/services/digital-library/publications/publication.html/125487. Last accessed July 19, 2020.
Kavka, G. (1982). The paradox of future individuals. *Philosophy and Public Affairs, 11*(2), 93–112.
Kolm, S. C. (2006a). Introduction to the economics of giving, altruism and reciprocity. In S. C. Kolm & J. M. Ythier (Eds.), *Handbook of the economics of giving, altruism and reciprocity, volume 1: Foundations*. North-Holland.
Kolm, S. C. (2006b). Reciprocity: Its scope, rationales, and consequences. In S. C. Kolm & J. M. Ythier (Eds.), *Handbook of the economics of giving, altruism and reciprocity, volume 1: Foundations*. North-Holland.
Kolm, S. C. (2008). *Reciprocity: An economics of social relations*. Cambridge University Press.
Kotlikoff, L. J., Persson, T., & Svensson, L. E. (1988). Social contracts as assets: A possible solution to the time-inconsistency problem. *American Economic Review, 78*(4), 662–677.
Kumar, R. (2009). Wronging future people: A contractualist proposal. In A. Gosseries & L. H. Meyer (Eds.), *Intergenerational justice* (pp. 251–272). Oxford University Press.
Kuroda, W. (1992). *Actions and norms*. Keiso-Shobo. (in Japanese)
Mauss, M. (1925, 1967). The gift: Forms and functions of exchange in archaic societies (I. Cunnison, Trans.). http://web.mit.edu/allanmc/www/mauss1.pdf. Last accessed on October 14, 2023.
Meyer, L. H. (2003). Past and future: The case for a threshold notion of harm. In L. H. Meyer, S.L. Paulson, & T. W. Pogge (Eds.), *Rights, culture, and the law, themes from the legal and political philosophy of Joseph Raz* (pp. 143–160). Oxford University Press, Oxford.
Narveson, J. (1967). Utilitarianism and new generations. *Mind, 76*(301), 62–72.
Offerman, T., Potters, J., & Verbon, H. (2001). Cooperation in an overlapping generations experiment. *Games and Economic Behavior, 36*(2), 264–275.
Oxford Leaner's Dictionaries. (2019). Available from: https://www.oxfordlearnersdictionaries.com/. Last accessed December 24, 2019.
Parfit, D. (1984). *Reasons and people*. Oxford University Press.
Rawls, J. (1971a, 1999). *A theory of justice* (Revised). Harvard University Press.
Rawls, J. (1971b, 1999). Justice as reciprocity. In S. Freeman (Ed.), *Collected papers: John Rawls* (pp. 190–224). Harvard University Press.
Rawls, J. (1993). *Political liberalism*. Columbia University Press.
Roberts, M. A. (2003). Is the person-affecting intuition paradoxical? *Theory and Decision, 55*(1), 1–44.
Roberts, M. A. (2019). *"The nonidentity problem," The Stanford Encyclopedia of philosophy archive* (Summer). In E. N. Zalta (Ed.). Retrieved from, https://plato.stanford.edu/archives/sum2019/entries/nonidentity-problem/. Last accessed June 17, 2020.
Saijo, T. (2020a). Future design: An introduction. In *Future design: Incorporating preferences of future generations for sustainability*. Springer.
Saijo, T. (2020b). Future design: Bequeathing sustainable natural environments and sustainable societies to future generations. *Sustainability, 12*(16), 1–21.
Samuelson, P. (1958). An exact consumption: A loan model of interest with or without the social contrivance of money. *Journal of Political Economy, 66*(6), 467–482.
Scheffler, S. (1985). Agent-centered restrictions, rationality, and the virtues. *Mind, 94*(375), 409–419.
Scheffler, S. (2013). *Death and the afterlife*. Oxford University Press.
Scheffler, S. (2018). *Why worry about future generations?* Oxford University Press.
Sen, A. K. (1977). Rational fools: A critique of the behavioral foundation of economic theory. *Philosophy and Public Affairs, 6*(4), 317–344.
Sen, A. K. (2018). Our obligation to future generations. In S. Rangan (Ed.), *Capitalism beyond mutuality? Perspectives integrating philosophy and social science* (pp. 131–138). Oxford University Press.

Sikora, R. I. (1996). Is it wrong to prevent the existence of future generations? In R. I. Sikora & B. Barry (Eds.), *Obligations to future generations* (pp. 112–166). White Horse Press.
Slovic, P. (2010). If I look at the mass I will never act: Psychic numbing and genocide. In S. Roeser (Ed.), *Emotions and risky technologies* (pp. 37–59). Springer.
Solow, R. M. (1986). On the intergenerational allocation of natural resources. *Scandinavian Journal of Economics, 88*(1), 141–149.
Suzumura, K., & Tadenuma, K. (2007). Normative approaches to the issues of global warning: Responsibility and compensation. In J. Roemer & K. Suzumura (Eds.), *Intergenerational equity and sustainability* (pp. 320–336). Palgrave MacMillan.
Usami, M. (2006). The moral basis of consideration for future generations: Sustainability, rights, and fairness. In K. Suzumura (Ed.), *The logic and ethics of intergenerational equity* (pp. 255–282). Toyo-Keizai. (in Japanese)
Woodward, J. (1986). The non-identity problem. *Ethics, 96*(4), 804–831.

Chapter 3
Developing Intergenerational Cooperation Based on Public Reciprocity: Intergenerational Cooperation Through the Kantian Categorical Imperative

Abstract This chapter points out that intergenerational cooperation is possible, but not always sufficient, under public reciprocity. The focus of interest in this chapter and the Chap. 4 is to find methodologies to encourage further cooperation. The methodologies discussed in this chapter are fund establishment (constitutionalization), the Kantian categorical imperative, and intergenerational negotiation (discussed in Appendix 3.1). An experiment shows that the preceding generation morally inspires subsequent generations through its behavior (endogenization of preferences of subsequent generations). When there is moral inspiration, if the preceding generation wishes the cooperation of the subsequent generations, it will in fact cooperate itself. This logic is interpreted by the Kantian categorical imperative. Although the Kantian categorical imperative has excellent properties, its drawback is that it fixes cooperation in a low state throughout the generation when the preceding generation has only a low interest in cooperation.

3.1 Introduction

Chapter 2 (Sect. 2.5) discussed the concern for life after death as an opportunity to introduce reciprocity between generations. For example, when climate change threatens the survival of humankind, and when this survival is a value (objective) that can be shared among different generations, it is argued that reciprocity in terms of public reciprocity can be established between generations through the shared rule of fulfilling one's duty for the survival of humankind.

This chapter deepens the discussion of the multi-generational model under this public reciprocity and identifies where the possibilities and difficulties of intergenerational cooperation lie. It points out that intergenerational cooperation is possible through public reciprocity, but the degree of cooperation is not always sufficient. In addition to elucidating the reasons why intergenerational cooperation is not sufficient, several methodologies are proposed to promote the same. One of these is fund establishment (constitutionalization), in which the preceding generation directly binds the actions of the subsequent generations. This chapter then reports the results of

T. Hiromitsu, *Resolving Intergenerational Conflicts*, Advances in Japanese Business and Economics 33, https://doi.org/10.1007/978-981-97-0614-3_3

an economic experiment that mimics the model and provides insight into what can actually occur between generations. The experiment is structured such that subjects are asked to make successive donations. First, the first subject entrusts the second with the amount of money they intend to donate. Then, the second subject decides the final amount to be donated from the sum of the amount entrusted by the first, and the amount of money in the possession. The results of the experiment show that first-mover donations do not decrease as much as the model predicts, but they do decrease for those who have a strong interest in donating. A more interesting result is that the behavior of the first mover influences the second mover, indicating that the former was providing moral inspiration to the latter.

The second half of this chapter will be directed toward incorporating this relationship of influence into the model and expanding the potential for intergenerational cooperation. Building on previous studies, such as those by Andreoni (1998, 2006), which have examined the impact of other donors' behavior on donations, this chapter will deepen the understanding of the impact of first player on second player. It is then shown that when the preceding generation takes into account this influence, it increases the degree of its own cooperation. If the preceding generation wants the subsequent generation to cooperate, it should cooperate itself, and now it actually does so. One should take only those actions that one would advocate for (all) others to also take. That cooperation follows this path is interpreted in this chapter with reference to previous economic research on the Kantian categorical imperative.

This chapter is organized as follows: Sect. 3.2 summarizes previous studies; Sect. 3.3 identifies the possibilities and difficulties of intergenerational cooperation; Sect. 3.4 conducts an economic experiment that mimics the model and interprets the results; Sect. 3.5 extends the model by incorporating the inspiration of the preceding generation on the following generation, and raises the possibility of intergenerational cooperation through the Kantian categorical imperative. Finally, Sect. 3.6 summarizes the conclusions and remaining issues. Appendix 3.1 discusses the possibilities and problems of a different methodology than the ones addressed in the main part of the chapter, which intends to improve Pareto efficiency through intergenerational negotiation. Appendix 3.2 examines the role of personality in intergenerational issues, based on the experimental results.

3.2 Previous Studies and Methods of this Chapter

In this section, in addition to looking at studies dealing with intergenerational relations, those on public goods provision, such as donations, are also discussed, because an experiment simulating intergenerational decision-making through sequential donation behavior is conducted in Sect. 3.4. The latter half of this section refers to previous studies that examine the sequential contribution setting in particular.

3.2.1 Intergenerational Relationships

The main lines of previous research dealing with intergenerational issues, including Barro's (1974) work were reviewed in Chap. 2. In this chapter, an experiment mimicking an intergenerational model by means of sequential donation behavior is considered in Sect. 3.4. Although actual intergenerational behavior can only be observed for very long periods of time, research has been conducted in laboratories where subjects make sequential decisions, to gain insight into intergenerational issues (e.g., Kamijo et al., 2015, 2017). As for Samuelson's (1958) type of ascending reciprocity, which was discussed in Chap. 2 (Sect. 2.4), Offerman created a setting in which the choice of subjects in the subsequent generation role increases or decreases the gain of subjects in the preceding generation, and tested whether cooperation through ascending reciprocity can actually be observed (Offerman et al., 2001). The important question is whether the settings are appropriate for the targeted intergenerational issues. The relevance of emulating the intergenerational relationship through sequential donations model is discussed in Sect. 3.4.

3.2.2 Public Goods

In interpreting the sequential donations experiment, it is necessary to refer to previous studies on donation and provision of public goods at large. What is commonly noted about provision of public good is the theoretical predictions that there is an incentive to free-ride, leaving the supply of public goods to others, and that public goods are only underprovided.[1] Various proposals have been made to correct for the undersupply of public goods. Richard Cornes and Todd Sandler (1984) question the assumption of Nash that considers the behavior of others a given. They term the effect of an increase in one's own payment for a public good on the total payments of other individuals "conjectural variations". They point out that when the variation is positive, a public good supply above the Nash equilibrium may be realized.[2] Cornes and Sandler captured the idea that one's own actions come to conform to the desirable actions of others through conjectural variations, and described this in terms of the

[1] Experimental studies have shown that people supply more public goods than theory predicts. The pioneering experimental study on the voluntary provision of public goods was conducted by Marwell and Ames (1981), in which multiple subjects were asked to simultaneously divide their resources between private goods and payments for public goods. Resources provided to the public good are combined with those provided by other subjects, and converted to the public good using specific formulas (the production functions of the public good). The public good is returned to the subjects equally, regardless of their respective payments for the public good. What was observed by Marwell and Ames, and in more well-designed later studies (e.g., Kim & Walker, 1984) in which the absence of payment for the public good was designed to be the dominant strategy, was that the level of payment for the public good did not reach the Pareto optimum, and that there was a free ride in this range; however, the payments were found to be made at a significant level.

[2] Cornes and Sandler (1984, pp. 377–378).

Kantian categorical imperative. The Kantian categorical imperative is formulated, according to Kant himself, as to "Act only according to that maxim whereby you can at the same time will that it should become a universal law" (Kant, 1785). John Roemer formulated this as "one should take those actions and only those actions that one would advocate all others take as well."[3] Kantian categorical imperative is a maxim that goes hand-in-hand with the Golden Rule discussed in Chap. 1 (Sect. 1.3.2). The Golden Rule is a maxim that requires one to do to others what one would want others to do to oneself. Although it is constructed with the relationship between oneself and a particular person in mind, it is similar to the Kantian categorical imperative in its requirement to only take actions that one would advocate others take as well. In fact, Kant himself states that the Golden Rule is not categorical imperative itself, but is derived from the categorical imperative under various limitations (Kant, 1785).

The work of Cornes and Sandler is an interesting discussion that brings up the Kantian categorical imperative in considering solutions to the undersupply of public goods. Unfortunately, Robert Sugden (1985) presents a persuasive criticism of their argument. The criticism is that an optimist who increase their supply in the belief that others will also supply, will immediately be betrayed by people who reduce own their supply.[4] Sugden offers his own solution to such a situation: "Suppose that *I* is the group of individuals who benefit from the public good, and consider any person *i* who is a member of *I*. Let *i* choose the level of effort that she would most prefer that every member of *I* should make (the same effort for each person). Then *i* is obliged to make at least this effort" (p. 774). Under this rule (together with other certain conditions) Pareto efficient provision of public goods is realized (Sugden, 1984). However, Toru Mori points out that this rule is too demanding as an ethical requirement because it forces individuals to make unconditional payments regardless of whether others actually contribute (Mori, 1996).[5]

In addition to the work of Cornes and Sandler, economists have studied the Kantian categorical imperative in two approaches. One is the study by Roemer, mentioned earlier, which assumes that players have a protocol based on the Kantian categorical imperative (Roemer, 2010, 2015). His study shows that the solution to public goods game by such players—Roemer specifically solves the problem of commons—is Pareto efficient. In the first research approach, the categorical imperative is an assumption, and Roemer does not speculate further on its origin. He provides examples such as the fact that people educate their children to imprint Kantian ethics, and magical thinking like "if I donate, all others like me will also donate,"[6] but does not go into depth on the same. The issue with the first approach is that simply assuming the categorical imperative does not avoid the same shortcomings of intergenerational ethics as duty, as discussed in Chap. 2. There is no guarantee for the implementation of the categorical imperative, and there is no way for Kantian ethics to become a reality.

---

[3] Roemer (2010, p. 2).

[4] Sugden (1985, pp. 118–122).

[5] Mori (1996, p. 225).

[6] Roemer (2010, p. 18).

Another approach addresses the manner in which people come to have preferences that follow the Kantian categorical imperative. Alger and Weibull (2013, 2016) examine whether Kantian preferences survive the evolutionary process, and draw positive conclusions.[7] This second approach provides an evolutionary answer as a path to guarantee the implementation of the categorical imperative. Evolutionary theory can be a powerful weapon to explain peoples' motives.[8] However, this book does not rest on the evolutionary explanation or cease to think. As discussed in Chap. 1 (Sect. 1.1), the intergenerational problem is a new one that has emerged with the increase in human power. If this understanding is correct, then the explanation that humans have come to possess Kantian ethics as part of their nature through the process of evolution alone does not guarantee that the new problem of intergenerational issues can be adequately addressed. Rather, it is important to offer a way to actualize the Kantian categorical imperative, even under the strict assumption that the players do not have Kantian ethics, and this chapter is devoted to this consideration. In doing so, the focus will be on what Roemer calls magical thinking, and Cornes' and Sandler's conjectural variations, which have a similar logic.

3.2.3 Sequential Decision

A study by Varian (1994) outlines a theoretical framework for the provision of public goods with sequential settings. Varian models a situation in which two players make sequential payments for a public good, noting that under sequential settings, the supply of the public good is reduced by the same amount or less, as compared to the simultaneous settings case. Simon Gächter also conducted an experiment mimicking Varian's model, and found that the provision of public goods does indeed decrease under sequential settings when compared to simultaneous ones (Gächter et al., 2010). However, he found that the reduction was smaller than that predicted by the model, which was attributed to the fact that when the first mover pays less, the second mover can punish in the form of reduced payments. An experiment by Hans-Theo Normann and Holger Rau introduced steps in the gains from public goods and established a setting in which higher gains are obtained when payments above a certain level are collected (Normann & Rau, 2014). Under this setting, the results show that the introduction of sequentiality improved the provision of public goods. The first mover's payment slightly below the step threshold induces the second mover to pay for the public good. An experiment by Anat Bracha also tested donation behavior when there is a fixed cost for the project to be donated and obtained positive results,

---

[7] Alger's recent work has attempted to show by experimentation that Kantian preferences, whose existence she theoretically affirmed, are in fact real among people (van Leeuwen & Alger, 2021).

[8] Chapter 2 suggests that the evolution through group selection is a useful explanation for why the interest in life after death exists in humans (2.5.1, Note 37). In this chapter, too, group selection is suggested as an explanation for conformity to the predecessors (3.4.3, note 23).

which can be interpreted as being based on the same logic as the introduction of a step for gains (Bracha et al., 2011).

It is also useful to look at previous studies with sequential donation settings. Theoretically, in a situation where others make large donations, one would expect to see a reduction in one's own donations. In other words, donations from oneself and others are substitutive. However, through a field experiment dealing with public radio donation, Jen Shang and Rachel Croson report that social information that others are donating a lot tends to increase subjects' donations; self- and other-donations are complementary rather than substitutive (Shang & Croson, 2009). Andreoni reports that obtaining seed money at the beginning of a charity can help to obtain more donations (Andreoni, 1998, 2006). Promises of refunds in the event that sufficient contributions are not collected are known to encourage donations as well (List & Lucking-Reiley, 2002). Andreoni's explanation for the effectiveness of the seed money is the economic rationale that donors want the charity to succeed, and the seed money brings it closer to success (Andreoni, 1998). This economic explanation is based on the same logic as the effect of the introduction of steps to the gains from public goods in Norman and Lau's experiment. At the same time, Andreoni also points out that the seed money provides information that ensures the quality of the charity, suggesting the importance of focusing on the sequential nature of donation decisions. The sequential nature of decision-making and the flow of information linking decisions will be noted in this chapter as particularly important to intergenerational issues involving sequential decisions. Based on the results of the experiment, this chapter will present a way to utilize Cornes and Sandler's idea of conjectural variations, which was criticized by Sugden, as well Roemer's magical thinking in intergenerational issues.

3.3 Possibilities and Difficulties of Intergenerational Cooperation

3.3.1 Intergenerational Savings Succession Model

As discussed in Chap. 2, Barry (1996) pointed out that punishment does not work and there are no circumstances of justice between generations. In response to this problem, as seen in Chap. 2, finding direct reciprocity as public reciprocity between generations restores circumstances of justice, but this restoration is not always sufficient. First, the preceding generation cannot punish the one that follows it in time. Even if the preceding generation wants to save for the survival of the community, they will be discouraged from saving if they anticipate wastage of their savings by the subsequent generation. The obstruction of cooperation through this channel is called "anticipation of betrayal by subsequent generations." The second, which shall be called "dependence on subsequent generations," stems from the difficulty of subsequent generations in punishing the preceding generation. The preceding generation believes that the subsequent one will be cooperative, and because of this, tries to rely only on this cooperation, without cooperating itself. Below, it is shown how intergenerational cooperation is hindered through these two pathways.

Here, the "intergenerational savings succession model" that introduces direct reciprocity between generations is presented. Specifically, under a situation in which each generation makes decentralized decisions, the preceding generation passes savings to the subsequent generation, and both are interested in the final savings left by the subsequent generation.

First, assume the following utility function and the constraint for the preceding generation (Generation 1)

$$u_1^A = u_1^A(c_1^A, s_1^A). \tag{3.1}$$

$$s.t. c_1^A + s_1^A = y_1, y_1 \geq 0. \tag{3.2}$$

Below, a homothetic function is assumed as the utility function of Generation 1.[9]

$$u_1^A = (1 - \alpha_1)\log c_1^A + \alpha_1 \log s_1^A, 0 \alpha_1 1. \tag{3.3}$$

"A" on the right shoulder of the symbol represents this game where only Generation 1 is its player (Game A),[10] and distinguishes it from the multi-generation chained game described immediately below. Generation 1, who receives the income y_1 allocates it for its own consumption c_1^A and saving for the future s_1^A. Generation 1 receives utility from savings s_1^A directly. Equation 3.3 is assumed to be maximized, yielding the following solution

$$c_1^{A*} = (1 - \alpha_1)y_1, s_1^{A*} = \alpha_1 y_1. \tag{3.4}$$

A subsequent generation (Generation 2) shall be introduced. Each generation is assumed to be a chained generation, with no overlap in life. In Samuelson's (1958) overlapping generations model, which was discussed in Chap. 2 (Sect. 2.4.2), generations have overlapping life periods, such as old age and prime age. However, in the intergenerational savings succession model, each generation does not have any overlapping life periods. This not only simplifies the model, but also eliminates the overlapping periods, thereby eliminating the room for intergenerational cooperation based on indirect reciprocity. Generation 1 receives income y_1 for its own consumption and savings for the future. However, the savings are not directly realized as savings for the future, but are temporarily entrusted to Generation 2. Generation 2 receives its own income y_2 and adds s_1^B from Generation 1, and divides its resources

---

[9] In a homothetic utility function, when indifferent consumption vectors are arbitrarily chosen, the consumption vectors θx, θy, …, obtained by increasing the consumption of all goods by the same fraction θ, are also indifferent.

[10] Although only a single generation exists in Game A, it is labelled "game" for comparison with Game B, and even though Generation 2 does not exist, it is labelled "Generation 1".

$(y_2 + s_1^B)$ into Generation 2's own consumption c_1^B and final savings for the future S_3^B. The utility functions of Generations 1 and 2 are given by Eqs. 3.5 and 3.6, respectively.

$$u_1^B = u_1^B\left(c_1^B, S_3^B\right) = (1 - \alpha_1)\log c_1^B + \alpha_1 \log S_3^B. \tag{3.5}$$

$$u_2^B = u_2^B\left(c_2^B, S_3^B\right) = (1 - \alpha_2)\log c_2^B + \alpha_2 \log S_3^B. \tag{3.6}$$

$$s.t. c_1^B + s_1^B = y_1, c_2^B + s_2^B = y_2 + s_1^B, S_3^B = s_2^B > 0, y_1, y_2 0. \tag{3.7}$$

Sign "B" denotes game B that chains the two generations. α_1 and α_2 are the degrees of the common interest in S_3^B of Generations 1 and 2, representing the degree of interest in their futures, respectively. In this section (Sect. 3.3), α_i is assumed to be constant.[11] The assumption of the degree of interest in the future as a constant is similar to the exhaustible natural resources model in Chap. 2, but is more flexible than the exhaustible natural resources model in allowing for differences in these constants across generations.

Equation 3.7 has $S_3^B = s_2^B > 0$, because when $S_3^B = s_2^B = 0$, the utility functions in Eqs. 3.5 and 3.6 cannot be defined. As seen later, when $\alpha_2 = 0$, $S_3^B = s_2^B = 0$. Equation 3.6 will be fine, because $\alpha_2 \log S_3^B$ will be erased; however, in Eq. 3.5, the problem arises that the utility of Generation 1 cannot be defined. For this reason, when $S_3^B = s_2^B = 0$ and $0 < \alpha_1 1$, Generation 1 shall maximize the following Eq. 3.8.

$$u_1^B = u_1^{B+}\left((1 - \alpha_1)\log c_1^B\right), S_3^B = s_2^B = 0, 0 < \alpha_1 1, u_1^{B+'} \geq 0. \tag{3.8}$$

The following relationship is then assumed to be satisfied as the preference relation

$$\left(c_1^B, S_3^B\right) \succ \left(c_1^{B+}, 0\right), S_3^B > 0, c_1^B > 0, c_1^{B+} > 0 \tag{3.9}$$

In other words, Generation 1 wants to avoid a final savings of zero at all costs (as long as $0 < \alpha_1$), but if savings S_3^B is zero, it prefers to increase its consumption c_1^B. Generation 1's utility is monotonically increasing with respect to its own consumption (except when $\alpha_1 = 1$).

Generations 1 and 2 maximize utilities in a decentralized manner. S_3^B is the asset remaining in the community at the end of Generation 2. This asset value is assumed to be related to the survival of the community. After the end of Generation 2, doomsday arrives, and the subjective probability that the community will continue to exist can be thought of as an increasing function of this asset. When the final savings are realized by Generation 2, Generation 1 has passed away. Generation 1 chooses its s_1^B according to its subjective prediction of choice of S_3^B by Generation 2. Generation 1 predicts α_2 and based on this prediction, forecasts the final savings S_3^B. From this

[11] α_2 Of Generation 2 will be extended to be an endogenous variables in Sect. 3.5.

subjective prediction, it obtains the utility of $\alpha_1 \log S_3^B$. The predication of α_2 by Generation 1 is a constant of $0\alpha_2 1$.

3.3.2 Subgame Perfect Equilibrium as a Reference Point

Generation 1 will leave the world without observing S_3^B. Even if Generation 2 consequently makes a decision that differs from the one predicted by Generation 1, this will not cause any problems. Therefore, the setting does not lead to an equilibrium of the game between Generations 1 and 2. However, Generation 1 anticipates the behavior of Generation 2 and maximizes its utility, including $\alpha_1 \log S_3^B$. Generation 1 has an idea of the eventual state of world (the value of S_3^B) as a result of its own decision and makes decisions based on this prediction. Generation 1, in its subjective view, makes its decisions in a strategic relationship with Generation 2, and its decisions can be described using the subgame perfect equilibrium as a reference point.

A subgame perfect equilibrium is a set of strategies that is a Nash equilibrium in all subgames. In this intergenerational savings session model, it refers to the equilibrium where Generation 1 acts rationally with the expectation that Generation 2 will also act rationally. For this reason, this subsection first obtains the optimal reaction of Generation 2, and then maximizes the utility of Generation 1 based on the optimal reaction that derives the savings of Generation 1 (s_1^{B*}) and final savings (S_3^{B*}). The followings include solutions with subscript "'" to equation number, which are adapted to the setting of the economic experiment to be conducted in Sect. 3.4, $y_1 = y_2 = 200$.

(1) when $\alpha_2 \neq 0$ (when Generation 1 expects Generation 2 to be interested in saving),

$$s_1^{B*} = \alpha_1 y_1 + (\alpha_1 - 1)y_2, if \frac{y_2}{y_1 + y_2} < \alpha_1 \leq 1. s_1^{B*} = 0, otherwise. \quad (3.10)$$

$$S_3^{B*} = \alpha_1 \alpha_2 (y_1 + y_2), if \frac{y_2}{y_1 + y_2} < \alpha_1 \leq 1. S_3^{B*} = \alpha_2 y_2, otherwise. \quad (3.11)$$

$$s_1^{B*} = 200(2\alpha_1 - 1), if \frac{1}{2} < \alpha_1 \leq 1. s_1^{B*} = 0, otherwise. \quad (3.10')$$

$$S_2^{B*} = 400\alpha_1 \alpha_2, if \frac{1}{2} < \alpha_1 \leq 1. S_3^{B*} = 200\alpha_2, otherwise. \quad (3.11')$$

(2) when $\alpha_2 = 0$ (when Generation 1 expects Generation 2 to be uninterested in saving), the optimal reaction of Generation 2 is $s_2^B = 0$ for any s_1^B, so anticipating this response in advance, Generation 1 leaves no savings.

$$s_1^{B*} = 0. \quad (3.12)$$

$$S_3^{B*} = s_2^{B*} = 0. \tag{3.13}$$

Because Eqs. 3.12 and 3.13 do not include income y_1, y_2, the solution is the same as in Eqs. 3.12 and 3.13 when $y_1 + y_2 = 200$.

If Generation 1 anticipates $\alpha_2 \neq 0$, the solutions are Eqs. 3.10 and 3.11, and if $\alpha_2 = 0$, the solutions are Eqs. 3.12 and 3.13.

This solution shows that if Generation 1 has enough interest in S_3^B, $\frac{y_2}{y_1+y_2} < \alpha_1$, and predicts Generation 2 to be $\alpha_2 \neq 0$, then Generation 1 will save. However, the level of saving is reduced from the case of Game A (Eq. 3.4), and if Generation 1's interest in the future (α_1) is not sufficient ($\alpha_1 < \frac{y_2}{y_1+y_2}$), the saving is zero. The higher the income of Generation 2 (y_2), the more Generation 1 reduces its own savings by relying on those savings of Generation 2. When Generation 2's income (y_2) is sufficiently high ($\frac{y_2}{y_1+y_2} \geq \alpha_1$), Generation 1 ultimately stops saving.

3.3.3 *Possibilities and Difficulties of Intergenerational Cooperation*

Here, it is necessary to obtain a solution that should be contrasted with the subgame perfect equilibrium, obtained as a reference point. The case of utilitarian maximization through Generations 1 and 2 is considered here. Decentralized decision-making by each generation is not allowed, and the choices made by Generations 1 and 2 are assumed to be decided at once. Assume that the utility functions of both generations are additive, and maximize the sum of the utility $u_1^B + u_2^B$ under the constraint Eq. 3.7, in terms of s_1^B and S_3^B. By solving the simultaneous equations, the followings are obtained as the optimal solutions through generations.

$$s_1^{B\dagger} = \frac{(\alpha_1+1)y_1 + (\alpha_1-1)y_2}{2}, \text{ if } \frac{y_2 - y_1}{y_1+y_2} < \alpha_1 \leq 1. s_1^{B\dagger} = 0, \text{ otherwise.} \tag{3.14}$$

$$S_3^{B\dagger} = \frac{(\alpha_1+\alpha_2)(y_1+y_2)}{2}, \text{ if } \frac{y_2 - y_1}{y_1+y_2} < \alpha_1 \leq 1. S_3^{B\dagger} = \frac{(\alpha_1+\alpha_2)y_2}{\alpha_1+1}, \text{ otherwise.} \tag{3.15}$$

$$s_1^{B\dagger} = 200\alpha_1. \tag{3.14'}$$

$$S_3^{B\dagger} = 200(\alpha_1+\alpha_2). \tag{3.15'}$$

Because decentralized decisions are not allowed, Generation 1 may save even if $\alpha_1 = 0$, and Generation 2 may save even if $\alpha_2 = 0$.

Comparing Eqs. 3.10, 3.12 and 3.14, and furthermore comparing Eqs. 3.11, 3.13 and (3.15), we get $s_1^{B*} s_1^{B\dagger}$, $S_3^{B*} S_3^{B\dagger}$. In subgame perfect equilibrium, both Generation 1's savings and final savings are reduced from the optimal solution. Note that Eq. ((3.14') coincides with Eq. 3.4 at $y_1 = 200$. When $y_1 = y_2 = 200$, Generation 1 entrusts the same amount of savings to Generation 2, as it does in Game A. Moreover, Eq. (3.15') is equal to the sum of the savings of Generations 1 and 2 playing Game A separately. From Eqs. 3.10 and 3.14, $\partial s_1^{B*}/\partial y_2 (= \alpha_1 - 1) \leq \partial s_1^{B\dagger}/\partial y_2 (= (\alpha_1 - 1)/2) \leq 0$. Both s_1^{B*} and $s_1^{B\dagger}$ are decreasing functions of y_2 (income of generation 2). As Generation 1's interest in the future α_1 is weaker, the stronger the degree to which they are decreasing functions of y_2. It is noteworthy that the subgame perfect equilibrium decreases even faster than the optimal solution, with the increase of y_2. In other words, there is a dependence on the subsequent generation, which means relying on the income of the subsequent generation and reducing preceding generation's own savings.

What about the other pathway of noncooperation, the anticipation of betrayal by subsequent generations? This path can be confirmed by *fund establishment* of the savings of Generation 1. Fund establishment is the process of making the transfer of Generation 1's savings to Generation 2 irreversible, and ensuring that they are passed on as final savings (S_3^B). When $\alpha_2 \neq 0$, under fund establishment, $S_3^B = s_1^B + \varsigma_2$, $\varsigma_2 \geq 0$. ς_2 is the savings added by Generation 2. As Generation 2 cannot reverse the savings entrusted to it by Generation 1, $\varsigma_2 \geq 0$. Generation 1 seeks the optimal reaction of Generation 2 under this constraint, based on which it maximizes its own utility. In this case, the following holds.

$$s_1^{B**} = \alpha_1 y_1, if \frac{\alpha_2 y_2}{(1-\alpha_2) y_1} < \alpha_1 \leq 1. \tag{3.16}$$

When $0 \leq \alpha_1 \leq \frac{\alpha_2 y_2}{(1-\alpha_2) y_1}$, the solution is the same as in Eq. 3.10. Equation 3.16 is more likely to be the solution when Generation 1 is more concerned about the future, Generation 2 is less concerned about the future, and Generation 2 has lower income. In other words, fund establishment works. When $\alpha_2 = 0$, the optimal reaction of Generation 2 is rewritten from $S_s^{B*} = s_2^{B*} = 0$ to $S_s^{B**} = s_2^{B**} = s_1^B$. As Generation 1 maximizes $u_1^B = (1-\alpha_1) \log c_1^B + \alpha_1 \log s_1^B$, $s_1^{B**} = \alpha_1 y_1$ is obtained. This savings is the same as in the case of Game A, which is played by Generation 1 alone. When $\alpha_2 = 0$, fund establishment prevents Generation 1 from saving less. That is, there are cases in which fund establishment enables Generation 1 to save more than in the subgame perfect equilibrium. On the flip side, this implies that the anticipation of betrayal by the subsequent generations prevents cooperation by the preceding generation.

Figure 3.1, under $y_1 = y_2 = 200$, shows the relationship between Generation 1's interest in the future (α_1) (horizontal axis) and its savings in game B (s_1^B) (vertical axis). Line 1 corresponds to the subgame perfect equilibrium of Eq. (3.10'). The savings stick to zero between $\alpha_1 = 0$ and 0.5, and is an increasing function above 0.5. Line 2 (the 45-degree line) is the savings (optimal solution) for Generation 1 in Eq. (3.14'). Line 2 is also the relationship between α_1 and the savings in Game A on the vertical axis (s_1^A). When Generation 1 has a high interest in S_3^B ($\alpha_1 > 0.5$), and if it anticipates Generation 2 to be $\alpha_2 \neq 0$, then Generation 1 will save. However, the saving of Generation 1 is less than the optimal solution (also savings in Game A) and is zero when Generation 1's interest in the future is not sufficient. Line 3 in Fig. 3.1 depicts the savings by Generation 1 in the fund establishment case, especially for $\alpha_2 = 0.4$. When α_1 greater than 2/3 ($= \alpha_2 y_2/(1-\alpha_2)y_1$, $y_1 = y_2 = 200$), the reduction in savings is prevented by fund establishment.

Figure 3.2 depicts the final savings from Generations 1 and 2 in Game B at the time of $\alpha_2 \neq 0$ (when $\alpha_2 = 0$, the final savings are zero in any α_1). As in Fig. 3.1, the case with $y_1 = y_2 = 200$ and $\alpha_2 = 0.4$ is depicted. Line 1 corresponds to the subgame perfect equilibrium of Eq. (3.11'). Compared to line 1 in Fig. 3.1, when Generation 1's interest in the future is $\alpha_1 = 0.5$, it does not save at all (marked with x). However, 80 points of savings are realized in the end (marked with x). Generation 1 is dependent on Generation 2. Line 2 is the final savings (optimal solution) according to Eq. (3.15'). Line 2 also depicts the total savings when each

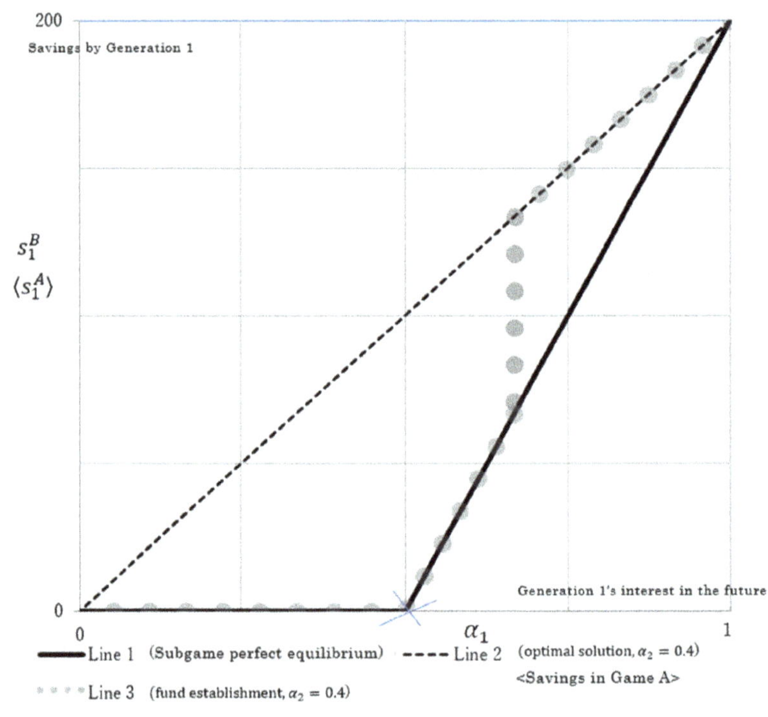

Fig. 3.1 Savings by Generation 1 (subgame perfect equilibrium) ($y_1 = y_2 = 200$). *Note* When Generation 1 has a high interest in final savings, and if it anticipates Generation 2 to also have some interest in the same, Generation 1 will save. However, the saving of generation 1 is less than the optimal solution (also savings in Game A) and is zero when Generation 1's interest in the future is not sufficient. Line 3 depicts the savings by Generation 1 in the fund establishment case. The reduction in savings is prevented by fund establishment as depicted in the right-hand of the domain

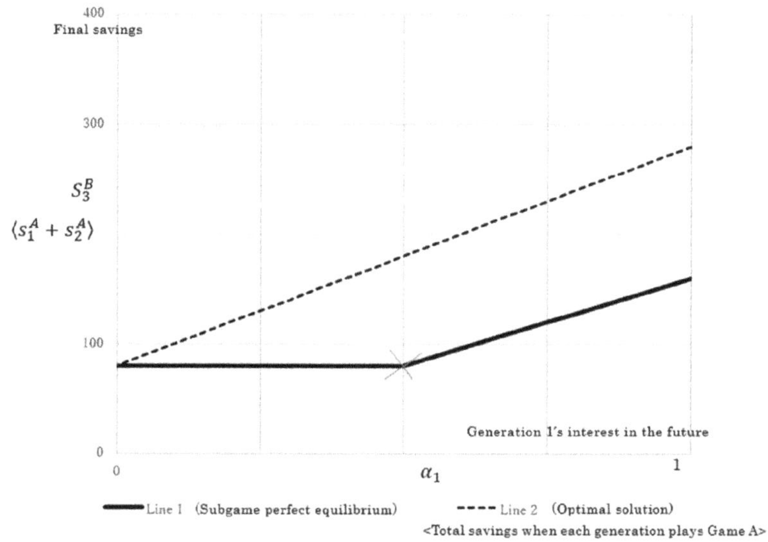

Fig. 3.2 Final savings (subgame perfect equilibrium) ($y_1 = y_2 = 200, \alpha_2 = 0.4$). *Note* Line 1 corresponds to the subgame perfect equilibrium of Eq. 3.11'. Line 2 is the final savings (optimal solution) according to Eq. 3.15'. Line 2 is also the line depicting the total savings when each generation plays Game A separately. A comparison of Lines 1 and 2 shows that the subgame perfect equilibrium achieves only smaller savings, relative to the optimal solution (also the total savings when each generation plays Game A separately), i.e., there is insufficient cooperation

generation plays Game A separately. A comparison of Lines 1 and 2 shows that the subgame perfect equilibrium achieves only smaller savings, relative to the optimal solution (also the total savings when each generation plays Game A separately), i.e., there is insufficient cooperation.

The point clarified through the intergenerational savings succession model in this section is summarized as Theorem 3.1.

Theorem 3.1 (Two pathways that impede intergenerational cooperation) *Intergenerational cooperation is impeded by the two following pathways:*

(1) *Anticipation of betrayal by subsequent generations: Even if the preceding generation has a preference for cooperation for the sake of the community's survival, it will refrain from cooperation if it anticipates that cooperation will be wasted by subsequent generations.*
(2) *Dependence on the subsequent generations: If the preceding generation believes that the subsequent generations will be cooperative, the preceding generation will rely on the cooperation of the subsequent generations and refrain from cooperating itself.*

While intergenerational cooperation is possible under public reciprocity, the degree of cooperation is not necessarily sufficient. The intergenerational savings succession model is structured as a trust game[12]. In the anticipation of betrayal by subsequent generations, the sequential nature of intergenerational relations makes it ineffective for the preceding generation to punish such betrayal. From the perspective of the preceding generation, it would be nice to claim damages for betrayal, but the path to claim and enforce such reparations between generations is blocked. From the perspective of the subsequent generations, if they could effectively commit themselves to saving enough in advance, before the preceding generation's choice, they would have the advantage of extracting more savings from the preceding generation. However, subsequent generations that have yet to come into existence cannot commit. In the dependence on subsequent generations, the sequential nature of intergenerational relations makes it ineffective for them to punish the preceding generation for not handing over sufficient savings. From the perspective of the subsequent generation, it is not possible to make any demands on the preceding generation, who are in the past. If the game is repeatable, cooperation can be encouraged, but intergenerational relations are one-time affairs.

Chapter 2 (Sect. 2.3) pointed out that intergenerational ethics as duty has difficulties in its actualization. In doing so, it was argued that when the present generation consists of multiple individuals, an incentive problem arises in terms of who among them will be the bearers of duty (a problem separates from *akrasia*). The two paths in Theorem 3.1 are also related to the incentive problem, which now arises not between individuals within the present generation, but between generations.

Next is Theorem 3.2, which is the finding on fund establishment through the intergenerational savings succession model in Sect. 3.3.3.

Theorem 3.2 (Fund establishment) *The non-cooperation of the preceding generation, stemming from the anticipation of betrayal by the subsequent ones, can be prevented through fund establishment.*

Fund establishment is a way to allow the preceding generation to act in its own interest in the future by eliminating concerns about betrayal by subsequent generations. Note that it is not necessary to limit fund establishment to its literal meaning. Large-scale (high-quality) public investment is an example of fund establishment. The essence of fund establishment is binding across generations. Directly binding the choices of subsequent generations through constitutional measures that cannot be easily amended has the same effect as fund establishment. For example, a constitutional rule that forbids the present generation to mine exhaustible natural resources alone, requiring instead for generations to mine slowly over several generations. Of course, an irreversible fund even after the preceding generation has passed away is "easier said than done." It is not enough to ban by law, because the possibility of reversal through legislations is always open. Nevertheless, fund establishment (constitutionalization) is a meaningful way to encourage intergenerational cooperation.

It should be noted that the character of fund establishment (constitutionalization) is incompatible with public reciprocity, which allows cooperation through shared

[12] The trust game considers a collaboration in which Player 1 works first and Player 2 works later. If Player 2 skips work, then Player 1's work is wasted.

rules based on mutual respect. In the process of fund establishment (constitutionalization), the preceding generation imposes on the subsequent generation a constitutional rule or prohibition on withdrawal of funds, but there is no mutual respect in such an imposition. Fund establishment (constitutionalization) moves away from reciprocity. The ineffectiveness of fund establishment (constitutionalization) on dependence on subsequent generations is also a serious drawback. It should be noted that important parts of the intergenerational issues are due to the dependence on subsequent generations. People are not willing to let humanity die out, but tend to be grateful if subsequent generations do the work of reducing fossil fuel consumption.

3.4 Economic Experiment

3.4.1 Setting, Hypotheses

This section conducts an economic experiment that mimics the intergenerational savings succession model. Following the experiment simulating Game A (Experiment A), the experiment simulating Game B (Experiment B) is conducted. Since it is not possible to reproduce the generations that replace each other over a long period of time in the laboratory, the experiment will observe subjects' behaviors as they make sequential decisions. What requires attention in the laboratory is how to reproduce the values shared by different generations. In the experiment, the subjects are tasked with dividing a certain source of funds into a private share and a donation. The donation is given to the Central Community Chest of Japan (CCCJ), which uses the fund to promote social welfare. The donations represent value shared by the different subjects. In the model presented in Sect. 3.3, c is regarded as the subject's private share, and s and S are regarded as donations.

The experiment was conducted in January 2018 with 74 s- and third-year students in the Faculty of Economics of the Josai University, Japan (the average age was 20.2 years, with 68 male and 6 female students). The procedure is as follows (a more detailed experiment description is provided in Attachment 1).

(General guidance)

(1) Ask the participants to respond freely according to their own ideas. Explain that there is no correct answer and that it will not be revealed to the audience how individuals answered the questions. Also, explain that points earned or responses given in the experiment will not be reflected in students' grades.
(2) Explain that each subject will be rewarded according to the points that they have earned through the experiment, and that the rewards will be made by drawing lots at the conversion of 10 points to 10 yen (approximately, 10 cents).

(Experiment A)

(3) Give 200 points to all the respective subjects. Then, all the subjects are asked to simultaneously divide the 200 points between their own share and a donation (to the CCCJ, the same as below). (The allocation was chosen in 10-point increments. (The same below). The subjects are not informed of any of the results of the allocation in Experiment A; neither the allocation by any individuals,' nor the overall decisions among the subjects (e.g., the donation mean).

(Experiment B)

(4) The subjects are then randomly divided into two groups. One subject from the first group (hereafter referred to as "the first player") and one subject from the second group (hereafter referred to as "the second player") are combined (37 pairs in total). All the subjects are again given 200 points each. The first player is then instructed to divide the 200 points between their share and a donation. Here, the first player is informed that the points for donation are not donated directly, but are entrusted to the second player.
(5) The second player is informed of the points entrusted to them by the first player paired with them. The second player is then instructed to divide the sum of their own 200 points and those entrusted to them, into two parts: their own share and the final donation. The decision by the second player is not communicated to the first player, and both are aware of this missing of communication.

(Procedures for termination)

(6) The subjects are asked to complete a survey of their basic attributes (age, gender, etc.) and a test to measure prosociality (van Lange et al., 1997).[13] Note that the series of arrangements does not ask for a name and ensures the subjects' anonymity.
(7) Payment of rewards is by lottery (drawing of subjects' serial numbers and coin toss, with a 1/2 chance of winning; payment will be made in points that have been set aside as the players' share through Experiments A and B).[14] In addition, donations made in Experiment A and the portion of Experiment B that was ultimately deemed to be allocated to donations are donated by the experimenter.

The experiment took approximately 40 min. As a result of the lottery, rewards were paid to 37 participants (maximum value 480-yen, minimum value 0-yen, average value 230 yen; subjects with even ID numbers were eligible for payment, and those with even ID numbers played the role of the second player in Experiment B. There was no payment for participation).

[13] For an overview of the prosociality test, see the instructions to subjects cited in Attachment 2. In the example in the instructions, B is the option chosen by the prosocial subject. Subjects answer nine similar questions, and those who give prosocial answers to six or more questions are judged to be prosocial.

[14] Narrowing the list of those eligible for reward payments by lottery is a standard procedure implemented to save research funds.

The CCCJ was chosen, because it is the most familiar fundraising campaign in Japan,[15] having started in 1947, soon after World War II, as a private citizen-driven movement.[16] The subjects' familiarity with the CCCJ is thought to contribute to making them believe that they were really making a donation (the subjects were told that the experimenter would be responsible for the donation, and that the experimenter actually donated the indicated amount). Furthermore, the CCCJ is supposed to be used for a wide range of social welfare, and it would be a more appropriate for the experiment whose ultimate goal is to examine the issue of intergenerational cooperation, an issue that concerns society as a whole, than other donations that focus on narrow areas such as specific diseases, regional development, or foreign aid. In light of "induced value theory" (Smith, 1976, 1982), which emphasizes the payment of monetary rewards to subjects in proportion to their payoffs, it could be argued that the rewards are too small to provide sufficient inducement. However, the amount paid by individuals to the CCCJ is not large,[17] and providing large rewards may inadvertently distort natural donation behaviors. Keeping the reward amounts reasonable would also be beneficial in convincing subjects that the experimenter really does donate.

The above is similar to the setup of the savings succession model in Sect. 3.3. The first player is Generation 1 and the second player is Generation 2; the donation corresponds to the common interest of Generations 1 and 2, the final savings (S_3^B), Assuming a homothetic function like Eq. 3.3 as the subjects' utility function is debatable, however this point will be addressed in Sect. 3.4.2. Consider the share allocated to each subject's donation in Experiment A as representing the degree of interest in the intersubject shared value of the subject in question. From Eq. 3.4, when $y_{ij} = 200$, define $\alpha_{ij} = \frac{s_{ij}^{A*}}{200}$, which is regarded as each subject's interest in the donation (i is the role number of the first [1] and second [2] players given in experiment B, and j is the subject's ID). Each subject is assumed to have interest in the donation, observed in Experiment A and to proceed to Experiment B. Note that, strictly speaking, the first player 's prediction about second player's interest in donating may not be a constant, but may be a random variable with a range. However, in the previous analysis with the model (Sect. 3.3), as a first-order approach to analyze the behavior of the preceding generation, the discussion proceeds by assuming that the prediction made by the first player is constant.

From the model presented in Sect. 3.3, the following hypotheses are formulated

[15] According to the Cabinet Office (2019), in a nationwide survey using a two-stage random sampling method for districts and age groups, 1263 of the 3072 valid responses indicated that they had made donations in 2018. Of those 1254 who mentioned the target of their donations, those who mentioned the CCCJ placed first (37.2%) (multiple responses were allowed). The Japanese Red Cross Society came in second (29.5%) and neighborhood associations placed third (28.9%).

[16] Central Community Chest of Japan (2021).

[17] For example, in one area, the estimated donation per household in FY2020 is 255 yen (Kanagawa Community Chest Association, Kohoku-ku Branch, Yokohama City, Social Welfare Corporation, 2020).

Table 3.1 Summary of results of the experiment (points turned into donations)

	s_1^A, s_2^A	s_1^A	s_1^B	$s_1^A + s_2^A$	$S_3^B \langle = s_2^B \rangle$	$s^A{}_2$	$200S_3^B/(200 + s_1^B)$ (share of donations: 200 points conversion)
Third quartile	150	155	120	250	200	130	140.4
Mean	108.2	116.2	105.4	216.5	168.9	100.3	108.5
Median	100	100	100	210	150	100	100
First quartile	80	100	80	170	125	60	82.9

Note Experiment A, n = 74; Experiment B, n = 37

Hypothesis 1: First player donations in Experiment B will decrease relative to donations in Experiment A. In particular, for the first player who is less interested in donating, there are zero donations entrusted by the first player to the second player: $s_{1j}^B < s_{1j}^A, s_{1j}^B = 0 if \alpha_{1j} \leq 0.5$.
Hypothesis 2: The final donations made through the first and second players in Experiment B will be less than the sum of the donations made by each of the first and second players in Experiment A: $S_3^B < s_{1j}^A + s_{2k}^A, (k \neq j)$.

Hypothesis 1 describes the comparison of Lines 1 and 2 in Fig. 3.1. Line 2 is the donation of the first player in the optimal solution and also coincides with the donation in Game A. Hypothesis 2 describes the comparison between Lines 1 and 2 in Fig. 3.2.[18] This Line 2 is the final donation in the optimal solution, and coincides with the donation in Game A.

3.4.2 *Summary of Results*

A summary of the results is presented in Table 3.1. First, Consider results of Experiment A. The mean of donations is 108.2. There is no significant correlation between donations and subjects' attributes (gender and prosociality) (correlation coefficients are 0.09, 0.09; two-sided p-values = 0.46, 0.44; male = 1, prosocial = 1). Forty-eight of the 74 subjects are judged to be prosocial.

Now, examine the results of Experiment B. The first is the first player's decision. Comparing Experiments A and B, the difference in mean donations is not significant (two-sided p-value = 0.35, t-value = 0.95), although it seems that donations are slightly reduced in Experiment B (on average, from 116.2 to 105.4). Compared to experiment A, 35.1% (13 subjects) reduced their donations, 60.0% (21 subjects) did not change, and 8.1% (3 subjects) increased their donations. Only one subject is

[18] In Fig. 3.2, the interest in the future of Generation 2 α_2 is specified as 0.4, but the final donation varies with the value of α_2.

$s_1^B = 0$, therefore $s_{1j}^B = 0$, $if \alpha_{1j} \leq 0.5$, is not established. At first glance, Hypothesis 1 seems to have been rejected.

From Fig. 3.3, however, one can read that the first players were making complex decisions. Figure 3.3 shows a scatter plot of the first players' donations in Experiment A (horizontal axis) and the same first players' donations in Experiment B (vertical axis) superimposed on Fig. 3.1. The linear line (experimental results) is a linear regression line with the donation in Experiment B as the explained variable, and the donation in Experiment A as the explanatory variable. This regression line is close to the 45-degree line (Line 2). This is consistent with the insignificance of the difference between the means of donations in Experiments A and B. However, this regression line is below the 45-degree line on the right-hand side of the figure, where the interest in donations of the first player (α_1) is strong. The stronger the first player's interest in donation, the more it tends to reduce its donation in Experiment B. Subjects in the area circled by the dotted line in the figure fall into this category. As predicted by Hypothesis 1, the subjects who are relatively more interested in donating are more likely to reduce their donations.

Now consider the decisions of the second player. Comparing s_2^B (mean 168.9) with s_2^A (mean 100.3), it is clear that $s_2^B > s_2^A$ (two-sided p-value = 0.00, t = 4.05). In comparison with donations in Experiment A (total for the same pairs as in the experiment, $s_{1j}^A + s_{2k}^A$) (mean 216.5), the final donations in Experiment B (S_3^B) (mean 168.9) is reduced. The difference is significant (two-sided p-value = 0.01, t-value = 2.60). Hypothesis 2 is not rejected.

To understand the choices of the second players, it is useful to focus on two statistics. The first is the final donation in Experiment B minus the donation entrusted by the first player, i.e., the net donation by the second player. This is the donation, so to speak out of its own pocket in Experiment B. The other statistics is the share of the final donation allocated from the resources in the hand of the second player. In Experiment A, the subject who is later assigned the role of the second player donates s_2^A from 200 points given by the experimenter. In Experiment B, the resource in the hand of the second player is $200 + s_1^B$. The share of points allocated to the final donation by the second player is $\frac{S_3^B}{200+s_1^B}$. In order to scale with the donation in Experiment A s_2^A, this ratio is converted to 200 points, yielding $\frac{200S_3^B}{200+s_1^B}$. Based on these preparations, the mean of s_2^A is 100.3, while the mean of $\frac{200S_3^B}{200+s_1^B}$ is 108.5, and the difference is not significant (two-sided p-value = 0.48, t-value = 0.70). On average, this means that throughout Experiments A and B, the second players (the subjects who are assigned the role) did not change their allocation proportions of private shares and donations. Therefore, the use of the homothetic utility function adopted in the model in Sect. 3.3 is appropriate to evaluate the economic experiment in this chapter. In the homothetic utility function, both the private share and the donation increase at a rate θ in proportion to the growth (θ) in the allocation source.

An interesting fact can be discerned from these two statistics. Table 3.2 traces the relationship between (1) "the points obtained by deducting the 'donation of the second player in Experiment A' from the 'donation of the first player observed by

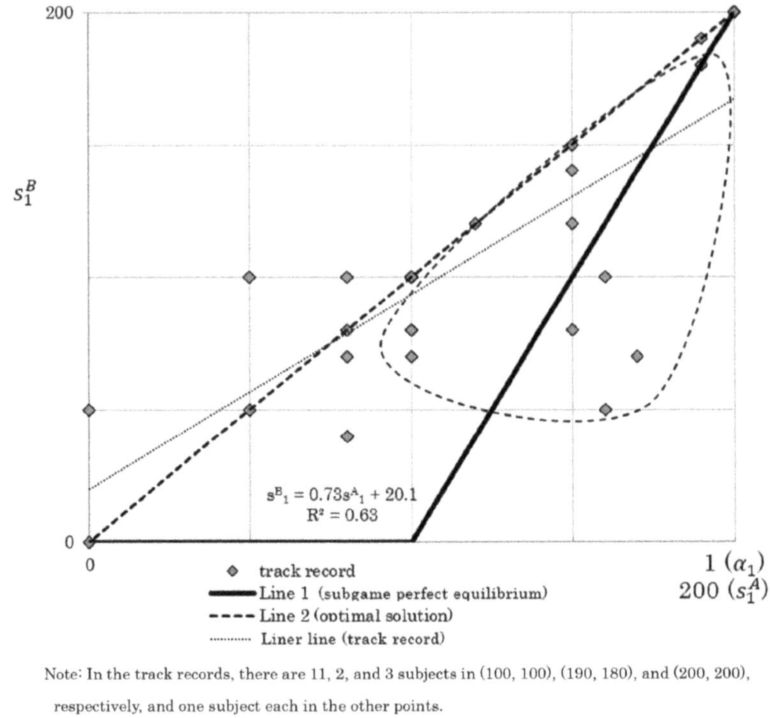

Fig. 3.3 Donations in Experiment A (horizontal axis) and Experiment B (vertical axis) ($y_1 = y_2 = 200$). *Note* This is a scatter plot of the first players' donations in Experiment A (horizontal axis) and the same first players' donations in Experiment B (vertical axis) superimposed on Fig. 3.1, which has subgame perfect equilibrium and optimal solution. The linear line (experimental results) is a linear regression line with the donation in Experiment B as the explained variable and the donation in experiment A as the explanatory variable. This regression line is below the 45-degree line on the right-hand side of the figure, where the interest in donations of the first player (α_1) is strong. The stronger the first player's interest in donation is, the more they tend to reduce they donation in Experiment B

the second player in Experiment B'" (the impression of the first player to the second player),[19] (2) the change from the donation in Experiment A to the net donation in Experiment B by the subject who becomes the second player, and (3) the change from Experiment A to Experiment B in the share of donations by the same subject. If the number in (1) is positive, the first player gives the second player the impression of being "generous"; if the number is zero, it is "neutral"; if negative, the impression is "stingy"; if the number in (2) is increasing, the second player is regarded "generous"; if it is the same, "neutral"; if it is decreasing, they are seen as "stingy"; and if the

[19] $s_1^B - s_2^A$ The first hand is more generous to the second hand than the second hand is to the first hand. From the perspective of the backer, the more donations entrusted by the first mover compared to the donations made by himself in Experiment A, the more generous he feels toward the first mover.

number in (3) is increasing, the second player is regarded as "generous"; if it is the same, "neutral"; if it is decreasing, they are considered "stingy." Table 3.2 organizes the relationship between (1) the impression of the first player to the second player, and (2) and (3) in terms of the corresponding number of players. The "(i) Correlation coefficient" in Table 3.2 is the correlation coefficient between (1) and (2), and (1) and (3), with "generous" and "neutral" receiving 1 point, and "stingy" receiving 0 points. The "(ii) mean" in Table 3.2 is the mean of the scores in the sense of (2) and (3) of the second player's actions when the impression of the first player is "generous" and "neutral," and the mean of the scores in the sense of (2) and (3) of the second player's actions when the impression of the first player is "stingy." The test of the difference between the mean when the impression of the first player is "generous" or "neutral," and when the impression of the first player is "stingy," is performed.

In (2), the change from donation in Experiment A to net donation in Experiment B (the second player), it appears that the second player also tends to act generously when they get an impression of generosity from the first player. However, the relationship is not statistically significant due to the limited number of samples, The trend is clear in (3). When the second player observes the donation entrusted by the first player and gets the impression that the first player is generous, the second player increases their share allocated to the donation. Moreover, when the first player is regarded as stingy, the second player decreases their share allocated to the donation.

The regression analysis in Table 3.3 (with the Tobit model) confirms the same trend.[20] Figure 3.4 shows the scatterplot of the impression of the first player to the second player (horizontal axis) and the change in the share of the second player's donation to their resources (vertical axis). It is seen that the players who perceive the first players as generous tend to be more generous themselves. However, the more the first player's donation increases, the more the second player's resources $(200 + s_1^B)$ increases. It is possible that when the income elasticity of donations is high, the second player may increase the proportion of their donation. However, the regression analysis in Table 3.3 does not show that the increase in the resources has an effect on the increase in donations by the second player. Model 1 fits better in the models that do not include prosociality as an explanatory variable, whereas Model 4 fits better in the models that include prosociality. Neither model include the resources as an explanatory variable. It is reasonable to assume that the impression of the first player to the second player has positive impact on the donation by the second player.

Another interesting finding of the regression analysis is that prosocial subjects tend to increase the share of donations (Models 4 and 5). For prosocial subjects, participation in Game B itself has the effect of increasing the share of donations. This point will be addressed again in Appendix 3.2.

[20] Tobit model is used, because the dependent variable $\frac{200S_3^B}{200+s_1^B} - s_2^A$ takes only the limited range of values, with a maximum of 200 and a minimum of − 200.

Table 3.2 Relationship between the impression of the first player to the second player and the actions of the second player (persons)

(2) The change from donation in Experiment A to net donation in Experiment B (the action of second player)		(3) The change from Experiment A to Experiment B in share of donation (the action of second player)	
(1) Impression of the first player → (2) Action of the second player	(i) Correlation coefficient (ii) Mean	(1) Impression of the first player → (3) Action of the second player	(i) Correlation coefficient (ii) Mean
Generous → generous, 4 persons Generous → neutral, 3 persons Generous → stingy, 11 persons Neutral → generous, 1 person Neutral → neutral, 2 persons Neutral → stingy, 3 persons Stingy → generous, 2 persons Stingy → neutral, 1 person Stingy → stingy, 10 persons	(i) 0.19 (ii) 0.42/0.23	Generous → generous, 12 persons Generous → neutral, 2 persons Generous → stingy, 4 persons Neutral → generous, 3 persons Neutral → neutral, 3 persons Neutral → stingy, 0 person Stingy → generous, 2 persons Stingy → neutral, 2 persons Stingy → stingy, 9 persons	(i) 0.53** (ii) 0.83/0.13***

Note (1) n = 37. ***1% significant, **5% significant, *10% significant
Note (2) "Correlation coefficient" is the correlation coefficient between (1) Impression of the first player and (2) Action of the second player, and (1) Impression of the first player and (3) Action of the second player, with "generous" and "neutral" receiving 1 point and "stingy" receiving 0 points
Note (3) "Mean" is the mean of the scores in the sense of (2) and (3) of the second player's actions when the impression of the first player is "generous" and "neutral," and the mean of the scores in the sense of (2) and (3) of the second player's actions when the impression of the first player is "stingy." The test of the difference between the mean when the impression of the first player is "generous" or "neutral" and the mean when the impression of the first player is "stingy" is performed

Table 3.3 Regression analysis of changes in share donated (Tobit)

	$\frac{200S_3^B}{200+s_1^B} - s_2^A$ (donation share change: 200 points conversion)				
	Model 1	Model 2	Model 3	Model 4	Model 5
Const.	– 7.82	– 108.69	32.47	– 41.26**	7.04
$s_1^B - s_2^A$ (impressions of the first player)	0.44***	–	0.50**	0.40***	0.47**
$200 + s_1^B$ (resources)	–	0.34	– 0.13	–	– 0.16
Prosociality	–	–	–	57.41***	57.93***
AIC	208.8	214.9	210.6	200.4	201.9

Note n = 37. ***1% significant, **5% significant, *10% significant

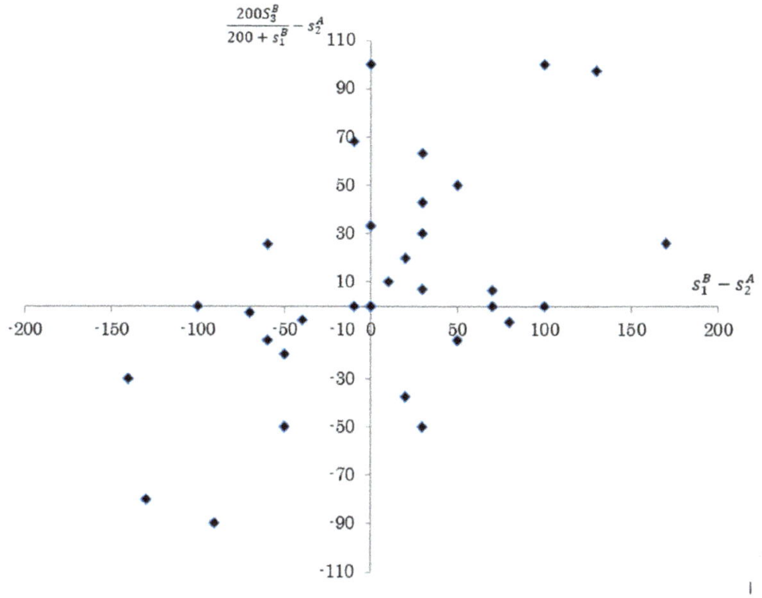

Fig. 3.4 Impressions of the first player to the second player (horizontal axis) and changes in the share of the donation by the second player to the resource (vertical axis). *Note* This figure illustrates scatterplot of the impression of the first player to the second player (horizontal axis) and the change in the share of the second player's donation to their resources (vertical axis). It is seen that the players who perceive the first players as generous tend to be more generous themselves

3.4.3 Interpretation

Although the difference-in-means test seems to reject Hypothesis 1, subjects who were more interested in donating tended to reduce their donations in Experiment B. This can be interpreted as subjects who only donated small points in Experiment A not originally finding a large stake in donating, even if they were subjected to Experiment B. They would therefore be more likely to make the same decision as in Experiment A. However, subjects who were more interested in donating were more likely to make a decision to reduce their donations when subjected to Experiment B, because they were more interested in the difference from the situation in Experiment A, in which they could directly decide points to be donated. The first player who sees a stake in the donation does not want to be betrayed and exploited by the second player. This means that those who had found strong value in their donations were forced to reduce their donations.

Hypothesis 2 is not rejected. As far as the test of difference in means was concerned, Hypothesis 1 was rejected; so, the main origin of the reduction in final donations in Experiment B was due to the decision of the second player. As discussed in the summary of results, on average, the second player did not change the ratio of private share to donations throughout Experiments A and B. In this case, they did not reduce their donation compared to their own in experiment A ($S_3^B \geq s_{2k}^A$), however Hypothesis 2 holds ($S_3^B < s_{1j}^A + s_{2k}^A$). If Generations 1 and 2 had cooperated, the final donation would have increased further, but under the decentralized decision of each generation, the donation ended up being subdued.

First, it is useful to place the results of the experiment among the previous studies on public goods with sequentiality raised in Sect. 3.2.3. The present results are in line with Gächter's experiment that mimics the analysis based on Varian's model and reports that the supply of public goods is reduced under sequential decisions compared to the case of simultaneous decisions (Gächter et al., 2010). To avoid this decrease, Normann and Rau's (2014) experiment showed that the introduction of steps to the gains from public goods is effective. The effectiveness of the introduction of steps in the context of donations has already been discussed, where Andreoni gives the economic rationale that the presence of seed money brings the charity closer to success. However, as will be seen below, what is important in this chapter's experiment is another effect of the seed money pointed out by Andreoni, namely, the effect of information in the sequentiality of decision-making; this point needs to be examined in depth.

In this regard, an interesting finding in the decision of the second player is that the behavior of the first player had an influence on the second player, as shown in Tables 3.2 and 3.3, and Fig. 3.4. The first player inspired the second player.[21] Since this case was an experiment involving donations, it is safe to say that this was a moral inspiration. This finding is consistent with the results of Shang and Croson's (2009) study, according to which social information that others are donating a lot increases the subjects' donations. Since the target of the donations in the current experiment is the CCCJ, this is different from the situation discussed by Andreoni (1998), where the seed money lures subsequent donors in a setting where the charity is not sure if it will be successful or not. The success or failure of the project, the CCCJ, has nothing to do with the behavior of the first player in the laboratory. It is natural to see the influence of the first player's behavior on the second player as another explanation suggested by Andreoni, the effect of information on the sequentiality of decision-making.

There is a wider body of research on the existence of inspiration that goes beyond donation. Classic psychological studies use the term conformity, especially from the perspective of the recipient of inspiration. Studies by Sherif (1937) and Asch's (1955), and derivative experiments by Crutchfield (1955) have found conformity in a wide range of matters, from fact recognition to normative judgments. In one of Crutchfield's examples, only 19% of the control group agreed with the statement that free speech was a privilege, not a right, and society could suspend free speech whenever it felt threatened; whereas, in a situation where those around them unanimously agreed, 58% of subjects agreed. In the experiments in this chapter, the subject

[21] A note should be made on the relationship between the assumption of homothetic utility function and the inspiration. The mean of the impression of the first players to the second players $\left(s_1^B - s_2^A\right)$ is insignificant, averaging 5.1 (to 18 s players they were positive, to 6 zero and to 13 negative). In total, the inspirations given by the first players offset each other. Thus, it makes sense to assume the homothetic function as the utility function of the second player before the first player's influence.

who is referred to is a single subject (rather than many), however it is not difficult to find the same motif of conformity with others.[22]

A study by management scientist Wade-Benzoni (2002) addresses the effects of the preceding generations on subsequent generations in experiments. Wade-Benzoni reported the results of the experiments in which she found that subsequent generations that were treated well by their predecessors treated their successors well. Wade-Benzoni attributes the chain of favorable treatment to the logic that (1) the preceding generations serve as a role model for the subsequent generation, and (2) when one is treated kindly, one is inclined to treat others kindly. In the experiment in this chapter, it is explicitly stated that the donation entrusted by the first player is not for the second player, but for the final donation. Insofar as the second player understands this setup correctly, it can be considered the first role model, or logic of inspiration, which is at work in the experiments of this chapter.

It should be noted that by extending the discussion to moral inspiration, the discussion in this chapter moves away from the position that preferences for subject of subsequent generation roles are fixed. In economics, the discussion is usually based on the assumption of fixed preferences. Here, the argument is based on the results of economic experiments, and allows for limited endogenous determination of preferences under the particularized logic of influences from the behavior of preceding generations' subjects.

3.5 Intergenerational Cooperation Through the Kantian Categorical Imperative

3.5.1 Model Extensions

It is valuable to extend the intergenerational savings succession model to consider what happens when the preceding generation is aware of its moral inspiration on the subsequent generations.[23] In this case, the utility function of the subsequent generation is not constant, but influenced by the behavior of the preceding generation. In the utility function of Generation 2 (Eq. 3.6), the degree of interest in the future α_2 is now an endogenous variable (while the degree of interest in the future in Generation 1 α_1 remains fixed). Assuming the inspiration from the preceding generation, α_2 is defined as an endogenous variable, as follows.

[22] A full explanation of the rationale for conformity from the perspective of the followers must be left for another study. A prime explanation could be that conformity is an efficient method with low cognitive load in discovering strategies that work well. Conformity is also rational when similar behavior among several persons generates a positive externality (Katz & Shapiro, 1986; Ross & Nisbett, 1991). See Bernheim's (1994) study for prior research on this issue.

[23] The solution obtained through the extension of the model in this section also describes the subjective solution of the preceding generation with the game solution as the reference point, just as in the subgame perfect equilibrium in Sect. 3.3.2.

$$\alpha_2 = \frac{s_1^B}{y_1}. \tag{3.17}$$

$$u_2^B = u_2^B(c_2^B, S_3^B|\alpha_2) = (1-\alpha_2)\log c_2^B + \alpha_2 \log S_3^B. \tag{3.18}$$

Equation 3.17 determines α_2 of Generation 2, and under the α_2, Generation 2 maximizes Eq. 3.18. In Eq. 3.17, α_2 is assumed to be the proportion of savings that Generation 1 entrusts to Generation 2 from its own income. In this case, if generation 1 is aware of its moral inspiration on Generation 2, it tries to maximize its own utility while taking this inspiration into account. Generation 1 knows that Generation 2 will divide consumption and saving in the ratio of $1 - \frac{s_1^B}{y_1} : \frac{s_1^B}{y_1}$, and the followings are obtained as the savings and final savings of Generation 1 (The solution at $y_1 = y_2 = 200$ is shown with a subscript ' in the equation number).

$$s_1^{B**} = \sqrt{\frac{\alpha_1 y_1 y_2}{\alpha_1 + 1} + \frac{(y_2 - 2\alpha_1 y_1)^2}{4(\alpha_1 + 1)^2}} + \frac{2\alpha_1 y_1 - y_2}{2(\alpha_1 + 1)}. \tag{3.19}$$

$$S_3^{B**} = \frac{\left(y_2 + s_1^{B**}\right)s_1^{B**}}{y_1}. \tag{3.20}$$

$$s_1^{B**} = \frac{100\left(\sqrt{8\alpha_1^2 + 1} + 2\alpha_1 - 1\right)}{\alpha_1 + 1}. \tag{3.19'}$$

$$S_3^{B**} = \frac{50\left[\left(\sqrt{8\alpha_1^2 + 1} + 2\alpha_1 - 1\right)\left(\sqrt{8\alpha_1^2 + 1} + 4\alpha_1 + 1\right)\right]}{(\alpha_1 + 1)^2}. \tag{3.20'}$$

In Eqs. 3.20 and 3.19 should be substituted for s_1^{B**}. However, for the sake of simplicity, the equation before the substitution is shown.

Note that while Eq. 3.17 is an easily understood formulation of the moral inspiration, it is not necessarily an accurate representation. Generation 1 is concerned with private consumption and final savings, as indicated by its utility function Eq. 3.5. The share of saving for subsequent generations to private consumption, as assumed in Eq. 3.17, does not express the degree of interest in the future of Generation 1. To put this in perspective, α_2 should be given by

$$\alpha_2 = \frac{S_3^B}{c_1^B + S_3^B}. \tag{3.21}$$

$\frac{S_3^B}{c_1^B + S_3^B}$ is the ratio of final savings divided by the sum of private consumption of Generation 1 and the final savings. Generation 2 is inspired by Generation 1's behavior, as indicated by this ratio.

Generation 1 maximizes its own utility, while taking into account this precise inspiration in Eq. 3.21. The followings are solutions.

$$s_1^{B***} = \frac{(\alpha_1 + 1)y_1 + (\alpha_1 - 1)y_2}{2}, \text{ if } \frac{y_2 - y_1}{y_2 + y_1} < \alpha_1 \leq 1. s_1^{B***} = 0, \text{ otherwise.} \tag{3.22}$$

$$S_3^{B***} = (y_1 + y_2)\alpha_1, \text{ if } \frac{y_2 - y_1}{y_2 + y_1} < \alpha_1 \leq 1. S_3^{B***} = y_2 - y_2, \text{ otherwise.} \tag{3.23}$$

$$s_1^{B***} = 200\alpha_1. \tag{3.22'}$$

$$S_3^{B***} = 400\alpha_1. \tag{3.23'}$$

Equation 3.22 coincides with Eq. 3.14. When Generation 2 is precisely inspired by the behavior of Generation 1, and the latter takes this inspiration into account, the savings of Generation 1 coincide with the optimal solution.

Line 4 in Fig. 3.5. indicates the savings of Generation 1 (Eq. 3.19') after taking into account imprecise inspiration according to Eq. 3.17. Line 5 shows the savings of Generation 1 (Eq. 3.22') when precise inspiration according to Eq. 3.21 is taken into account. Comparing Lines 4 and 5 with Line 1, it is shown that the moral inspiration and taking it into account, significantly increase Generation 1's savings. The comparison of Lines 4 and 5 with Line 2 shows that when imprecise inspiration is taken into account (Line 4), the savings of Generation 1 exceed the optimal solution, whereas when precise inspiration is taken into account (Line 5), these savings coincide with the optimal solution. Line 4 exceeds Line 5 because comparison of Eqs. 3.17 and 3.21 shows that (as long as $s_1^B \leq S_3^B$) $\frac{s_1^B}{y_1}\left(= \frac{s_1^B}{c_1^B + s_1^B}\right) \leq \frac{S_3^B}{c_1^B + S_3^B}$), it follows that when Generation 2 is inspired imprecisely through Eq. 3.17, Generation 1 is forced to cooperate more, in order to ensure that Generation 2 is cooperative as well.

Figure 3.6 depicts the final savings realized through Generations 1 and 2. Line 4 shows the final savings after taking into account imprecise inspiration according to Eqs. 3.17 (3.18'), whereas Line 5 indicates the final savings after taking into account precise inspiration according to Eq. 3.21 (Eq. 3.23'). In Lines 4 and 5, Generation 2's interest in the future α_2 is endogenously determined. Comparing Lines 4 and 5 with Lines 1 and 2, the moral inspiration and its prior consideration increase final savings (over optimal as well as subgame perfect solutions) when Generation 1's interest in the future is strong; however, they reduce final savings (below subgame perfect as well as optimal solutions) when Generation 1's interest in the future is weak (the elliptical region). When Generation 1's interest in the future is weak, Generation 2's interest in the future is also weakened, through moral inspiration, and final savings are suppressed.

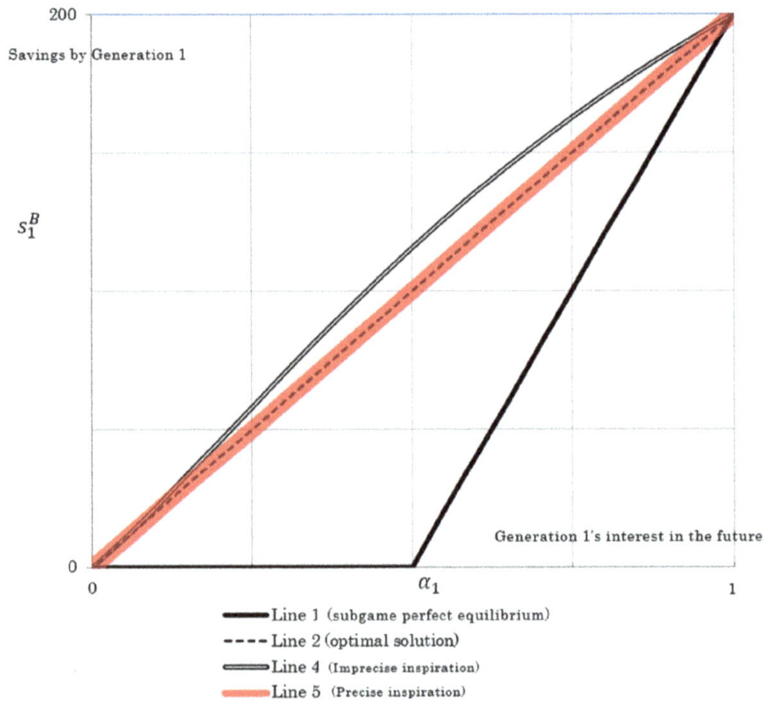

Fig. 3.5 Savings by Generation 1 (the Kantian categorical imperative) ($y_1 = y_2 = 200$). *Note* Line 4 shows the savings of Generation 1 after taking into account imprecise inspiration. Line 5 shows the savings of Generation 1 when precise inspiration is taken into account. Comparing Lines 4 and 5 with Line 1, it is shown that moral inspiration, and taking it into account, significantly increase Generation 1's savings

3.5.2 Discussion 1 (The Kantian Categorical Imperative)

If Generation 1 wishes for Generation 2 to cooperate, it should cooperate itself, and indeed it does. It should be pointed out that, in acting according to Eqs. 3.19 and 3.22, Generation 1 can be interpreted as acting according to the Kantian categorical imperative. In Sect. 3.2.2, the Kantian categorical imperative formulated by Roemer (2010) was presented. Excluding the stiff tone from his formulation, the Kantian categorical imperative is represented as follows:

> One should take an action that one can support, if (all) others take it.

The "all" is placed in brackets because the model discussed in this chapter is a two-generation model, and "all others" refer to one generation, that is, Generation 2, in the model. The action taken by Generation 2 that Generation 1 supports is cooperation. Such cooperation should be undertaken by Generation 1 as its own action.

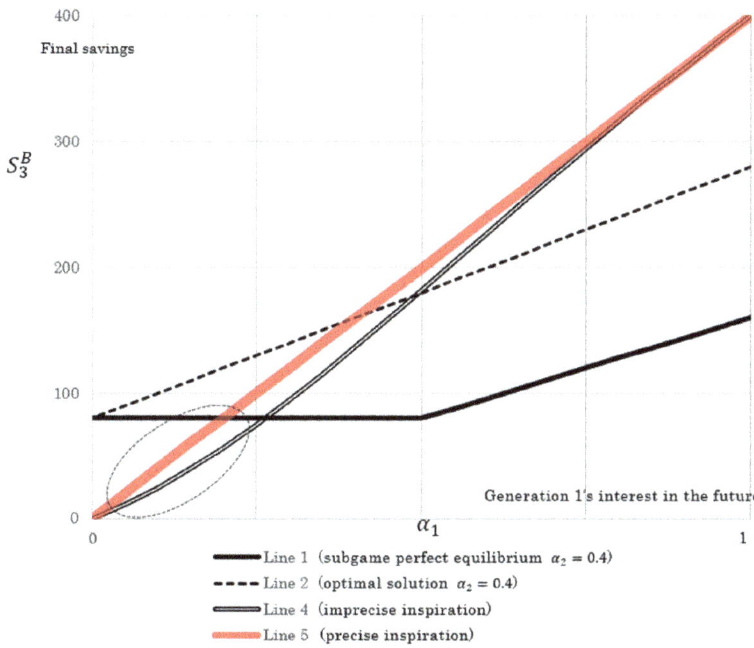

Fig. 3.6 Final savings (the Kantian categorical imperative) ($y_1 = y_2 = 200$). *Note* Line 4 shows the final savings after taking into account imprecise inspiration, whereas Line 5 shows the final savings after taking into account precise inspiration. Comparing Lines 4 and 5 with Lines 1 and 2, moral inspiration and its prior consideration increase final savings when Generation 1's interest in the future is strong, and they reduce final savings when Generation 1's interest in the future is weak

Most interesting is that the Kantian categorical imperative is not merely stated as a maxim, but that within the framework of moral inspiration and its consideration, Generation 1 actually takes cooperative actions. The ineffectiveness of punishment among successive generations makes intergenerational cooperation difficult, as has been seen in Theorem 3.1. First, subsequent generations cannot punish the preceding generation that has left the world before them. However, under inspiration and its consideration, if the preceding generation is not cooperative itself, it will be confronted with the prospect that its own interests S_3^B will be reduced. Indeed, in their subjective view, subsequent generations are merely acting according to their own utility function. However, the preceding generation perceives the subsequent generations as threats. Second, the preceding generation cannot punish the subsequent generation because it leaves the world first. However, when the preceding generation exerts moral inspiration, cooperation from the succeeding generation is guaranteed as long as the preceding generation behaves cooperatively. Through its own behavior, the preceding generation decides the kind of people that the future will consist of.

Previous studies that refer to the Kantian categorical imperative include that of Cornes and Sandler (1984). This study questions Nash's assumption that considers the behavior of others as given. They call the effect of an increase in one's own payment for a public good on the total payments of others conjectural variations, and point out that when the variations are positive, the supply of the public good above the Nash equilibrium level may be realized. Although their study is based on good intuition, it has already been noted in Sect. 3.2.2 that Sugden (1985) has a compelling criticism of this study. Every optimist who increases their payments because they believe that others will pay, will be betrayed by people who reduce their own payments. Intergenerational cooperation through the Kantian categorical imperative, in the sense of this chapter, also leads to an increase in the supply of public goods (final savings) by assuming non-Nash behavior. However, unlike the work of Cornes and Sandler, it has the mechanism to generate positive conjectural variations through inspiration by previous generations, thus escaping Sugden's criticism. Sugden points out that if positive conjectural variations occur, individuals are simply not maximizing their utilities (p. 123). The argument in this chapter leads to positive conjectural variations through the transformation of the utility function[24] and is different from simple utility maximization, which assumes stable preferences. The moral inspiration associated with sequential decisions has the implication of expanding the possibilities for cooperation over public goods in general, and not just between generations. As Andreoni suggested in his study of donations, the sequentiality of decision-making has important implications. Another advantage of the argument presented in this chapter is that it does not require the preceding generation to behave excessively ethically. According to the rule suggested by Sugden, as seen in Sect. 3.2.2, "suppose that I is the group of individuals who benefit from the public good, and consider any person i who is a member of I. Let i choose the level of effort that she would most prefer that every member of I should make (the same effort for each person). Then i is obliged to make at least this effort." (Sugden, 1984, p. 774). This is a strict ethical requirement on the agents, however in the discussion of this chapter, it is sufficient for the preceding generation to know that subsequent generations will be inspired by their actions.

Thus, moral inspiration and its consideration succeed in giving a reasonable logic to the intuition of conjectural variations in the context of sequential decision-making. Moreover, they also give logic to the intuition of what Roemer calls "magical thinking." Magical thinking was one of the reasons Roemer enumerated, without explanation, for why people act in accordance with Kantian ethics: "if I donate, all others like me will also donate." By giving the logic of moral inspiration and

[24] Chapter 1 (Sect. 1.3.5) has already seen that Saijo (2020a, 2020b) has been working on the endogenous determination of preferences under the policy of designing institutions to change individual preferences. Many other studies have engaged in explicitly making variables that are usually neglected the subject of consideration. For example, in Botond Kőszegi and Matthew Rabin's "reference point-dependent preferences," the evaluation of choices is dependent not only on preference for the choice itself, but also the contrast with the reference point (Kőszegi & Rabin, 2006). The reference point is formed by one's own and others' past consumption, etc., and changes in the reference point in response to the situation affect the subject's behavior. George Akerlof and Rachel Kranton have incorporated identity, such as the gender, as a variable in their model, and have attempted to elucidate phenomena that were previously considered difficult to explain, such as differences in contributions to household (Akerlof & Kranton, 2000, 2005).

its consideration, this magical thinking actually works. Rather than showing that the preference for Kantian ethics survives the evolutionary process, as Alger and Weibull's (2013, 2016) work tells us, even under the simplistic assumption of a generation with only an interest in the survival of the community, there is a way to ensure the Kantian categorical imperative works in practice.

The point clarified through the extension of the model in Sects. 3.5.1 and 3.5.2 is summarized in Theorem 3.3.

Theorem 3.3 (Intergenerational cooperation through the Kantian categorical imperative) *When different generations share a concern for the survival of a project (e.g., humanity, community) and when the subsequent generation is morally inspired by the behavior of the preceding generation, the preceding generation behaves itself as it wants the subsequent generation to behave. Intergenerational cooperation through this pathway is effective against both anticipation of betrayal by the subsequent generation and dependence on the subsequent generation.*

While intergenerational cooperation is indeed possible under public reciprocity, the degree of cooperation has not always been sufficient. The intergenerational cooperation through the Kantian categorical imperative, presented here, increases the degree of cooperation by increasing the degree of rule-sharing between the preceding and subsequent generations. In this sense, intergenerational cooperation through the Kantian categorical imperative can be understood as an extension of public reciprocity, which promotes the complete fulfillment of the function of the reciprocity. Where moral inspiration and its consideration work, the degree of rule-sharing increases. The increased degree of rule-sharing binds a series of generations together like a community with shared purpose, and encourages the preceding generation to act in accordance with the Kantian categorical imperative.

3.5.3 Discussion 2 (Welfare Analysis)

Next, this subsection considers the welfare implications. Figure 3.7 depicts the preceding generation's interest in the future (α_1) on the horizontal axis and the utility of the preceding generation on the vertical axis.[25] Line 1 depicts utility based on the subgame perfect equilibrium of Game B (Eqs. 3.10' and 3.11'), when $\alpha_2 = 0.4$), Line 4 is the utility based on imprecise inspiration (Eqs. 3.19' and 3.20'), Line 5 is the utility based on precise inspiration (Eqs. 3.22' and 3.23'), and Line 6 is the utility from Game A. Comparing Line 1 (subgame perfect equilibrium) with Lines 4 and 5 (inspiration) shows that there is more welfare improvement by the Kantian categorical imperative when the preceding generation is more interested in the future. For

[25] As Sect. 3.3.2 has discussed, S_3^B the value in the utility function of Generation 1, predicted by Generation 1. The utilities of the preceding generations are computed based on solutions like subgame perfect, but these solutions are just reference points that represent the subjective solutions of the preceding generations rather than the solutions of the game.

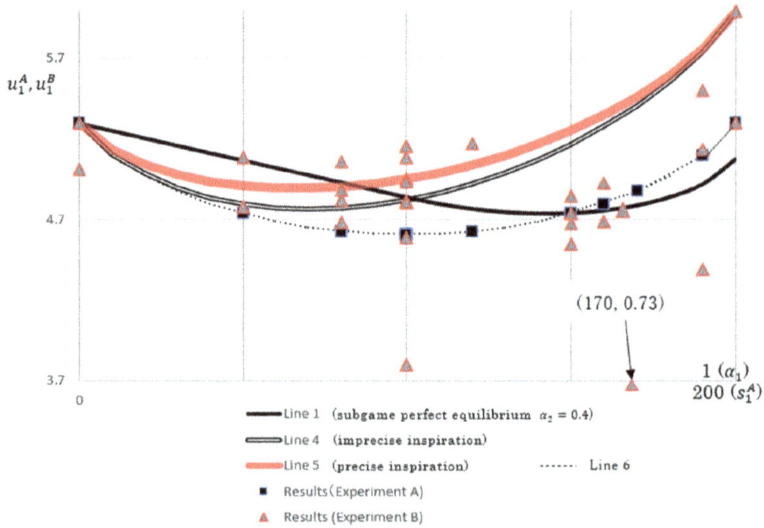

Fig. 3.7 The utility of the first player. *Note* This figure depicts the preceding generation's interest in the future (α_1) on the horizontal axis and the utility of the preceding generation on the vertical axis. From a comparison of Line 1 (subgame perfect equilibrium) with Lines 4 and 5 (inspiration), it is shown that there is more welfare improvement by the Kantian categorical imperative when preceding generation is more interested in the future. However, the welfare of the less future-oriented generation deteriorates

the preceding generation that is more concerned about the future, it can increase its own utility by increasing the final savings through the inspiration of the subsequent generation. However, the welfare of the less future-oriented generation deteriorates. This is because it will no longer be able to take the selfish approach of consuming to its heart's content, while asking the subsequent generation to save for itself.

Figure 3.7 only addresses the utility of the preceding generation and not that of the subsequent generation. This is because when moral inspiration is taken into account, the utility function of the subsequent generation changes, making it impossible to discuss the impact of the Kantian categorical imperative on the welfare of the subsequent generation. However, it is worth noting that in the solution through Kantian categorical imperative (Eq. 3.22), compared with the subgame perfect equilibrium (Eq. 3.10), the savings (s_1^B) of the preceding generation to be entrusted to the subsequent generation increases. Behaving according to the Kantian categorical imperative succeeds in giving more resources to subsequent generations. In sum, intergenerational cooperation through the Kantian categorical imperative not only improves the welfare of the preceding generation but also improves the resources of the subsequent generation, when the former's interest in the future is strong. When the preceding generation is less concerned about the future, its welfare worsens, but the resources improve in the subsequent generation; so, the welfare evaluation through the two generations is indeterminate.

It is necessary to make a note to prevent possible misunderstandings in the welfare analysis. It has already been pointed out that Lines 4 and 5 are below Lines 1 and 2 (the ellipse) in the left-hand region of Fig. 3.6, where the preceding generation is less interested in the future. The necessary annotation is that the existence of the elliptical area does *not* represent a flaw in the Kantian categorical imperative. As long as the preceding generations place low value on the survival of the community, and the subsequent generations are inspired by this value, there is no welfare problem in the sluggish allocation of resources for the survival of the community. If anyone sees a problem with the sluggish allocation, it is the observer, who is looking at the game from the outside.

However, the pros and cons of dismissing the discussion by ignoring this assessment from the outside observer should be considered carefully, given the reality of intergenerational issues. Whether climate change or financial sustainability, intergenerational issues are now becoming problematic because the present generation (the preceding generation) continues to prefer dangerous policies even such polices put the survival of humanity and the community at risk. It is inappropriate to ignore the assessments of outside observers. From an outside observer's point of view, it is disadvantageous that moral inspiration and its consideration fixes cooperation at a low level through the inspiration of subsequent generations to the preceding generation's low level of cooperation. Our generation's reluctance to take action on certain issues (e.g., climate change, fiscal sustainability) may be the result of our being inspired by the behavior of our predecessors, who were not enthusiastic about these issues. Moral inspiration takes into account the endogenous determination of the preferences of subsequent generations, leaving the preferences of preceding generations exogenously fixed. No way to break out of this negative situation endogenously can emerge from intergenerational cooperation through the Kantian categorical imperative. In order to break out of this situation, it is necessary to problematize the preferences of the preceding generation, which remain fixed in the discussion in Chaps. 3, and 4 will take up the issue as the discussion of deliberation.

Finally, it is useful to shed light once again on the experimental results seen in Sect. 3.4. Figure 3.7 overlays the scatter plots of the first player's actual utility (■, ▲) in Experiments A and B. Here, utility in Experiment B is defined as the utility obtained by substituting the actual value of the final donation determined by the second player into the utility function of the first player. Comparing the actual utility in Experiments A and B, eight subjects had better utility in Experiment A, 26 in Experiment B, and three in the tie. Although the overall results were better in Experiment B, it is noteworthy that of the eight subjects who were below in Experiment B, indeed seven of them were plotted on the right-hand side of the figure, $\alpha_1 \geq 0.5$. Of these seven, five reduced their donations in Experiment B compared to Experiment A. These reductions point to the same fact that the first player tended to reduce donations in the right-hand region of Fig. 3.3. The first player who was more interested in donating had a better chance of improving welfare through the Kantian categorical imperative, but in reality, this chance was not fully exploited.

It is important to note that the actual utility (▲) in Experiment B, plotted in Fig. 3.7, is *counterfactual*. In reality, the first player *never* knows the decisions of the second player.[26] What is considered utility in Experiment B is the first player's utility had they learned of the second player's decision, and not the actual utility of the first player. Thus, those who assess that the first player had a good chance to improve welfare, but did not fully take advantage of this chance are observers who were looking at the game from the outside. If such an outside observer can teach the first player that initiating cooperation will inspire cooperation by the second player, the observer will be able to encourage cooperation on the part of the first player.

3.5.4 Discussion 3 (Application to Public Policies, Business Managements)

It is also important to point out that *generations* need not be limited to groups of people of different eras. The administrations and managers in charge of national policies and corporate management, and those who are replaced over time, can be seen as different generations making sequential decisions. Moral inspiration and its consideration can function as a logic to ensure the policy implementation and management, in line with the Kantian categorical imperative. In other words, it can function as a mechanism to sustain good policy and business management over the course of different administrations and managers. Administrations or managements could want to engage in wasteful spending. However, when moral inspiration from the preceding administration or management works, they foresee that once wasteful spending starts, the bad practice will continue over a long period of time, and the survival of the country or company will be undermined; so, the wasteful spending will be discouraged. Such logic can work. The problem domain in which the Kantian categorical imperative can work is not limited to public policies and corporate management. The time-different self is also a subsequent generation. There are a series of arguments by the behavioral economist Richard Thaler, in favor of viewing the future self as a stranger and subject to control (Thaler & Shefrin, 1981). If one lives a life of moderation to discourage the future self from following bad habits such as smoking or overeating, which would harm one's future health, then the Kantian categorical imperative is at work in this situation.

3.5.5 Discussion 4 (Points to be Noted)

The last point is to leave the theoretical considerations made in Sect. 3.5 and return once again to the results of the economic experiment (Sect. 3.4). It should be noted that Kantian categorical imperative does not work as well as the theoretical considerations

[26] By the time the final savings by Generation 2 are realized, Generation 1 has already passed away. Even in the experimental setting, the first players are never informed of the second player's decision, and the first players are aware of this.

suggest if the inspiration exerted by the preceding generation is not certain and sufficient. As the results of the economic experiment reveal, not all subjects in the second player were reliably inspired by the first player. As can be seen in Fig. 3.4, the subjects plotted in the second and fourth quadrants of the figure behave differently than expected after being inspired. In addition, the second player was not necessarily fully inspired by the first player. As Fig. 3.4 and Table 3.3 suggest, for every one-unit improvement in first player impressions, the 200-point equivalent percentage of second-mover donations on the vertical axis improves by less than one unit (the regression coefficient is only about 0.5–0.4). Even though inspiration exists, adhesion to one's original preferences also exists. Because of this, it is possible that the impact of the preceding generation's behavior on subsequent generations may be interrupted or diminished, especially when the chain of generations spans multiple generations.

3.6 Conclusions and Remaining Issues

This chapter discusses the possibilities and difficulties of intergenerational cooperation based on the intergenerational savings succession model, which incorporates direct reciprocity between generations through public reciprocity discussed in Chap. 2. While intergenerational cooperation is indeed possible under public reciprocity, the degree of cooperation is not always sufficient. Two pathways were found to hinder intergenerational cooperation: anticipation of betrayal by subsequent generations and; dependence on subsequent generations. Although fund establishment (constitutionalization) is a countermeasure against betrayal by subsequent generations, it is incompatible with public reciprocity. This chapter then conducted an economic experiment to simulate the model and gain insight into what might happen in real intergenerational situations. The results of the experiment revealed that although the preceding generation does not reduce donations as much as the model predicted, subjects who placed higher value on donations (a common intergenerational value) were more likely to curb their donations. One of the most interesting findings is that the subsequent generation was influenced by the behavior of the preceding one. The preceding generation morally inspires the subsequent generation. There is room to treat the degree of interest in the future of the subsequent generation as an endogenous variable, although it had been treated as an exogenous variable previously. The discussion in the latter half of this chapter was directed toward incorporating this inspiration into the model and expanding the possibilities for intergenerational cooperation. When the preceding generation takes into account that the subsequent generation will be inspired, it will increase its degree of cooperation. If the preceding generation wants the subsequent generation to cooperate, it should cooperate itself, and indeed it does; here, cooperation is realized in accordance with the Kantian categorical imperative. Intergenerational cooperation through the Kantian categorical imperative increases the degree of cooperation by increasing the degree of sharing of rules among generations. In this sense, intergenerational cooperation through the Kantian categorical imperative is an extension of public reciprocity and promotes its full functioning.

Three issues still need to be addressed. The first concerns the limitations of intergenerational cooperation through the Kantian categorical imperative, as pointed out in Sect. 3.5.3. From an outside observer's point of view, the drawback of the Kantian categorical imperative is that it fixes cooperation at a low level when the preceding generation has only a low interest in cooperation. To resolve this difficulty, it is necessary to address the preferences of the preceding generation. This issue is addressed in Chap. 4, which examines whether the preferences of the preceding (present) generation can be changed through deliberation among them.

The second issue, also in Sect. 3.5.3, concerns the fact that teaching the preceding generation about the role of moral inspiration may enhance intergenerational cooperation. This point is a hypothetical one that states a logical consequence. In Sect. 3.5.4, it is also pointed out that Kantian categorical imperative can function in situations ranging from public policy to individual lifestyles; however, whether such a function can be observed in actual situations needs to be verified.

The third issue concerns the concept of moral inspiration. In this chapter, from the perspective of the predecessor, they inspire the subsequent generation, but the same situation can be seen from the perspective of the subsequent generation, which is attuned to the behavior of the predecessor. However, such conformity ranges from mechanically imitating the predecessor to actively learning from the predecessor, even though the appearance of behaving like the predecessor is the same. As Wade Benzoni pointed out, there is another logic that is a bit more complex, in which, if one receives a kindness, one will want to be kind to another person. These various variances in conformity lead directly to the complexity of the concept of moral inspiration, and a precise consideration of the conformity must be the subject of future work.

This final issue is related to the main point of this chapter's argument that intergenerational cooperation through the Kantian categorical imperative is an extension of public reciprocity. That is, when the conformity in response to moral inspiration is regarded as mere mechanical imitation, a tension arises between such conformity and the public reciprocity of recognizing subsequent generations as persons and sharing rules. This is a problem that can be set aside when considering the practical function of the Kantian categorical proposition in intergenerational relations. Regardless of the logic by which subsequent generations are attuned, intergenerational cooperation is realized if only by the fact that it exerts inspiration. However, as a philosophical and theoretical issue, this is a problem that cannot be overlooked. Philosophically, in order to locate intergenerational cooperation through the Kantian categorical imperative in public reciprocity, we must consider the situation in which the subsequent generation behaves like the preceding one as a result of the subjective choice of persons. In the words of Wataru Kuroda, discussed in Chap. 2 (Sect. 2.3.1), the subsequent generation will not only have "causal necessity" in the sense that "knowledge of a principle has a power in a person's mind, and if it is encountered within certain circumstances, that power activates proper conducts" (Kuroda, 1992,

p. 95). Rather, it also has "normative necessity" in the sense that "one who accepts a certain practical principle should always act in accordance with that principle in appropriate circumstances" (p. 95), and the preceding generation must understand this. In order to trace such complex thinking, precise examination based on the various conformities is necessary.

Attachment 1: Experimental description

(General guidance)

- In modern economics, empirical research that incorporates experimental methods called "experimental economics" is being actively conducted. We would like to ask for your cooperation in conducting research using experimental methods.
- In the following, there are two experiments. Please follow the instructions and respond to the questions below.
- Please feel free to answer as you see fit. There is no correct answer, nor will we be able to show the audience how you answered the questions after the session.
- Never chat with others or signal to each other during the experiment. Also, please switch off your cell phone.
- In the two experiments, you will be rewarded by drawing lots after the experiments are completed for the points you have earned with 10 points = 10 yen". In Experiments A and B, your partner's share of the points will also be paid actually on the outcomes of the lot.
- Your points earned and responses in this experiment will not affect your grade.

(Experiment A)

- You are to divide the 200-point reward between yourself and the donation for the public. You are the one who decides the distribution.
- The organizer of the experiment promises to donate the share of the public donation to the Central Community Chest of Japan (CCCJ).

(Experiment B)

(For the first player)

- You are to divide the 200 points reward between yourself and the donation for the public. You are the one who decides the distribution.
- However, this time, there will be another person paired with you, between you and the donation for the public, as shown below.

$$\begin{aligned} \text{You(endowment: 200 points)} &\Rightarrow \text{Your pair(endowment: 200 points)} \\ &\Rightarrow \text{Donation for the public} \end{aligned}$$

- The points that you have set as your share will become your points as they are.
- However, the points that you have taken as the share of the public donation will not become a public donation as it is, but will be passed on to your pair once.

- The points received from you, plus the points your pair has as endowment (200 points), will then be divided between the pair themself and the donation for the public. (Note that your pair will not tell you what their final allocation decision will be.)
- The organizer of the experiment promises to donate to the CCCJ the share of the final public donation.

(For the second player)

- You are to divide the reward between yourself and donations for the public. You determine the distribution.
- However, this time, the other person you are paired with will enter before you, as shown below.

$$\text{Your pair (endowment: 200 points)} \Rightarrow \text{You (endowment: 200 points)}$$
$$\Rightarrow \text{Donation for public}$$

- Your pair will determine their share between themself and the public donation, and give you the portion of the donation that they have made as the share of the public donation.
- You decide how you will allocate the points given to you by your pair, plus the points you have (endowment: 200 points), between yourself and the donation for the public. (Note that you are not to tell your pair your decision.)
- The organizer of the experiment also promises to donate to the CCCJ, the share of the final public donation.

(Procedures for closure)

(Survey on basic attributes, conduct of prosociality tests, pay rewards, etc.)

Attachment 2: Instructions to Subjects in the Prosociality Test (van Lange et al., 1997)

In this task we ask you to imagine that you have been randomly paired with another person, whom we will refer to simply as the "Other." This other person is someone you do not know and that you will not knowingly meet in the future. Both you and the "Other" person will be making choices by circling either the letter A, B, or C. ^bur own choices will produce points for both yourself and the "Other" person. Likewise, the other's choice will produce points for him/her and for you. Every point has value: The more points you receive, the better for you, and the more points the "Other" receives, the better for him/her.

Here's an example of how this task works:

	A	B	C
You get	500	500	550
Other gets	100	500	300

In this example, if you chose A, you would receive 500 points and the other would receive 100 points; if you chose B, you would receive 500 points and the other 500; and if you chose C, you would receive 550 points and the other 300. So, you see that your choice influences both the number of points you receive and the number of points the other receives.

Before you begin making choices, please keep in mind that there are no right or wrong answers—choose the option that you, for whatever reason, prefer most. Also, remember that the points have value; The more of them you accumulate, the better for you. Likewise, from the "other's" point of view, the more points s/he accumulates, the better for him/her.

Appendix 3.1: Intergenerational Negotiation

The subgame perfect equilibrium in the intergenerational savings succession model is not Pareto optimal. This chapter has already discussed fund establishment (constitutionalization) and the Kantian categorical imperative as paths to a more appropriate solution, and this Appendix argues a way of intergenerational negotiation.

A study by Suzumura and Tadenuma (2007) examines the idea of intergenerational negotiation to resolve intergenerational issues. They refer to the resolution of pollution externalities through negotiation between parties, as proposed by Coase (1960) and discuss its possible application to intergenerational issues. They raise the difficulty of intergenerational negotiation due to the temporal disconnect between originators of harm and victims, but point out that it is still possible to envision imaginary negotiations in hypothetical setting in which all parties come together.

Suzumura and Tadenuma ultimately dismiss this imaginary negotiation because of the plasticity of future generations, which is brought about by the non-identity problem[27]. However, from the standpoint of this book, which has already discussed the non-identity problem in Chap. 2, it is possible for the present generation to assume hypothetical future persons who claim "such events like harms should be avoided." This is because such claims share a common understanding within the present generation about events like harm to the future generations that established intergenerational ethics through duty. Because the concern for life after death, such as the survival of the human race, has fundamental value and is not subject to change over time, the difficulty of having hypothetical future persons make such claims may be reduced.

It is useful to considers the negotiation between Generations 1 and 2 in the model of Eq. 3.5–3.10. Generation 2 is a hypothetical agent assumed by the present generation. Assume $y_1 = y_2 = 200$ and, due to the fundamental nature of the interest in life

[27] The plasticity of future generations referred to by Suzumura and Tadenuma is the kind of preference plasticity in which people raised in an automobile-intensive society will produce generations that prefers the use of automobiles in the future. See Chap. 2 (Sect. 2.2.1) for my view of this plasticity.

after death, in this appendix, the degrees of that interest of Generations 1 and 2 are assumed to be equivalent to α. The starting point for negotiation is here the subgame perfect equilibrium solution of Eqs. (3.10') and (3.11'), and the bargaining assumes that.

Generation 2 asks Generation 1 for addition of s_1^B (savings passed on to Generation 2). At this time, Generation 1 will comply with the demand on the condition that it does not reduce its own utility, and therefore, Generation 1 asks Generation 2 to increase allocation to S_3^B (final savings).

When c_1^B (consumption of Generation 1) is reduced and S_3^B (final savings) is increased, the following must hold for constant the utility condition from the standpoint of Generation 1.

$$(1-\alpha)\log c_1^{B*} - (1-\alpha)\log\left(c_1^{B*} - x\right) = -\left[\alpha\log\left(S_3^{B*}\right) - \alpha\log\left(S_3^{B*} + z\right)\right]. \tag{3.24}$$

where the left-hand side is the reduction in utility of Generation 1 by reducing c_1^B by x, and the right-hand side is the (negative sign of) increase in the utility of Generation 1 by increasing S_3^B by z. These are connected by an equal sign. Solving Eq. 3.24 yields the relationships between x and z, which are indifference curves of Generation 1, starting from the subgame equilibriums. In the bargaining, from the combinations of (c_1^B, S_3^B), Generation 2 chooses the point that maximizes its own utility. The negotiations are concluded there and Pareto improvements are realized.

Figure 3.8 depicts the path of the negotiations. The cases of $\alpha = 1/4$, 1/2, and 3/4 are depicted. The upper panel shows the vertical axis S_3^B (final savings) and the horizontal axis c_1^B (consumption of Generation 1), and the curves are the indifference curves for Generation 1. The equilibriums are marked by ■, and from these starting points, c_1^B is reduced, and S_3^B is increased according to indifference curves. In the lower panel, the vertical axis is u_2^B (the utility of Generation 2) and the horizontal axis is c_1^B, and the curves are the utility of Generation 2 corresponding to the points on the indifference curves of Generation 1. Generation 2 chooses the points ▲ that maximize its utility, and Generation 1 moves from ■ to ▲ on the indifference curves, thus concluding negotiations. In any case, the probability of community survival increases in exchange for Generation 1's reduced consumption, Generation 1's utility remains unchanged, and Generation 2's utility improves.

Intergenerational negotiations suggest two important points. The first concerns the starting points for negotiations. In Fig. 3.8, the subgame perfect equilibriums are assumed to be the starting points for negotiations. When the starting points contain some injustice on the part of the preceding generation directed to the subsequent generation, there is reason to doubt the value of the outcomes that succeed the starting points. For example, Point A is $\left(c_1^{B*}, c_2^{B*}\right) = (200, 100)$, which is the equilibrium when $\alpha = 1/4$. Generation 1 consumes more than Generation 2, even though the two generations have the same utility function. If one doubts the fairness of this solution, that doubt hurts the value of Point B, which is the negotiation outcome. Generation 1 allows negotiations on the condition of not reducing its utility, which narrows the

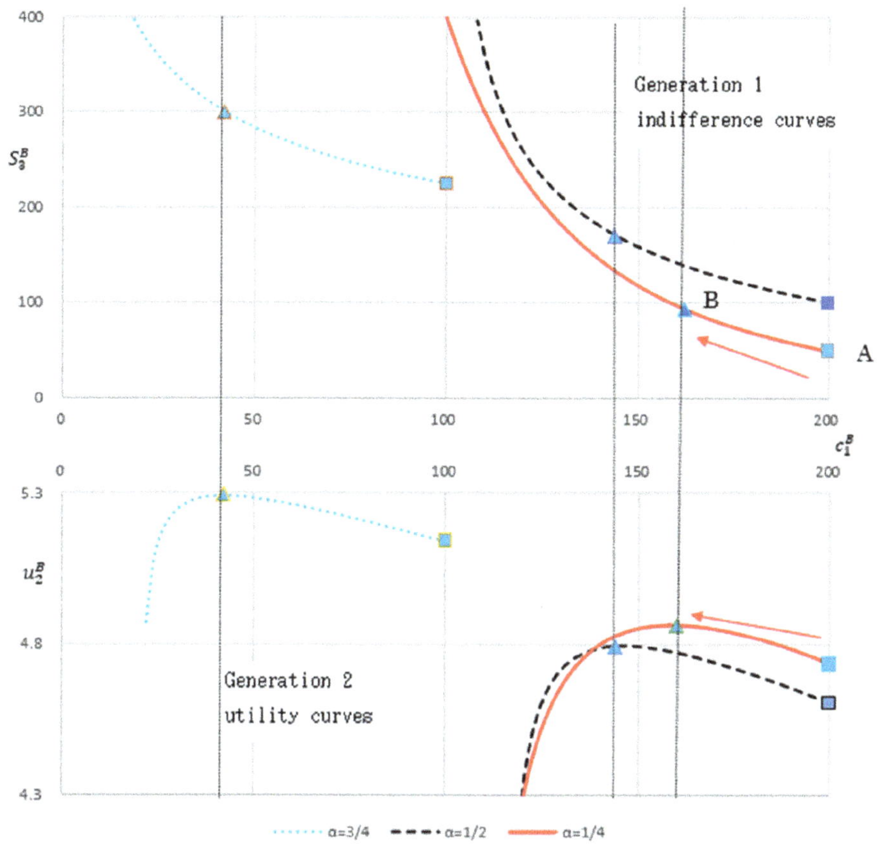

Fig. 3.8 Pareto improvement through intergenerational negotiations. [■ (subgame perfect equilibrium) → ▲ (negotiation conclusion), ($y_1 = y_2 = 200, \alpha_1 = \alpha_2 = \alpha$)]. *Note* The upper panel shows the vertical axis S_3^B (final savings) and the horizontal axis c_1^B (consumption of Generation 1), and the curves are the indifference curves for Generation 1. The subgame equilibriums are marked by ■, and from these starting points, c_1^B is reduced, and S_3^B is increased according to indifference curves. In lower panel, the vertical axis is u_2^B (the utility of Generation 2) and the horizontal axis is c_1^B and the curves are the utility of Generation 2 corresponding to the points on the indifference curves of Generation 1. Generation 2 chooses the points ▲ that maximize its utility, and Generation 1 moves from ■ to ▲ on the indifference curves, thus concluding negotiations

usefulness of the negotiations, particularly when Generation 1 has low preference for cooperation.

The second point is the necessity to assume that Generation 2 will comply with the negotiated agreement. Generation 2 does not necessarily have an incentive to comply with the negotiated outcome. For example, in Fig. 3.8, in $\alpha = 1/4$, it would be better for Generation 2 to break the agreement with Generation 1 and consume three quarters of the added resources ($s_1^B + 200$). It is natural for Generation 1 to think that without the means to constrain subsequent generations through fund establishment (constitutionalization), as seen in Theorem 3.2, it will be betrayed even after intergenerational agreements are reached. It has already been seen that fund establishment (constitutionalization) is incompatible with public reciprocity (Sect. 3.3.3). To introduce negotiations between generations is to move intergenerational relations away from the reciprocity to the relationship of exchange. It is useful to refer to Table 2.1 in Chap. 2 (Sect. 2.4.1) in which Kolm makes the distinctions between exchange and reciprocity. Exchange and reciprocity share the character of interrelated two-way transfers. However, exchange is based on self-centered motivations, and the reason for the exchange is because it is beneficial. Reciprocity, however, is based on other-oriented motivations, since it is left to the initiative of the recipient to give back. In exchange, individual exchanges must be carried out, whereas in reciprocity this is left to the spontaneity of the parties involved. Considering intergenerational negotiations, while bearing this distinction in mind, it becomes clear that intergenerational negotiations have transformed cooperation through intergenerational reciprocity into that through exchange. Since it is now the exchange, it becomes necessary for Generation 2 to comply with the outcomes of the negotiations. Now, is it possible to ensure the feasibility of intergenerational negotiations solely within the framework of reciprocity? In this case, it is turn of the Kantian categorical imperative presented in this chapter, where subsequent generations that observe the preceding generation taking the initiative to comply with the negotiated outcome will voluntarily comply with the outcome themselves.

Following Suzumura and Tadenuma study on addressing intergenerational issues through intergenerational negotiations, we have studies by Sajio (2020a, 2020b) and Kamijo et al. (2017). These studies ask members of the present generation to pretend hail from the future generation, and name them the "imaginary future generation" (IFG). They then propose that policies with long-term impacts be determined through negotiations and deliberations between the present generation and IFG. While the intergenerational negotiations in Fig. 3.8 fixes the preferences (utility function) of Generation 1, the series of studies using the IFG are unique in that they discuss a situation in which the preferences of Generation 1 can change endogenously as a result of negotiations and deliberation. Based on finding moral inspiration, this chapter endogenizes the interest in the future of subsequent generations, but the series of studies on the IFGs is concerned with how to determine the interest in the future of the present (preceding) generation. Chapter 4 of this book reexamines the methodology for encouraging intergenerational cooperation through intergenerational negotiation, including through the use of the IFG.

Appendix 3.2: The Role of Personality in Intergenerational Issues

An interesting finding of the regression analysis of changes in share donated, in Table 3.3, shows, besides the moral inspiration, the tendency for prosocial subjects to increase their share of donations (Models 4 and 5),[28] Based on the Akaike Information Criterion (AIC), the models with prosociality as an explanatory variable fit better, and prosociality is a factor that cannot be ignored in the interpretation of second players' behaviors.

Prosociality here is the personality as measured by the test developed by psychologist Paul von Lange and his colleagues, given in Attachment 2 (van Lange et al., 1997). The test defines prosocial individuals as possessing "tend(ency) to maximize outcomes for both themselves and others (i.e., cooperation)" (p. 733). The experiment in this chapter suggests is that, for prosocial subjects, participation in Game B itself has inspired an increase of donations.

Figures 3.9 and 3.10 are boxplot created to visually capture the influence of prosociality. First, as Fig. 3.9 shows, there is no evidence that either the prosocial or the unsocial second players received biased impressions from their predecessors' behavior (the mean impression received by the prosocial second players was 11.9 and that by the unsocial second players was -3.8). Nevertheless, there was a marked tendency for the prosocial second players to increase the share of donations, and for the unsocial second players to decrease the share.

However, as reported in the main part of this chapter (Sect. 3.4.2), there was no correlation between prosociality and the amount of donations in Experiment A, where each subject decides to donate independently (the correlation coefficient is 0.09). In order to test the relationship between the behaviors of first players and their prosociality, Table 3.4 presents the results of regression analysis (Tobit) of the first player's donation in Experiment B (s_1^B) as the dependent variable, and the first player's donation (s_1^A) in Experiment A and player's prosociality as independent variables. Clearly, prosociality has no influence on the first player's behaviors.

When moved from the setting in which people are simply asked about their personal preference for donation (Experiment A) to that in which they are asked to donate in cooperation with others (Experiment B), the prosocial subjects increase their cooperative behavior and the unsocial one decreases the same. These effects were observed in the second players, but not in the first. The reason for this can only be guided by interpretation, but it is possible that the second players, rather than the first players, are more likely to perceive themselves as being placed in a situation where they cooperate with others. Compared to the first players, who are never informed of the final results of their entrusted donations, the second players are in the position to be more aware of the presence of others, considering that the first players have actually entrusted their donations to the second players.

---

[28] The lower the AIC value, the better the model is judged to fit.

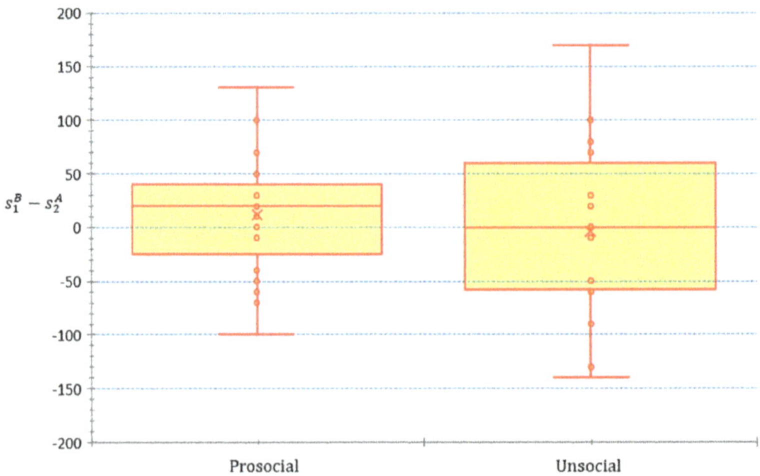

Fig. 3.9 Relationship between the prosociality/unsociality of the second players (horizontal axis) and the impression of the first players to the second players axis): boxplot. *Note* There is no evidence that either the prosocial or unsocial second players received biased impressions from their predecessors' behaviors. Note that in the boxplot, the horizontal line in the box indicates the median and × indicates the mean. The bottom of the box represents the 25th percentile of data from the smaller bottom, and the top of the box represents the 75th percentile of data from the larger top. The thin horizontal line at the bottom represents the minimum value, and the thin horizontal line at the top represents the maximum value

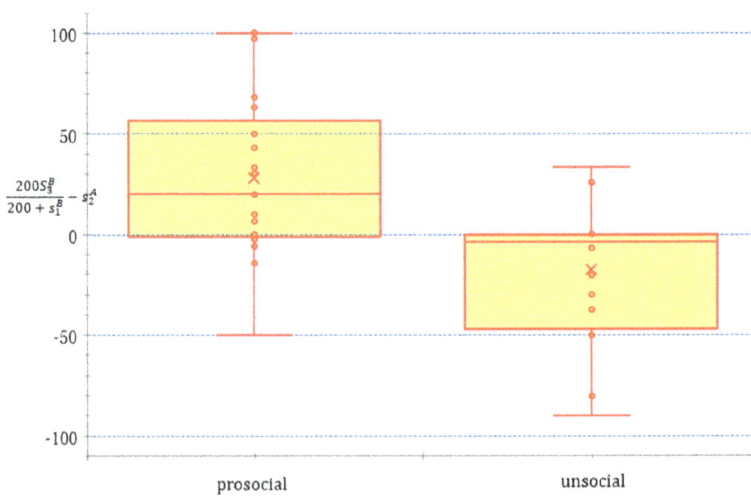

Fig. 3.10 Relationship between sociability/unsociability of the second players (horizontal axis) and changes in the share of the second players' donations to their resources (vertical axis): boxplot. *Note* There is a marked tendency for the prosocial second players to increase the share of donations, and for the unsocial second players to decrease the share

Table 3.4 Regression analysis of first players' donations (Tobit)

	Model 1	Model 2
Const.	17.05	14.61
The first players' donations in Experiment A (s_1^A)	0.76***	0.75***
Prosociality	–	4.22
AIC	352.14	353.99

Note n = 37. ***1% significance, **5% significance, *10% significance

The results found by the experiments in this chapter on prosociality are ambivalent in terms of the goal of this book, which is to encourage intergenerational cooperation. If a society is composed of prosocial people, it will be able to encourage cooperative behavior by promoting recognition that issues such as climate change are not simply matters of personal preference, but challenges that involve continued, long-lasting efforts from the preceding to future generations. However, societies are not composed entirely of prosocial people. One way of thinking about this is that the proportion of prosocial members in a society determines the direction in which forces work more strongly. Von Lange and his colleagues themselves conducted a test on 1728 people in the Netherlands and reported that the proportion of prosocial subjects increases with age from a bottom of 55.9% of those aged 15–29–81.5% of those aged 60 and older.[29] Looking at the subjects treated in the experiments in this chapter, 64.9% (48 of 74) were judged to be prosocial. The relatively high percentage of those who were prosocial suggests that a bias may operate in the direction of enhancing cooperative behavior. However, it is reasonable to limit our discussion to pointing out the possibility, since complex dynamics between the distribution of personalities and social decisions in society can be expected.

A natural question would be whether increasing the number of prosocial members in a society would encourage intergenerational cooperation. Indeed, one of the characteristics of this book's approach is that it does not necessarily treat preferences as fixed. Although the term personality implies more stability than preference, and concerns the whole of the individual, it is not necessary to think of personality as entirely different from preference. Personality is the more stable of the preferences, and relates to the individual as a whole; it is, so to speak, a subset of preferences. From this understanding, one need not assume that personality is also fixed. However, the policy of this book requires that preferences be supported by certain logic and experimental results when considering them as changeable. This book does not find a logic for changing prosociality. Therefore, it has no choice but to keep the prosocial personality as fixed. The possibility of promoting intergenerational cooperation through increasing the number of prosocial members is interesting, but it is appropriate to place it outside the scope of this book.

[29] Van Lange et al., (1997, p. 743).

References

Akerlof, G. A., & Kranton, R. E. (2000). Economics and Identity. *Quarterly Journal of Economics, 115*(3), 715–753.

Akerlof, G. A., & Kranton, R. E. (2005). Identity and the economics of organization. *Journal of Economic Perspectives, 19*(1), 9–32.

Alger, I., & Weibull, J. (2013). Homo Moralis—Preference evolution under incomplete information and assortative matching. *Econometrica, 81*(6), 2269–2302.

Alger, I., & Weibull, J. (2016). Evolution and Kantian morality. *Games and Economic Behavior, 98*, 56–67.

Andreoni, J. (1998). Toward a theory of charitable fund-raising. *Journal of Political Economy, 106*(6), 1186–1213.

Andreoni, J. (2006). Leadership giving in charitable fund-raising. *Journal of Public Economic Theory, 8*(1), 1–22.

Asch, S. E. (1955). Opinions and social pressure. *Scientific American, 193*(5), 31–35.

Barro, R. J. (1974). Are government bonds net wealth? *Journal of Political Economy, 82*(6), 1095–1117.

Barry, B. (1996). Circumstances of justice and future generations. In R.I. Sikora & B. Barry (Eds.), *Obligations to future generations* (pp. 204–248). White Horse Press.

Bernheim, B. D. (1994). A theory of conformity. *Journal of Political Economy, 102*(5), 841–877.

Bracha, A., Menietti, M., & Vesterlund, L. (2011). Seeds to succeed? Sequential giving to public projects. *Journal of Public Economics, 95*(5–6), 416–427.

Cabinet Office, Japan. (2019). *Survey on citizens' contributions to society.* (in Japanese)

Central Community Chest of Japan. (2021). Red feather community chest. https://www.akaihane.or.jp/bokin/. Last accessed May, 22, 2021.

Coase, R. (1960). The problem of social cost. *Journal of Law and Economics, 3*, 1–44.

Cornes, R., & Sandler, T. (1984). The theory of public goods: Non-Nash behavior. *Journal of Public Economics, 23*(3), 367–379.

Crutchfield, R. S. (1955). Conformity and character. *American Psychologist, 10*(5), 191–198.

Gächter, S., Nosenzo, D., Renner, E., & Sefton, M. (2010). Sequential vs. simultaneous contributions to public goods: Experimental evidence. *Journal of Public Economics, 94*(7–8), 515–522.

Kamijo, Y., Hizen Y., & Saijo, T. (2015). *Hearing the voice of future generations: A laboratory experiment of 'demeny voting'*. SDES-2015-8, Kochitec.

Kamijo, K. A., Mifune, N., & Saijo, T. (2017). Negotiating with the future: Incorporating imaginary future generations into negotiations. *Suitability Science, 12*(3), 409–420.

Kanagawa Community Chest Association, Kohoku-ku Branch, Yokohama City, Social Welfare Corporation. (2020). Notes regarding the implementation of community chest campaign. https://www.city.yokohama.lg.jp/kohoku/kurashi/kyodo_manabi/kyodo_shien/jichikai/r2/202009kurenkai.files/0105_20200918.pdf. Last accessed May 22, 2021. (in Japanese)

Kant, I. (1785, 1998). *Groundwork of the metaphysics of morals* (M. Gregor & J. Timmermann, Trans.). Cambridge University Press. https://assets.cambridge.org/97811070/08519/frontmatter/9781107008519_frontmatter.pdf. Last accessed October 14, 2023.

Katz, M. L., & Shapiro, C. (1986). Technology adoption in the presence of network externalities. *Journal of Political Economy, 94*(4), 822–841.

Kim, O., & Walker, M. (1984). The free rider problem: Experimental evidence. *Public Choice, 43*(1), 3–24.

Kőszegi, B., & Rabin, M. (2006). A model of reference-dependent preferences. *Quarterly Journal of Economics, 121*(4), 1133–1165.

Kuroda, W. (1992). *Actions and norms.* Keiso-Shobo. (in Japanese)

Van Leeuwen, B., & Alger, I. (2021). *Estimating social preferences and Kantian morality in strategic interactions*, July 14, 2021, the paper presented at the American Economic Association, January, 7, 2022.

List, J. A., & Lucking-Reiley, D. (2002). The effects of seed money and refunds on charitable giving: Experimental evidence form a university capital campaign. *Journal of Political Economy, 110*(1), 215–233.

Marwell, G., & Ames, E. (1981). Economists free ride, does anyone else? Experiments on the provision of public goods IV. *Journal of Public Economics, 15*(3), 295–310.

Mori, T. (1996). *The effectiveness of public goods supply mechanisms: An experimental economic approach.* Taga-Publishing. (in Japanese)

Normann, H.-T., & Rau, H. A. (2014). Simultaneous and sequential contributions to step-level public goods: One vs. two provision levels. *Journal of Conflict Resolution, 1–28*, 1–28.

Offerman, T., Potters, J., & Verbon, H. (2001). Cooperation in an overlapping generations experiment. *Games and Economic Behavior, 36*(2), 264–275.

Roemer, J. (2010). Kantian equilibrium. *Scandinavian Journal of Economics, 112*(1), 1–24.

Roemer, J. (2015). Kantian optimization: A microfoundation for cooperation. *Journal of Public Economics, 127*, 45–57.

Ross, L., & Nisbett, R. (1991). *The person and the situation: Perspectives of social psychology.* McGraw-Hill.

Saijo, T. (2020a). Future design: an introduction. In *Future design: Incorporating preferences of future generations for sustainability*. Springer.

Saijo, T. (2020b). Future design: Bequeathing sustainable natural environments and sustainable societies to future generations. *Sustainability, 12*(16), 1–21.

Samuelson, P. (1958). An exact consumption: A loan model of interest with or without the social contrivance of money. *Journal of Political Economy, 66*(6), 467–482.

Shang, J., & Croson, R. (2009). A field experiment in charitable contribution: The impact of social information on the voluntary provision of public goods. *The Economic Journal, 119*(540), 1422–1439.

Sherif, M. (1937). An experimental approach to the study of attitudes. *Sociometry, 1*(1/2), 90–98.

Smith, V. L. (1976). Experimental economics: Induced value theory. *American Economic Review, 66*(2), 274–279.

Smith, V. L. (1982). Microeconomic systems as experimental science. *American Economic Review, 72*(5), 923–955.

Sugden, R. (1984). Reciprocity: The supply of public goods through voluntary contributions. *Economic Journal, 94*(376), 772–787.

Sugden, R. (1985). Consistent conjectures and voluntary contributions to public goods: Why the conventional theory does not work. *Journal of Public Economics, 27*(1), 117–124.

Suzumura, K., & Tadenuma, K. (2007). Normative approaches to the issues of global warning: Responsibility and compensation. In J. Roemer & K. Suzumura (Eds.), *Intergenerational equity and sustainability* (pp. 320–336). Palgrave MacMillan.

Thaler, R. H., & Shefrin, H. M. (1981). An economic theory of self-control. *Journal of Political Economy, 89*(2), 392–406.

Van Lange, P. A. M., De Bruin, E. M. N., Otten, W., & Joireman, J. A. (1997). Development of prosocial, individualistic, and competitive orientations: Theory and preliminary evidence. *Journal of Personality and Social Psychology, 73*(4), 733–746.

Varian, H. R. (1994). Sequential contributions to public goods. *Journal of Public Economics, 53*(2), 165–186.

Wade-Benzoni, K. A. (2002). A golden rule over time: reciprocity in intergenerational allocation decisions. *Academy of Management Journal, 45*(5), 1011–1028.

Chapter 4
Considerations for Policy Decisions Involving Multiple Generations: An Examination Through an Economic Experiment on Fiscal Policy

Abstract As a methodology to encourage cooperation, this chapter discusses the function of deliberation. Through an experiment in which people are asked to select a fiscal policy, this chapter reveals what should be taken into account in policy decisions involving multiple generations. This chapter points out that policy selections do not necessarily depend solely on personal interests, but that consideration of the interests of society as a whole, and of immediate descendants play a certain role. The so-called "silver democracy theory" is overemphasized. The function of deliberation is verified by an experiment. While deliberation among the present generation alone does not necessarily promote desirable policy decisions, the policy preferences of the present generation can be changed through deliberation with the imaginary future generations (IFGs) (endogenization of the present generation's preferences). Appendix 4.1 clarifies what the IFGs say in deliberations. Appendix 4.2 examines the nature of fiscal policy as an intergenerational issue.

4.1 Introduction

Building on the previous chapters, this chapter will deepen our discussion of the issues to be considered in policy decisions involving multiple generations, through the example of a long-term fiscal policy. In doing so, this chapter provides empirical support for this discussion by conducting an economic experiment. In the experiment, subjects are asked to select from a set of hypothetical fiscal policy options, and then exchange opinions on them.

This chapter continues to assume a social planner who evaluates the stream of social states from the present to the future. The discussion here is empirical in nature. While it is desirable for social planners to give full consideration to social states, from the present to the future, this is not always the case in practice. As such, this is an issue that needs to be examined in practice. A particular problem is that the human life span has a beginning and end. Although future generations will be affected by policies, only the present generation can participate in policymaking. Even if policies that are desirable across generations exist, these may not be implemented

T. Hiromitsu, *Resolving Intergenerational Conflicts*, Advances in Japanese Business and Economics 33, https://doi.org/10.1007/978-981-97-0614-3_4

if they are incompatible with the interests of the present generation. When elderly people, representing a large portion of voters, stick to their own limited remaining interests and reject desirable policies, this situation is termed “silver democracy.”

To address the intergenerational issues, Chaps. 2 and 3 examined ways to find reciprocity, particularly public reciprocity, between different generations. Chapter 3 examined the situation in which the degree of interest in the future of each generation varied, and based on the results of an economic experiment, considered the situation in which the degree of interest in the future of subsequent generations is endogenously determined by moral inspiration derived from the preceding generation. However, in Chap. 3, the degree of interest in the future of the preceding (present) generation was considered a given. Therefore, it was pointed out that when the preceding generation’s interest in the future is low, through moral inspiration, the subsequent generation’s interest will also become low, resulting in limited intergenerational cooperation (this is an unfavorable outcome from the viewpoint of those outside the concerned parties).

The focus of this chapter shifts to the degree of interest in the future held by the present generation. This chapter will consider the relationship between the degree of interest in the future, and attributes such as age. It then considers the possibility that deliberation may influence the degree of interest in the future. Deliberation is an important channel for building consensus in democratic societies. As far back as Mill’s (1861) “Considerations on representative government,” deliberation among representatives in a representative democracy was expected to move away from mere aggregation of voters’ interests and improve the chances of obtaining more appropriate decisions. Chapter 3 (Appendix 3.1) examined ways of Pareto improvement through intergenerational negotiation. This chapter refers to the work of Tatsuyoshi Saijo (2020a, 2020b) and other relevant studies to examine how decisions can be made through deliberations between the present and imaginary future generations (IFGs) in addition to the conventional deliberations between the present generation.

Section 4.2 describes the approach of the chapter and previous research; Sect. 4.3 presents the experiment and the summary of the results; Sect. 4.4 interprets the results; Sect. 4.5 presents the considerations needed to solve long-term fiscal problems; Sect. 4.6 generalizes the findings on fiscal policy to multi-generational policymaking; and Sect. 4.7 concludes. Following these discussions, Appendix 4.1 examines what people actually say when they become IFGs, and the features that characterize their narratives, based on another experiment. Appendix 4.2 examines the structure of the long-term fiscal policy discussed in this chapter as an intergenerational issue.

4.2 Approach of This Chapter and Previous Studies

4.2.1 *Experiments*

In order to explore the issues that need to be considered in policy decisions involving multiple generations, this chapter discusses the results of an experiment in which fiscal policy decisions are used as an example. Subjects are asked to select from a set of hypothetical fiscal policy options and to exchange opinions about the same.

In experimental research on fiscal policy, the work of Cadsby and Frank (1991) is known as the study that spearheaded the testing of the Ricardian equivalence. The Ricardian equivalence, which is formulated by Barro (1974), reviewed in Chap. 2 (Sect. 2.5.4), states that even if debt is used to finance the consumption of the present generation, the debt burden is not transferred from the present to future generations. Knowing that their children will have to repay the debt, the parent generation does not consider the debt to be net asset and does not use the debt to increase consumption. Cadsby and Frank introduce the following altruistic utility function (U_1) of Generation 1 and ask subjects to act on this function.

$$U_1 = \left(C_1^A\right) * \left(C_1^B\right) * U_2. \tag{4.1}$$

$$U_2 = \left(C_1^B\right) * \left(C_1^C\right). \tag{4.2}$$

where C_1^A is the consumption by Generation 1 in Period A and U_2 is the utility function of Generation 2.

Cadsby and Frank tests whether consumption and savings change if Generation 1 issues public debt (to be redeemed from the income of Generation 2). Their results support the Ricardian equivalence (i.e., the consumption remains largely unchanged). Following Cadsby and Frank, various experiments have been conducted in different settings. For example, Stephen Slate et al (1995) test the equivalence under uncertainty, Ricciuti and Di Laurea (2003) under liquidity constraints, and Artidiatun Adji et al (2009) under the distortion by taxation, respectively, to find (as expected) that the Ricardian equivalence no longer holds under these additional conditions.

Importantly, if the utility function of Eq. 4.1 is given to Generation 1, then Generation 1 treats the utility of Generation 2 as equivalent to its own utility. So, the behavior of the subject assigned the role of Generation 1 can only be in line with Ricardian equivalence as long as the subject can calculate correctly. When considering the actual intergenerational relationship, it is doubtful whether Generation 1's utility function contains the utility of Generation 2 (U_2). In a setting where silver democracy applies, it is appropriate to consider the utility function for Generation 1 that removes the utility of Generation 2. It is also questionable whether the utility function of Generation 1 includes Generation 1's consumption in period B (C_1^B). Starting the study with Eq. 4.1 as a given would miss the important point of the intergenerational issue, and the experiments in this chapter do not give subjects a specific utility function. A study by Laurence Kotlikoff involves an experiment on finances using the method that does not give a specific utility function (Kotlikoff et al. 1988). Kotlikoff conducted the study using a questionnaire that asked subjects to respond to hypothetical situations. The study has found that subjects' responses indicate that they underestimate the resources they would use in the future, relative to the resources they would use in the present, suggesting that the Ricardian equivalence is not supported.

In experimental economics, Vernon Smith has emphasized the control of subjects' preferences by paying them monetary rewards proportional to their gains (induced-value method, Smith, 1976, 1982). No rewards were paid to subjects in this chapter's experiment;[1] it is not an experiment in Smith's sense, but the term "experiment has been used for convenience. As mentioned above, Kotlikoff's study also used a questionnaire that asked subjects to respond to hypothetical situations, but he too called the study an experiment, while declaring that the study was not an experiment in the sense of Smith. From a higher perspective, the Contingent Valuation Method (CVM) is one that uses expressed preference information to conduct economic evaluation. In the CVM, hypothetical policy scenarios are presented and subjects' ratings and votes on these scenarios are analyzed.[2]

A study using a survey instrument on fiscal policy in Japan was conducted by Kume et al. (2018), examining the relationship between individual attributes (age, years of education, employment status, public-mindedness, etc.) and fiscal and social security policy preferences based on the responses of 5324 individuals from an Internet monitor sample. They present their subjects with four qualitative options: "social security reduction and no tax increase," "social security expansion and no tax increase," "social security reduction and tax increase," and "social security expansion and tax increase." They report that support for "social security expansion and tax increases" is greater in the older respondents, while support for "social security reduction and no tax increases" is greater in the younger ones. Based on the degree of "public mindedness," measured by responses to the pros and cons of "unfair benefits" and "fare-free riding," they report that the lower the public mindedness, the more likely respondents are to support "social security expansion and no tax increase," and the lower their "unemployment anxiety," the more likely they are to support "social security reduction and no tax increase". Unlike Kume et al. (2018), this chapter presents policy options that have specificity with numerical values: based on the long-term fiscal projection by the government of Japan (Fiscal System Subcommittee Drafting and Review Committee, Fiscal System Council, Japan, 2015), policy options are created to eliminate those that are fiscally unfeasible (e.g., "social security expansion and no tax increase") in advance. Furthermore, this chapter introduces an opportunity for exchange of opinions among the subjects in order to examine the

[1] The experiments in this chapter examine policy choices over a period of more than 30 years. For fiscal policy choices, the people of 2046 could be either themselves or strangers in 2046, or both. This ambiguity in the identity of people in the future will affect policy choices, which is an issue we consider here. Assuming a particular utility function is not helpful for examining this issue.

[2] Hoyos and Mariel (2010) review the history and methodology of virtual valuation methods.

nature of collective decision-making, which is another unique feature of this chapter that has not been addressed in the Kume et al. study.

4.2.2 *Silver Democracy*

This chapter examines the relationship between individual attributes and policy preferences by allowing subjects to select among hypothetical fiscal policy options. The relationship with age, in particular, concerns the question of the relevance of the so-called silver democracy.

Silver democracy theory can be broken down into two issues. One is whether the elderly actually prefer policies that favor them. The second is whether the societal aging leads to the adoption of policies favorable to the elderly in the real world. Regarding the first issue, Japan's Ministry of Health, Labor and Welfare reports the results of a questionnaire survey in Japan, showing that as the age of respondents increases, a greater number of them support raising/maintaining social security benefit levels (Office of the Director for Policy Evaluation, Ministry of Health, Labor and Welfare, 2015). The percentage of support is 44.8% for respondents aged 65 and older, and only 35.3% of respondents in their 20 s. In an international survey, the sociologists Blekesaune and Quadagno (2003) note, from a database of social surveys in developed countries including Japan, that support for helping the sick and elderly increases with an increase in age.

Regarding the second issue, that is, the impact on policies adopted in the real world, a study by Shimasawa et al. (2014) found that per capita welfare expenditures for the elderly in 47 prefectures in Japan increase with the median age of the prefecture. In an international study, Richard Disney's (2007) analysis of data from the 1970s to the 1990s in developed countries shows that aging is associated with a larger welfare state.

Since this chapter is based on a laboratory study, the second issue, the examination of the effects on policies adopted in the real world, is outside its scope. The interest of this chapter is limited to the first issue, that is, the relationship between age and policy preferences. Compared to the survey conducted by the Ministry of Health, Labor and Welfare and others, this chapter attempts to understand the relationship between age and policy preferences in greater detail by presenting specific policy options in a controlled laboratory setting. The hypotheses to be tested are as follows.

Hypothesis 3 (Silver democracy)

People prefer policies based on their interests for the rest of their limited life expectancy.

4.2.3 Deliberation, Intergenerational Negotiations

This chapter not only focuses on the selections of individual subjects, but also examines the function of collective decision-making, especially deliberation, by arriving at the policy decision through an exchange of opinions among the subjects.

While the scope of collective decision-making extends from cognitive to social issue, it has been noted that collective decisions generally result in better decisions than individual decisions (e.g., Surowiecki, 2004). Regarding decision-making on social issues, especially through deliberation, James Fishkin, a political scientist of Stanford University, has reported the results of a number of deliberative practices (Fishkin, 2011). Fishkin notes that through deliberation, one can expect to improve civic competence. He argues that deliberation strengthens attributes, such as public mindedness, that help citizens solve group problems, and leads to better decisions.[3] However, there is a more cautious view of the function of deliberation. In the 2000 study subtitled "Why groups go to extremes," Cass Sunstein points out that through deliberation, the discussions are biased toward extreme views, and termed these phenomena *polarization* (Sunstein, 2000). Based on the results of experiments on collective decision-making, the psychologist Kameda Tatsuya points out that in decision-making scenarios where the correctness of the solution is not objectively or socio-politically guaranteed, subjects are likely to make decisions led by the majority view (initial majority) from among the views they held prior to the collective decision-making process (Kameda, 1997, p. 44). If the deliberation is dominated by the initial majority, then it does not function as well as one might expect.

This chapter examines social decisions involving multiple generations, and decisions about fiscal policy as an example of such social decisions. These decisions differ in important ways from those about common issues among contemporaries. Social decisions involving multiple generations are not about selecting policies that are good for people who are alive today. The focus is on the possibility of selecting policies that might negatively affect people living in the present, but have a positive impact on people in the future. The hypothesis to be tested are as follows.

Hypothesis 4 (deliberative democracy)

Through deliberation, more appropriate policy decisions through generations can be obtained.

In some of the deliberations conducted in this chapter, "representatives of the future generation" are artificially created and participate in the deliberations. This book first discussed the idea of negotiation between the present generation and the imaginary future generation in Chap. 3 (Appendix 3.1), through Suzumura and Tadenuma's (2007) budding study. This idea has been fully developed in a series of studies on *Future Design* proposed by Saijo (2020a, 2020b). This chapter follows Saijo, and refers to representatives of this future generation as *imaginary future generations (IFGs)*. The conception of hypothetical future generations is not a novel one. A similar idea can be found in the work of Michael MacKenzie, a political scientist

[3] Fishkin (2011, pp. 139–143).

at the University of Pittsburgh, who suggests intergenerational issues can be solved through "representing the future," which balances the present and the potential interests of the future. MacKenzie outlines three forms of representation: through the establishment of an independent commission to represent the interests of the future; through the establishment of a house of representatives elected for lengthy terms; and through the establishment of a house of representatives randomly selected from among the citizens.[4] Reiko Gotoh's (2018) study, discussed in Chap. 2 (Sects. 2.2.3, 2.5.2), also includes the idea of a soul/integrated personality advocating the need of preventing harm, on behalf of those yet to be born. Saijo himself states that he got the idea of IFGs from a story of the Native Iroquois people of the United States. who, when making important decisions, would pretend to be people seven generations in the future (Saijo, 2020a, pp. 45–46.). The IFGs are not isolated, much less novel. However, among these ideas, the series of studies of Future Design, led by Saijo and other experimental economists, is one-step ahead of the others, because they involve evidence-based arguments. For this reason, the following discussion will refer to the work of Saijo and his colleagues.

Yoshio Kamijo and his colleagues, including Saijo, present a representative study that tests the effects of introducing IFGs in laboratory settings (Kamijo et al., 2017). The study reports that with the introduction of IFGs in opinion exchanges, the group with IFGs' participation are more likely to make sustainable selections. While the subjects in their experiment are presented with simple numerical rewards, this chapter examines the function of the IFGs by presenting the subjects with concrete fiscal policy options.

The hypothesis to be tested is as follows

Hypothesis 5 (IFGs)

Through the introduction of IFGs into decision-making, more appropriate policy decisions can be obtained through generations.

[4] MacKenzie (2021, pp. 167–180).

4.3 Experiments on Fiscal Policy Decisions

4.3.1 Setup

The organizer of the experiment prepares a set of hypothetical fiscal policy options.[5] First, subjects made their individual policy selections, and then each group of three members decided, as a group, which fiscal policy to adopt in consultation with each other.[6] In some groups, a randomly selected person among the three is asked to take on the role of an IFG. In other words, they are asked to participate in an exchange of opinions on the selection of fiscal policy, from the standpoint of a person 30 years in the future (the year 2046). The subjects make their selections anonymously, and the selections made by any particular individual are not revealed to the experimenter and the experimental site.

Two hypothetical fiscal policy options, outlined Fig. 4.1, are developed on the basis of the *Long-term Fiscal Sustainability Analysis* in Japan, published by Fiscal System Subcommittee Drafting and Review Committee, Fiscal System Council (Japan).[7] Fiscal Policy 1 (FP1) postpones the burden to the future and favors the present generation. Fiscal Policy 2 (FP2) imposes equal burdens on the present and future. The options are subject to nearly identical budget constraints. For example, in 60 years (2016–2075), the total gross disposable income of FP1 is 104.04 million yen, while that of FP2 is 100.80 million yen.[8] The projection provides estimates of the fiscal gap that must be filled immediately in order to stabilize the debt-to-GDP ratio after 2060. The projection also includes estimates of the fiscal gap that would need to be additionally filled ("lagged cost") the more the stabilization is delayed. The options selected by the subjects are created by assigning the fiscal gap to the main items of household income and expenditure. In this sense, the two options are subject to the same macroeconomic and demographic constraints.

Fiscal Policy 1 maintains fiscal policies (e.g., tax rates and social insurance premium) similar to those in Japan today (at the time of the experiment) for 30 years starting in 2016, with a discontinuous increase in the burden after 2046 (e.g., the VAT rate is 10% in 2016 and 25% from 2046 onwards). Fiscal Policy 2 maintains

[5] Given the author's affiliation (Ministry of Finance), it might be pointed out that the participants could be induced to select FP2. However, the participants are gathered on the basis of units such as schools and workplaces, and are instructed that there is no correct answer to the selection of fiscal policies. While the ratio of selecting FP2 is around 70%, this paper does not draw meanings from the absolute level of this ratio. The focuses of analysis are the deviations from the average by attributes of the participants and the collective decision-making. Even if the participants felt such pressure, the findings in this paper would not have been affected.

[6] Because of rounding, there were groups with two or four persons.

[7] The methodology for the projection follows the guidance of the European Commission (2006). The European Commission publishes an annual Fiscal Sustainable Report for member countries using the same methodology.

[8] This does not necessarily mean that a person will live for 60 years, but rather, compares the disposable income that the economy will continue to generate over the same period of time, that is, 60 years.

- Imagine that you are in a hypothetical country that is similar to Japan but somewhat different. That country currently (2016) has a national debt of approximately 1,000 trillion yen (approximately 8 million yen per capita), population-aging rate of 26.0%, and a working-age population (15-64 years old) that is decreasing by over 1 million people each year.
- We assume the following two fiscal policy options. It should be noted that the fiscal policy and economy in 2046 is not necessarily certain, as they are based on projections.

<2016-2045>

Financial policy 1 (FP1)

*VAT (tax on consumption): 10%
*Income tax rate: 20%
*Insurance premium: 40,000 yen (monthly)
*30% of out-of-pocket medical expenses
*Pension benefit: 100,000 yen (monthly)

<Example>
Monthly salary: 300,000 yen (annually 6 million yen)
*VAT (tax on consumption): 15,000 yen
(150,000 yen purchase per month)
*Income tax: 60,000 yen
*Insurance premium: 40,000 yen
*Medical expenses: 3,000 yen (10,000 yen medical costs per month)
⇒ Approx. 180,000 yen remains on hand

Financial policy 2 (FP2)

*VAT (tax on consumption): 20%.
*Income tax rate: 25%
*Insurance premium 50,000 yen (monthly)
*35% of out-of-pocket medical expenses
*Pension benefit: 70,000 yen (monthly)

<Example>
Monthly salary: 300,000 yen (annually 6 million yen)
*VAT (tax on consumption): 30,000 yen
(150,000 yen purchase per month)
*Income tax: 75,000 yen
*Insurance premium: 50,000 yen
*Medical expenses: 3,500 yen (10,000 yen medical costs per month)
⇒ Approx. 140,000 yen remains on hand
⇒ Approx. 480,000 yen increase in annual burden compared to FP1

<After 2046>

<What it will look like in 30 years according to FP1>
*VAT (tax on consumption) : 25%
*Income tax rate: 30%
*Insurance premium: 60,000 yen (monthly)
*35% of out-of-pocket medical expenses
*Pension benefit: 50,000 yen (monthly)

<Example>
Monthly salary: 300,000 yen (annually 6 million yen)
*VAT (tax on consumption): 37,500 yen
(150,000 yen purchase per month)
*Income tax: 90,000 yen
*Insurance premium: 60,000 yen
*Medical expenses: 3,500 yen (10,000 yen medical costs per month)
⇒ Approx. 110,000 yen remains on hand
⇒ Approx. 360,000 yen increase in annual burden compared to FP 2

<What it will look like in 30 years according to FP 2>
*VAT (tax on consumption): 20%.
*Income tax rate: 25%
*Insurance premium 50,000 yen (monthly)
*35% of out-of-pocket medical expenses
*Pension benefit: 70,000 yen (monthly)

<Example>
Monthly salary: 300,000 yen (annually 6 million yen)
*VAT (tax on consumption): 30,000 yen
(150,000 yen purchase per month)
*Income tax: 75,000 yen
*Insurance premium: 50,000 yen
*Medical expenses: 3,500 yen (10,000 yen medical costs per month)
⇒ Approx. 140,000 yen remains on hand

*The above are estimates based on simplified assumptions. The fiscal policy and economy in 2046 are uncertain as they are based on projections.

Fig. 4.1 Options of fiscal policy

the same policy after 2016, and after 2046 as well; however, the burden from 2016 to 2045 is heavier than that of FP1, but lighter after 2046 (e.g., the VAT rate is constant at 20%). To facilitate understanding of the impact of the policies on individuals, information on individual-based tax and social insurance burden and disposable income is given in the "<example>" by converting from the macro burden rates. Some subjects were allowed to participate in the experiment without these individual-based burden information.

Figure 4.1 shows the specific presentation of options of fiscal policy.

The subjects respond individually to which fiscal policy they preferred, and then engage in a 10-min group discussion.[9] The subjects are asked to decide, as a group, which policy they preferred, either by a majority vote or consensus. During the discussion, those assigned the role of the IFGs are asked to inform the other two participants of the same.

Questionnaires are provided before and after the opinion exchange to collect data on age, optimism,[10] prosociality,[11] as well as other data and impressions from the experiment. After the exchange of opinions, most of the participants were asked about their viewpoints during the exchange of opinions (hereafter referred to as the "main questionnaire"). In some venues (three universities, two offices; 68 participants), the reasons for policy selections by individuals were collected before entering the opinion exchange, as well as after. The reasons for the change were collected for subjects who stated that they had changed their personal opinions after the opinion exchange (hereafter referred to as the "reason survey questionnaire").

4.3.2 *Summary of Results*

The experiment was conducted over 10 sites between December 2015 and April 2016,[12] with a total of 447 participants.[13] This period corresponds to the time when the consumption tax rate was legally scheduled to increase to 10% starting in April 2017. At the time of the experiment, the government had not made a final decision on whether to raise the consumption tax, and it was not until June 2016 that the

[9] In all, 148 groups were composed; 65 of the 148 groups included the IFG, and these 65 groups were allocated to all venues.

[10] The optimism test used is the Life Orientation Test-Revised (Scheier et al., 1994), and below is a sample of the test. "Please be as honest and accurate as you can throughout. Try not to let your response to one statement influence your responses to other statements. There are no "correct" or "incorrect." A = I agree a lot, B = I agree a little, C = I neither agree nor disagree, D = I disagree a little, E = I disagree a lot. 1. In uncertain times, I usually expect the best."

[11] The prosociality test is the Social Value Orientation Test (Van Lange et al., 1997), and the instructions for the subjects are included in Appendix 3.2 of Chap. 3.

[12] The venues include one high school, four universities (including student organizations), and five offices.

[13] One subject arrived late and did not complete any of the questionnaires. This subject is not included in the total number of 447 participants.

prime minister announced the government's policy to postpone the consumption tax rate increase for two and a half years, starting in October 2019. Against this background, it is possible to conclude that the period of the experiment was under a nearly homogeneous social environment regarding fiscal policy. Descriptive statistics are listed as Table 4.1.

Looking at the fiscal policy selected before the deliberation, Tables 4.2 and 4.3 reveal that about 70% of the subjects selected FP2. A regression analysis (probit) of the relationship between the selection of FP2 and the attributes of the subjects shows that age is a significant factor. Generally, support for FP2 declines by 0.5% as subjects age by one year. Providing subjects with information on the individual burden lowers support for FP2 by about 13%. Among occupations, non-regular employees and those in public service are negatively related with the support for FP2, although optimism and prosociality are not significant.

Tables 4.4 and 4.5 show the reasons for the selection of fiscal policy before the deliberations. In the responses to the main questionnaire in Table 4.4, 57.1% of those who selected FP1 made their choice "because the future (2046) is uncertain, present interests should be given priority," while 64.8% of those who selected FP2 did so because they felt that "both [our] (present generation) interests and the interests of the future generation should be fairly considered." In terms of responses to the reason survey questionnaire in Table 4.5, among the subjects who selected FP1, 39.1% each selected the reasons that "considering my own life, the policy of immediate burden increase is too harsh" and "depending on future population, economy, and science and technology, the future would be better than what is expected now". Among the subjects who selected FP2, more than half (51.1%) gave the reason as "not only

Table 4.1 Descriptive Statistics (n = 447)

Gender		Personality	
Male	Female	Optimistic	Prosocial
272	175	220	273

Occupation					
High school student	University and graduate student	Regular employee	Non-regular employee	Public service	Others No answer
115	137	70	51	64	10

Table 4.2 Those who selected FP2 before the deliberation, by age group

Age	15–19	20–24	25–29	30–34	35–39	40–44	45–49
Ratio (%)	80.4	74.3	66.7	61.1	80.0	65.2	62.5
Persons/population	140/174	55/74	12/18	11/18	8/10	15/23	25/40
Age	**50–54**	55–59	60–64	65–69	70–74	75–79	Whole
Ratio (%)	60.7	58.8	52.9	60.0	66.7	100	71.6
Persons/population	17/28	20/34	9/17	3/5	2/3	3/3	320/447

Table 4.3 Relationship between the selection of FP2 and the attributes of the subjects (probit regression; coefficients [marginal effects]; FP2 = 1, FP1 = 0)

	Model 1	Model 2	Model 3	Model 4	Model 5	Model 6
Female			0.067 [0.022]		– 0.165 [0.062]	– 0.793** [– 0.308]
Age	– 0.013*** [– 0.004]	– 0.013*** [– 0.004]	– 0.013*** [– 0.004]		– 0.005 [– 0.002]	0.278 [0.101]
Optimistic			– 0.137 [– 0.046]		– 0.327* [– 0.122]	– 0.155 [– 0.060]
Prosocial			0.125 [0.042]		0.370 [0.139]	0.438 [0.173]
Provision of personal burden information		– 0.439** [– 0.131]	– 0.434** [– 0.130]	– 0.493** [– 0.143]	– 0.364 [– 0.128]	– 0.782 [– 0.262]
High school student				0.232 [0.074]	-	-
University and graduate students				– 0.007 [– 0.002]	-	-
Non-regular employee				– 0.785*** [– 0.292]	– 0.594** [– 0.229]	
Public service				– 0.462** [– 0.166]	– 0.462** [– 0.166]	
Other/No answer				– 0.324 [– 0.116]	– 0.324 [– 0.116]	
AIC	524.9	522.5	526.2	522.5	–	–
BIC	533.1	534.8	550.8	563.5	–	–

Note ***1% significant; **5% significant; *10% significant. Dummy variables for optimistic = 1, prosocial = 1, with personal burden information = 1, high school student = 1, university/graduate student = 1, non-regular employee = 1, public service = 1, other/no response = 1; Model 5 excludes high school and university/graduate students from the sample; Model 6 covers only those 55 years and older. The correlation coefficient between age and optimism is 0.08, and 0.26 for age and prosociality (all samples)

my own interests but also interests of society as a whole, including those of future generations, should be considered." Slightly less than half of the respondents gave the following reasons: "considering my own life, a significant increase of burden after 30 years would be a major blow" or "considering the lives of my children and grandchildren, a significant increase of burden after 30 years would be a major blow," respectively.

Table 4.6 shows the selections made as a group as the result of the deliberation. Compared to the prior selection of fiscal policy (wherein the percentage of FP2 was 71.6%), after the deliberation, the percentage of selecting FP2 as a group has increased (79.1%). The lower panel classified groups into those that do not include the IFG, i.e., groups consisting only of the present generation, and those that include

Table 4.4 What were your points of view when you discussed the issue in the group? (multiple answers allowed) (Main Questionnaire)

Perspectives	Percentage of those who expressed their opinions from the perspective on the left (person who selected FP1)	Percentage of those who expressed their opinions from the perspective on the left (person who selected FP2)
(1) Interests of us (present generation) should come before those of future generations	20.9% (19 people)	1.7% (4 people)
(2) Both our (present generation) interests and the interests of the future generation should be fairly considered	29.7% (27 people)	64.8% (151 people)
(3) Interests of future generations should come before ours (present generation)	12.1% (11 people)	24.0% (56 people)
(4) Because the future (2046) is uncertain, present interests should be given priority	57.1% (52 people)	6.9% (16 people)
(5) We don't know what future generations will value, or what they will want	19.8% (18 people)	10.3% (24 people)
(6) It is important to obtain consensus among all participants, not just my own opinion	16.5% (15 people)	28.3% (66 people)
(7) As a democracy, it is natural to decide policy by majority vote	9.9% (9 people)	12.4% (29 people)
(8) Others (free description)	2.2% (2 people)	9.0% (21 people)
Number of respondents	91 people	233 people

the IFG. It shows the high percentage of the group that includes the IFG selecting FP2 (87.7%) behind the change through the deliberation.

Next is the effect of deliberation on individuals' policy preferences. There were 111 subjects who had selected FP1 in advance and 271 who had selected FP2 in advance (both excluding subjects who were assigned the role of IFGs). Of these subjects, those who said they changed their opinions after the deliberation are presented in Table 4.7 below. It is shown that the deliberation influenced individuals' opinions, especially increasing their support for FP2.

It is valuable to examine the process of collective decision-making in detail. Based on Table 4.6, Table 4.8 examines the relationship between individuals' prior

Table 4.5 Please select the two options below that most closely match your reasons for selecting 'FP1' or 'FP2' (Reason survey questionnaire)

Reasons	Percentage of those who selected FP1 for the reason on the left (person who selected FP1)	Percentage of those who selected FP2 for the reason on the left (person who selected FP2)
(1) My own interests should come first	21.7% (5 people)	4.4% (2 people)
(2) Not only my own interests but also interests of society as a whole, including those of future generations, should be considered	8.7% (2 people)	51.1% (23 people)
(3) The state and communities are semi-permanent beings, which have values beyond individuals, and the survival of the state and communities should come before my own interests	8.7% (2 people)	11.1% (5 people)
(4) Considering my own life, the policy of immediate burden increase is too harsh	39.1% (9 people)	2.2% (1 person)
(5) Considering my own life, a significant increase of burden after 30 years would be a major blow	0.0% (0 people)	46.7% (21 people)
(6) Considering the lives of my children and grandchildren, a significant increase of burden after 30 years would be a major blow	8.7% (2 people)	42.2% (19 people)
(7) Depending on future population, economy, and science and technology, the future would be better than what is expected now	39.1% (9 people)	4.4% (2 people)
(8) Depending on future population, economy, and science and technology, the future would be worse than what is expected now	13.0% (3 people)	11.1% (5 people)
(9) The actual fiscal situation may not be very bad and an increase of burden may not be necessary	4.3% (1 person)	0.0% (0 people)

(continued)

Table 4.5 (continued)

Reasons	Percentage of those who selected FP1 for the reason on the left (person who selected FP1)	Percentage of those who selected FP2 for the reason on the left (person who selected FP2)
(10) Considering future generations is not productive, because it is not knowable what future generations will value nor what they will really want	30.4% (7 people)	4.4% (2 people)
(11) It is doubtful whether the funds will be properly used, even if we accept an increased burden	17.4% (4 people)	4.4% (2 people)
(12) I would like to leave as rich and healthy a society as possible to future generations	8.7% (2 people)	17.8% (8 people)
Number of respondents	23 people	45 people

Table 4.6 Selections as groups

Selected fiscal policies	Number of groups	Percentage (%)	
FP1	31	20.9	
FP2	117	79.1	
Group of the present generation only	Number (Percentage)	Group containing IFG	Number (Percentage)
FP1	23 (27.7%)	FP1	8 (12.3%)
FP2	60 (72.3%)	FP2	57 (87.7%)

Table 4.7 Subjects who changed their personal opinions through the deliberation

	Persons (i)	People who changed their opinions (ii)	(ii)/(i) (%)
Those who selected FP1 before deliberation	111 people	39 people (changed from FP1 to FP2)	35.1
Those who selected FP2 before deliberation	271 people	21 people (changed from FP2 to FP1)	7.7

Table 4.8 Relationship between individual selections and selections as groups

Group of present generation only		Number of groups	Groups that contain IFGs		Number of groups
FP1		23 (27.7%)	FP1		8 (12.3%)
Individual selections → group decision	1,1,1 → 1 1,1,2 → 1 1,1,1,2 → 1 1,2,2 → 1 1,2,2,2 → 1	6 11 1 4 1	Individual selections → group decision	IFG(1),1,1 → 1 IFG(2),1,1 → 1 IFG(1),1,2 → 1 IFG(2),1,2 → 1	3 1 3 1
FP2		60 (72.3%)	FP2		57 (87.7%)
Individual selections → group decision	2,2,2 → 2 1,2,2 → 2 2,2,2,2 → 2 2,2 → 2 1,1,2 → 2 1,2,2,2 → 2 1,2 → 2 1,1 → 2	30 22 1 1 2 2 1 1	Individual selections → group decision	IFG(1),2,2 → 2 IFG(2),2,2 → 2 IFG(1),1,2 → 2 IFG(2),1,2 → 2 IFG(1),IFG(2),2,2 → 2 IFG(2),1,1 → 2	9 31 1 14 1 1

Note (1) In the "Individual selections → Group decision" column, for example, "1,1,2 → 1" means "two persons select FP1 and one selects FP2 as individuals. After deliberation, their decision as a group is FP1". (2) "IFG(1)" means "one whose individual selection as FP1 is assigned the role of IFG. (3) The underlined part indicates that the policy which was not in the majority at first, but has been selected by a group after the exchange of opinions. Those who are given the role of IFG are assumed to support FP2

selections and the selections by the groups in which the individuals are included. Comparing the individual preferences with the results of the deliberative process, it is clear that not only cases in which the majority opinion naturally became the group's selection, but, to a considerable extent, reversals by the minority also existed. Cases where policies that were not the majority selection at first, but have been selected by groups, are underlined. There were nine groups (4 + 1 + 3 + 1) in which the final group selection was FP1 and seven groups (2 + 2 + 1 + 1 + 1) in which the final group selection was FP2. In terms of groups including the IFGs, there were four groups (3 + 1) for FP1, and one group for FP2. Therefore, FP1 was more than evenly matched with FP2. The main reason for the increase in the percentage of the group including the IFG selecting FP2 is understood to be the direct effect of imposing the role of the IFGs, which increased the number of supporters of FP2.[14]

Figure 4.2 depicts the relationship between the prior individual selections and the group decision, based on Table 4.8. The horizontal axis shows the combination of individual selections. For example, "222 (or 22 IFG)" either means that all three individuals in the group selected FP2, or that two persons selected FP2 and the third played the role of the IFG. The subjects who were asked to play the role of IFGs are

[14] For example, in IFG(1),2,2 → 2, the chance for FP1 to win the group is destroyed in advance through the imposition of the IFG role on a supporter of FP1.

regarded as having selected FP2. The vertical axis shows the proportion of the groups that selected FP2. The solid line represents the group of the present generation only, and the thick dashed line represents the group including the IFG. As one moves to the right on the horizontal axis, the percentage of groups that chose FP2 as their group decision increases. The middle two—112 (or 11 IFG) and 122 (or 12 IFG)—indicate that the prior majority was not always the group's decision. For example, when the prior opinion is one for FP1 and two for FP2, a simple majority would result in the group choosing FP2, but in reality, only about 80% of the group selected FP2. There is no noticeable difference between the groups including only the present generations and the IFGs. The thin dashed line is the line redrawn based on prior individual selections in the group including the IFG. That is, for example, the group that was classified as "12 IFG" is reclassified as "112" if the prior individual selection of the subject in the IFG was FP1, and is reclassified as "122" if the prior individual selection of the subject in the IFG was FP2. This line implies that the reason for the stronger selections of FP2 among the group including the IFGs is the direct effect of the imposition of the role of the IFGs, which increased the number of FP2 supporters.

Furthermore, based on Table 4.7, the opponents of those who changed their opinions through opinion exchange are examined in Table 4.9. It is important to note the distinction between "adaptive opinion change to the majority" and "others." "Adaptive opinion change to the majority" refers to the opinion change toward the majority of the group. For example, a case in which one individual who had selected FP1 changed their opinion to FP2 after deliberating with two other participants who had selected FP2. Among the people who changed to FP2, nearly 80% [(15 + 12 + 4)/39] were cases of adaptive opinion changes, while 66.6% [(6 + 3 + 2 + 2)/21] of people who changed to FP1 were others. Fiscal Policy 1, even when supported by the minority, tends to demonstrate stronger persuasion, and is more than evenly matched against FP2.

What logic did supporters of FP1 and FP2 use to approach their opponents in the deliberations, respectively? Among those who changed their opinions, those who completed the reason survey questionnaire were asked why they changed their opinions, and the results are presented in Table 4.10. The most common reason given for changing from FP1 to FP2 was "considering my own life, a significant increase of burden after 30 years would be a major blow" (57.1%). However, the sample size for this survey was too small to make a full assessment.

Therefore, it is useful to focus on the cases in Table 4.8 where a policy that was not in the majority prior to the deliberation was selected after the deliberation (underlined part). Specifically, it is valuable to retrieve the logic of supporters of policies that were not in the majority prior to the deliberation. From the responses to the survey, the persuasiveness of logics is scored, according to the procedure in Attachment 3. The analysis focuses on those situations in which the logics were most effective in persuading. These results are given in Table 4.11.

When taking the position of FP1, the most persuasive logic is based on the uncertainty and agnosticism of the future: "the future would be better than what is expected now" or "It is not knowable what future generations will value nor what they will really want". Other influential logic is rooted in the reality of life: "Considering my

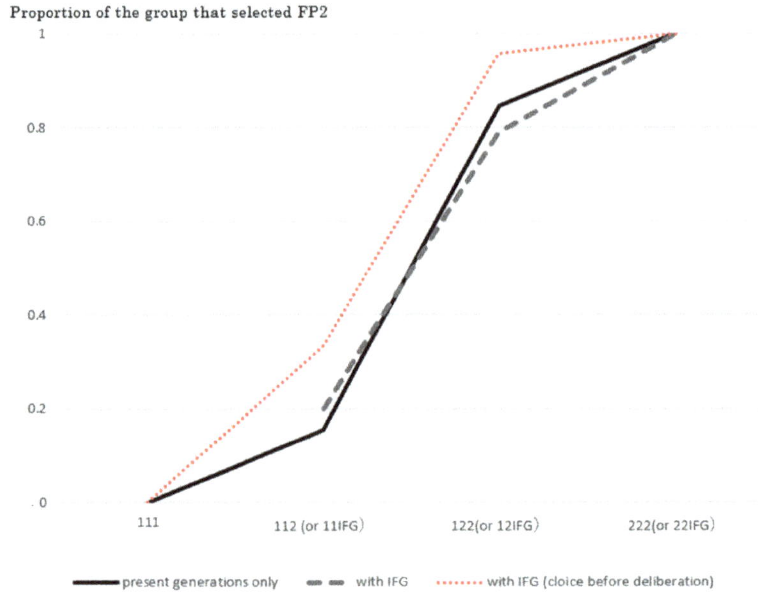

Fig. 4.2 Combination of individual selections in each group (horizontal axis) and group selection (vertical axis). *Note* The horizontal axis shows the combination of individual selections. For example, "222 (or 22 IFG)" means that all three individuals in the group selected FP2, or that two persons selected FP2 and third played the role of the IFG. The subjects who were asked to play the role of IFGs are regarded as having chosen FP2. The vertical axis shows the proportion of the groups that selected FP2. The solid line represents the group of present generation only, and the thick dashed line the group including the IFG. As one moves to the right on the horizontal axis, the percentage of groups that chose FP2 as their group decision increases. The middle two, 112 (or 11 IFG) and 122 (or 12 IFG), indicate that the prior majority was not always the group's decision. For example, when the prior opinion is one for FP1 and two for FP2, a simple majority would result in the group choosing FP2, but in reality, only about 80% of the group selected FP2. There is no noticeable difference between the groups including only the present generations and the IFGs. The thin dashed line is the line redrawn based on prior individual selections in the group including the IFG. That is, for example, the group that was classified as "11 IFG" is reclassified as "122" if the prior individual selection of the subject in the IFG was FP1, and is reclassified as "122" if the prior individual selection of the subject in the IFG was FP2. This line implies that the reason for the stronger selections of FP2 among the group including the IFGs is the direct effect of the imposition of the role of the IFGs, which increased the number of FP2 supporters

own life, the policy of immediate burden increase is too harsh." When taking the position of FP2, the persuasiveness of logics is not clearly expressed. The logics of "interests of society as a whole, including those of future generations, should be considered," and "considering my own life, a significant increase of burden after 30 years would be a major blow" were relatively persuasive.

Logics supporting FP1 are rated higher. The evaluation of the logics adopted a rule that gives additional points when the logic is described in the free response columns of both the persuader and the persuaded. In the case of logics in favor of FP1, it was effective because the persons who advocated the logics mentioned them in the free

Table 4.9 Opponents of those who changed their opinions through deliberation

	Adaptive change to the majority			Others		
Composition of opponents	2, 2	IFG, 2	2, 2, 1	2, 1	IFG, 1	1, 1
People who changed from FP1 to 2 (39 people)	15 people	12 people	4 people	5 people	2 people	1 person
	Adaptive change to the majority	Others				
Composition of opponents	**1, 1**	**1, 2**	**1, IFG**	**1, 2, 2**	**2, IFG**	**2**
People who changed from FP2 to 1 (21 people)	7 people	6 people	3 people	2 people	2 people	1 person

Note (1) For example, "2, 1" means "one supporter of FP2 and one supporter of FP1. (2) "Adaptive change to the majority" means the adaptive change of opinion to the majority of the group opponents

response section, and those who were persuaded also left comments agreeing with the logics.

4.4 Interpretation

4.4.1 Preparation of Interpretation

In preparation for interpretation, the utility function of Generation 1 by Cadsby and Frank (1991) is rewritten as follows.

$$U_1 = U_1^A\left(C_1^A\right) + \alpha U_1^B\left(C_1^B\right) + \beta U_2, 0 \leq \alpha \leq 1, 0 \leq \beta \leq 1. \tag{4.3}$$

where $U_1^{A'} > 0$, $U_1^{A''} < 0$, $U_1^{B'} > 0$, $U_1^{B''} < 0$. Period A is from 2016 to 2045 and Period B is after 2046. When subjects select FP1, several interpretations are possible. First, they can either ignore U_2 ($\beta = 0$), or U_2 may only have a low weight ($\beta < 1$) in their utility function. In such a scenario, they are considered *selfish*. Second, they may be getting older or less interested in the future. As they get older, or as they become less concerned about the future, the weight of U_1^B becomes smaller ($0 \leq \alpha < 1$). They are considered *shortsighted*. Third, they may have better economic prospects. Because they expect higher growth, they may believe that they will enjoy not only sufficient C_1^A but also enough C_1^B. They are considered *optimistic*. Fourth, they may not know the values of future generations. Since they do not know what future generations will want, they cannot know U_2 in their utility function. They have no other way to evaluate based on $U_1 = U_1^A\left(C_1^A\right) + \alpha U_1^B\left(C_1^B\right)$. They are considered *ignorant of future generations*.

In the discussion that follows, these four items will be used to interpret the results of the experiment. In addition to the results of the regression analysis presented in

Table 4.10 Please select the two reasons below that most closely match the reasons you came to believe that "FP2 (1)" would be better after the exchange of views

Reasons	Percentage of those who claimed the reason in the left among those who changed from FP2 to 1 (number of respondents)	Percentage of those who claimed the reason in the left among those who changed from FP1 to 2 (number of respondents)
(1) My own interests should come first	50.0% (1 person)	14.3% (1 person)
(2) Not only my own interests but also interests of society as a whole, including those of future generations, should be considered	0.0% (0 people)	14.3% (1 person)
(3) The state and communities are semi-permanent beings, which have values beyond individuals, and the survival of the state and communities should come before my own interests	0.0% (0 people)	0.0% (0 people)
(4) Considering my own life, the policy of immediate burden increase is too harsh	50.0% (1 person)	42.9% (3 people)
(5) Considering my own life, a significant increase of burden after 30 years would be a major blow	0.0% (0 people)	57.1% (4 people)
(6) Considering the lives of my children and grandchildren, a significant increase of burden after 30 years would be a major blow	0.0% (0 people)	14.3% (1 person)
(7) Depending on future population, economy, and science and technology, the future would be better than what is expected now	50.0% (1 person)	0.0% (0 people)
(8) Depending on future population, economy, and science and technology, the future would be worse than what is expected now	0.0% (0 people)	0.0% (0 people)
(9) The actual fiscal situation may not be very bad and an increase of burden may not be necessary	0.0% (0 people)	0.0% (0 people)

(continued)

Table 4.10 (continued)

Reasons	Percentage of those who claimed the reason in the left among those who changed from FP2 to 1 (number of respondents)	Percentage of those who claimed the reason in the left among those who changed from FP1 to 2 (number of respondents)
(10) Considering future generations is not productive, because it is not knowable what future generations will value nor what they will really want	50.0% (1 person)	0.0% (0 people)
(11) It is doubtful whether the funds will be properly used, even if we accept an increased burden	0.0% (0 people)	42.9% (3 people)
(12) I would like to leave as rich and healthy a society as possible to future generations	0.0% (0 people)	14.3% (1 person)
Number of respondents	2 people	7 people

Table 4.3, this section will use the responses to the questionnaire surveys in Tables 4.4 and 4.5. It should be noted that subjects are not always motivated to give real reasons in their questionnaire responses. However, the responses do provide an opportunity to access the motivation behind their choices, and the survey will be used as the resource in the analysis.

4.4.2 *Packaging of Policies*

Fiscal Policy 1 favors the present generation, while FP2 imposes equal burdens on the present and future generations. A surprisingly high number, of about 70% of the subjects, selected FP2 at the stage before the deliberation. This feeling is further reinforced in consideration of the political difficulties that consumption tax and other policies to increase the burden must face in Japan and other countries.

One of the reasons for the strong support for FP2 is that the setting itself makes it easier to select. Specifically, the selection is made by presenting the immediate and future burdens as a series of packages. Equation 4.3 shows that the fiscal policy options package has both C_1^A and C_1^B, and the subjects cannot enjoy both high C_1^A and high C_1^B.

Table 4.11 Persuasive logics (Logics that led to the final policy selections as groups)

Logic	In group of final decision FP1 (point)	In group of final decision FP2 (point)
(1) My own interests should come first	3 points	0 point
(2) Not only my own interests but also interests of society as a whole, including those of future generations, should be considered	3 points	4 points
(3) The state and communities are semi-permanent beings, which have values beyond individuals, and the survival of the state and communities should come before my own interests	0 point	1 point
(4) Considering my own life, the policy of immediate burden increase is too harsh	5 points	3 points
(5) Considering my own life, a significant increase of burden after 30 years would be a major blow	0 point	4 points
(6) Considering the lives of my children and grandchildren, a significant increase of burden after 30 years would be a major blow	0 point	2 points
(7) Depending on future population, economy, and science and technology, the future would be better than what is expected now	12 points	0 point
(8) Depending on future population, economy, and science and technology, the future would be worse than what is expected now	0 point	0 point
(9) The actual fiscal situation may not be very bad and an increase of burden may not be necessary	0 point	0 point

(continued)

Table 4.11 (continued)

Logic	In group of final decision FP1 (point)	In group of final decision FP2 (point)
(10) Considering future generations is not productive, because it is not knowable what future generations will value nor what they will really want	7 points	0 point
(11) It is doubtful whether the funds will be properly used, even if we accept an increased burden	0 point	2 points
(12) I would like to leave as rich and healthy a society as possible to future generations	0 point	3 points
(13) Discussion by IFG	4 points	1 point

4.4.3 *Personal Interests or Judgements Distinct from Personal Interests*

4.4.3.1 Personal Interests

First, it is not difficult to find evidence that the subjects made their selections based on their personal interests. As shown in Table 4.4, of the subjects who selected FP1, not a small number, that is, slightly more than 20% (20.9%), felt "Interest of us (present generation) should come before those of future generations." In Table 4.5, too, a little more than 20% (21.7%) argued that "My own interests should come first," and about 40% (39.1%) held that "Considering my own life, the policy of immediate burden increase is too harsh."

Interestingly, Table 4.5 shows that some of those who selected FP2 made this choice based on their long-term personal interests. As a matter of fact, just under half (46.7%) of the subjects who selected FP2 stated that, "Considering my own life, a significant increase of burden after 30 years would be a major blow," indicating that their choice of FP2 was on personal interests. Support for FP2 on the basis of personal interests is one explanation for it high support.

4.4.3.2 Judgements Distinct from Personal Interests

Another factor in the high support for FP2 is that participants made decisions that were not limited to their personal interests. In terms of Eq. 4.3, the utility of Generation 2, U_2, plays a larger role ($0 < \beta \leq 1$). The responses to the questionnaire survey in Tables 4.4 and 4.5 confirm the existence of judgements beyond personal interests behind the selection of FP2. As shown in Table 4.4, as many as 64.8% of the subjects who chose FP2 indicated that they expressed their opinion from the perspective that "both our (present generation) interests and the interests of the future generation should be fairly considered." Table 4.5 also shows that more than half (51.1%) of the subjects who selected FP2 cited "interests of society as a whole, including those of future generations, should be considered," as the reason for their choice.

Amartya Sen (1977, p. 326), borrowing words from Edgeworth, points out that there are two paths by which one can depart from "unsympathetic isolation abstractly assumed in Economics:" sympathy and commitment. Through sympathy, one rejoices and grieves at the happiness and misfortune of others and leaves one's own narrow interests behind. In commitment, Sen states "if it does not make you feel personally worse off, but you think it is wrong and you are ready to do something to stop it" (p. 326); hence, one acts for reasons that are clearly distinct from their personal interests. It is possible that the subjects participate in policy decisions out of sympathy and commitment, and not out of narrow personal interests, which may be one of the reasons for the high support for FP2.

Speaking of decisions beyond personal interests, they could be based on the interests of one's children and grandchildren, in addition to consideration of the interests of society as a whole. Table 4.5 shows that 42.2% of the subjects who selected FP2 chose "Considering the lives of my children and grandchildren, a significant increase of burden after 30 years would be a major blow." Consideration of the interests of one's own direct descendants, such as one's children and grandchildren, is another reason for choosing FP2. When individuals' interests, those of their immediate descendants, and societal interests as a whole are put into three categories, where the line is drawn between them depends on the purpose of the discussion. It is possible to classify the interests of immediate descendants in the same category as personal interests. This chapter, however, draws the line between personal interests and the interests of direct descendants. In terms of Eq. 4.3, the utility of direct descendants is included in U_2. The reason for this distinction is partly because the experiment did not collect information on whether the subjects had children, and also because the distinction between direct descendants and general future generations is more subjective and ambiguous than the distinction between personal interests and the rest, which is based on the objective fact of life expectancy.

4.4.3.3 Coexistence of Personal Interests and Judgments Distinct from Personal Interests

As Eq. 4.3 suggests, personal interests and decisions distinct from personal interests work simultaneously. In Table 4.6, from among those who selected FP2 and stated "interests of society as a whole, including those of future generations, should be considered" (23 respondents), six respondents simultaneously raised "Considering my own life, a significant increase of burden after 30 years would be a major blow."

The results of the prosociality test require a note. The test developed by the psychologist Paul Von Lange defines prosiciality as the "tend(ency) to maximize outcomes for both themselves and others (i.e., cooperation)" (Van Lang et al. 1997, p. 733); so, it would seem that those with higher levels of prosociality would be more likely to choose FP2. Table 4.3 shows that the sign of prosociality and the selection of FP2 is consistently positive, and although it is possible that subjects with higher prosociality tend to select FP2, the relationship is not statistically significant. In the previous study by Kamijo et al. (2017), the same test with this chapter was used to test prosociality. Although Kamijo's study did not enquire about personal choices prior to the exchange of opinions, and only the relationship between the choice as a group as a result of the exchange of opinions and prosociality is known, the study states that "in the control condition in this study (in the absence of IFGs), only groups comprised of three prosocial people selected the sustainable option" (p. 418); this suggests the relationship between prosociality and sustainable choice. Kume et al. (2018) also reports that the lower the public mindset, the more supportive of "social security expansion and no tax increase."

Two points that should be mentioned in comparison with Kamijo et al. (2018) regarding why the experiment in this chapter does not find a clear relationship between prosociality and the selection of FP2. First, the choice of FP2 is not only based on decisions distinct from personal interests, but is mixed with those based on personal interests. Such a mixture diminishes the relationship between high prosociality and selection of FP2. Second, the options in this experiment are fiscal policies with specificity, which is different from the simple payoffs presented in Kamijo's study. Although the prosociality test is a psychological test that identifies the personality of the subjects, the choice of fiscal policy is the complex issue influenced more by the attitudes developed in social experience, even if influenced by personality. Kume et al (2018) are concerned with the relationship between "public mindedness" and policy preferences. Their "public mindedness" is measured by attitudes in the social context of the pros and cons of "unfair benefits," "fare-free riding," etc. Therefore, it may be easier to find a relationship with policy choices than the prosociality measured in the test of Von Lange et al. (1997).

The two points discussed so far are opportune findings for the goal of this chapter, which is to solve long-term fiscal problems. If there was a strong relationship between personality and fiscal policy selections, then there would be little room for intervention. However, if decisions distinct from personal interests are the matter of attitudes developed through social experience, then it is possible to intervene in policy to strengthen the departure from personal interests. As an example of such an intervention, this chapter examines the effects of deliberative discussions, including those with IFGs.

4.4.4 Information Provided to Participants

The regression analysis in Table 4.3 shows that the selection of FP2 decreases considerably when subjects are given information, on an individual basis, regarding the amount of burden. Even those who would have chosen FP2 when judging solely on macro institutional information such as tax rates, chose to postpone the burden to the future as soon as they were presented with information on the amount of their individual burden. Before the experiment, I had expected that the provision of such information would encourage the subjects to choose FP2 because it would cause them to reflect on how heavy the future generations' burden would be. That prediction was borne out.

The situation described above (Sect. 4.4.3.3), in which personal interests and non-privatized judgments coexist is useful to understand this result. The provision of personal burden information encourages the privatization of public policy. In actual policymaking, the more important a policy is, the more detailed and privatized information will be provided through parliamentary deliberations and mass media reports. The provision of information that encourages this privatization may be one piece of the puzzle that bridges the gap between the 70% support for FP2 shown in this experiment and the strong resistance to increasing the burden in the real world.

4.4.5 Age and Selection of Fiscal Policy

It is necessary to examine the Silver democracy hypothesis described in Hypothesis 3. As shown in Table 4.3, there is a decreasing trend in the percentage of respondents selecting FP2 as they advanced in age. Hypothesis 3 is not rejected. However, the rate of progress was slow, decreasing by about 0.4 percentage points for each additional age year, with the percentage of respondents selecting FP2 decreasing by only about 12 percentage points as they progress over 30 years.

Behind the limited effect of age progress, it appears that the subjects are influenced by motivations beyond their personal interests. In other words, the proportion of older age groups choosing FP2 is bulked up. As seen in Tables 4.4 and 4.5, a majority of the subjects who selected FP2 indicated that they thought the interests of the present and future generations should be fairly considered. It is interesting to note that the relationship between policy selection and age appears to be lost at older ages, as Model 6 in Table 4.3 suggests. The hypothetical reason for this is that whether one is 60 or 70 years old, private interests can no longer reduce support for FP2 any further, since what occurs 30 years from now takes place after one's death.

At the same time, young subjects' support for FP2 is suppressed, in part, because they are making their choice out of personal interest: even those in their late teens or 20 s are likely to choose the less burdensome option for the next 30 years, which is the majority of their working lives.[15] As shown in Table 4.5, 39.1% of the subjects who selected FP1 felt "Considering my own life, the policy of immediate burden increase is too harsh."

Kume et al. (2018) reports that support for "social security reduction and no tax increase" is greater at younger ages. The study also finds that the support for "social

[15] Time preference, which discounts and evaluates future events, will facilitate such choices by younger generations.

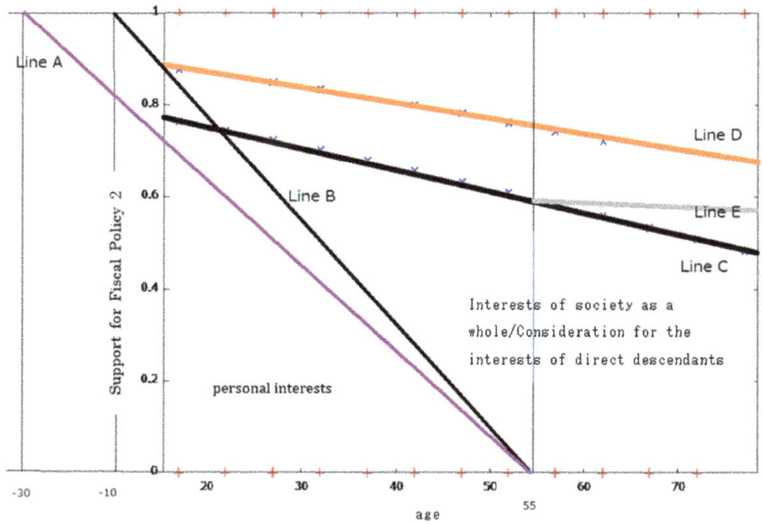

Fig. 4.3 Relationship between support for FP2 and age. *Note* If judged solely on the basis of personal interests, the support for FP2 for those aged 55 would be zero percent. There are two schools of thought regarding the age at which support for FP2 would be 100%: minus 30 or minus 10-year-old. The support of those between these two ages lies on Line A and Line B, which is the lines connecting 100% and zero percent. Lines A and B indicate support based on personal interests. The difference between Lines C and D is the presence or absence of personal burden information; giving personal burden information shifts Line D downward to Line C

security expansion and no tax increase" is also higher among those in their 20 s than other age groups. These reports are consistent with the finding that younger subjects select FP1 rather than FP2 because they make this choice based on personal interest.

Figure 4.3 summarizes the findings thus far.

Based on the life expectancy in the life table and the male–female ratio of the subjects,[16] the life expectancy at age 55 is 30 years. If judged solely on the basis of personal interests, the support for FP2 for those aged 55 would be zero percent.[17] There are two schools of thought regarding the age at which support for FP2 would be 100%: minus 30 or minus 10-year-old. First, one cannot enjoy the initial 30-year low burden of FP1 because it ends when one is born; then, the support for FP2 for a person who is conceptually minus 30 years old is 100%. Second, one cannot enjoy the initial 30-year low burden of FP1 because it ends when one enters the workforce; then, the support for FP2 is 100% for a person who is conceptually minus 10 years old. The support of those between the two ages lies on Line A and Line B, which are lines connecting 100% and zero percent. The support indicated by Lines A and B is based on personal interests.

---

[16] Life tables are tables in demography that show mortality rates and life expectancy for specific age groups and sexes. The life table used here is the 21st Complete Life Table (published in 2012), which was available at the time of the experiment.

[17] Risk aversion, in the sense of weighing the risk of living longer than average, is discarded here.

Model 2 obtained from the regression analysis (Table 4.3) is indicated by Lines C and D. The difference between Lines C and D is the presence or absence of personal burden information; providing personal burden information shifts Line D downward to Line C. The gap between Line C (D) and Lines A and B is the bulk of support for FP2 through judgments distinct from personal interests (i.e., consideration of the interests of society as a whole, and those of immediate descendants).

Figure 4.3 shows that the choice of FP2 is increasingly supported by judgments distinct from personal interests as one gets older. The silver democracy hypothesis (Hypothesis 3) is indeed not rejected. However, the experiment indicates that contrary to what is assumed in the hypothesis, older people make choices beyond their personal interests. As people get older, they begin to view things from the perspective of *nirvana*, that is, the position of detachment from individuality. In Chap. 2 (Sect. 2.5) of this book, drawing on the work of the philosopher Samuel Scheffler (2013, 2018), it has been pointed out that human beings value the continuation of projects, such as that of humanity, even after their own deaths. The experiment here has revealed that older subjects are more interested in life after death, and that the silver democracy theory is overemphasized.[18,19]

4.4.6 Occupation and Selection of Fiscal Policy

Table 4.3 shows that the percentage of respondents who select FP2 is considerably lower for non-regular employees and civil servants. One possible hypothesis for the unpopularity of FP2 for non-regular employees is that their income is less than that of regular employees, and their future prospects are less favorable. Since non-regular employees include a wide variety of workers, from part-time stay-at-home spouses to the so-called the working poor, it is still debatable to consider all non-regular employees as a disadvantaged group, but it is a plausible theory that the disadvantaged group will tend to avoid immediate increases in the burden. In Table 4.5, 39.1% of those who selected FP1 answered, "Considering my own life, the policy of immediate increases of burden is too harsh," suggesting that support for FP2 declines in accordance with the severity of life at present. Kume et al. (2018) also reports that the lower the hourly income, the more likely respondents are to support "social

[18] It is important to note, however, that support for FP2 based on judgments distinct from personal interests is expected to be more fragile than support based on private interests. Support for FP2 by the older age group is therefore more likely to shift.

[19] The discussion in this chapter does not cover risk aversion and time preference. However, these two factors may influence choice. When subjects are risk averse, they may prefer FP2 to avoid future difficulties in life. When their time preference is high, they may prefer FP1. However, a study by Ohtake and Tsutsui (2012) suggests, based on their experiment, that age has no significant effect on risk aversion. A study by Chao et al. (2009), through an examination of individuals, finds that age is not significantly associated with time preference. If this is true, then risk aversion and time preference would not affect the relationship between age and the policy selections examined in this chapter. However, the empirical evidence on the relationship between age and risk aversion, and time preference, is not necessarily convergent and can be considered as a topic for future research.

security expansion and tax increases," although the study finds that working styles, such as non-regular work, did not have any effect on policy preferences. Those from disadvantaged backgrounds may express their dissatisfactions with the experimental setting in the form of disapproval of FP2. This dissatisfaction would act as a force to shift Line C (or Line D) downward.[20]

4.4.7 Optimism Bias

Although the uncertainty includes both, the possibility that things will be better than expected and that things will be worse than expected, Table 4.4 shows that as many as 51.7% of the subjects selected FP1 states, "Because the future (2046) is uncertain, present interests should be given priority." It is important to note that the *economic views* of the participants seem to be mixed up in the evaluation of uncertainty. In Table 4.5, 39.1% of the participants who chose FP1 gave the following as the reason for their choice: "Depending on future population, economy, and science and technology, the future would be worse than what is expected now." If one doubts the validity of the package from one's own optimistic economic perspective, even though the question asks the subject to select either FP1 or FP2, one will select the package consistent with one's immediate interests, which are more certain.

In relation to Fig. 4.3, an optimistic economic view also acts as a force that shifts Line C (or D) downward. As Table 4.11 shows, the optimistic view of the economy is not only strong within individuals, but also has a strong persuasive effect on others. The logic of "Depending on future population, economy, and science and technology, the future would be better than what is expected now" works best in reverting from FP2 to FP1. Where logic relying on intergenerational equity can only win the reluctant consent from its opponents, an optimistic view of the economy evokes strong support.

The results of the optimism test imposed on the subjects require annotation. The regression analysis presented in Table 4.3 shows that the more optimistic the subjects, the less likely are they to select FP2; but this result does not reach clear statistical significance. The optimism test measures the degree of optimism in personal circumstances, for example, "In uncertain times, I usually expect the best." Although individuals with optimistic personalities may tend to hold optimistic economic views, it is believed that certain social experiences, and not just personality, contribute to the formation of economic views. The fact that there is not always a sufficient correlation between personality and the selection of fiscal policy, as was also the case in the test of prosociality, is a rather favorable finding for the goal of this chapter, which is to solve long-term fiscal problems. While there is limited room for intervention in optimistic personalities, it is conceivable to intervene in optimistic economic views

[20] Weak support for FP2 among public officials may stem from their understanding of the political difficulties of fiscal consolidation.

that have been developed through social experience. Providing exposure to more prudent views through deliberation is an example of one such possible intervention.

4.4.8 Excuse of "Agnosticism" on Future Generations

The optimism bias refers to an unfounded optimism about an uncertain future. The ignorance of future generations, as already discussed in Chap. 1 (Sect. 1.3.2), is the attitude toward an uncertain future, however, with a different logic: it is the attitude that it is unproductive to worry about the future now, because one does not know what people in the future will want.

Table 4.4 shows that 19.8% of the subjects who selected FP1 states that they expressed their opinion from the viewpoint that "we don't know what future generations will value, or what they want." Table 4.5 also shows that 30.4% of the subjects who selected FP1 give the following reason for their choice: "considering future generations is not productive, because it is not knowable what future generations will value nor what they will really want."

I included these choices in the survey on the suggestions by the philosopher Jonathan Glover. Glover argues that the people of the future who will be created by genetic engineering and brain control (the control of brain states through psychotropic drugs and information technology) will have very different values than us, and that we cannot decide whether or not to adopt these technologies based on our current discomfort with their application to humans (Glover, 1984).

As a matter of fact, I did not expect these options to be chosen very often, so the response results were a surprise. In a commentary on the Japanese translation of Glover's book, the philosopher Naotake Kato points out that "the so-called environmental problem is one in which the future generation will have fewer choices than the present generation, so the relativity of values that the present and the future generations have different values does not hold" (Kato, 1996, p. 329). Similarly, the long-term fiscal problem that the experiment in this chapter deals with is one in which "future generations will have less room for choice," i.e., it is merely a problem of the amount of resources, not a problem of value. Glover's point is that the human nature of future generations will be different from ours and that their value judgments will be unimaginable. For future generations, too, more resources are good and less are bad, just as they are for us now.

Here, ignorance about future generations serves as an insinuation, or excuse, for selecting FP1 instead of FP2. As Table 4.11 shows, this excuse is highly persuasive to others. The logic that "considering future generations is not productive, because it is not knowable what future generations will value nor what they will really want" is one of the logics that worked well in reverting from FP2 to FP1, which was in the minority in the prior personal selection.

In the framework of Fig. 4.3, the ignorance about future generations also shifts Line C (or line D) downward. Based on the previous discussion, Fig. 4.3 has been redrawn as Fig. 4.4.

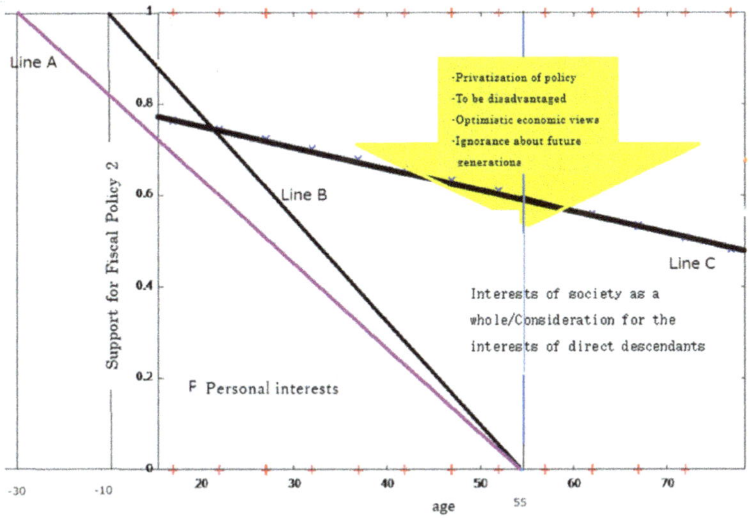

Fig. 4.4 Downward shift in support for FP2. *Note* Just as the privatization of policy pushed down support for FP2, the subjects' disadvantages, optimistic economic views, and ignorance about future generations shift support for FP2 downward

4.4.9 Deliberation, IFGs

Sections 4.4.2 through 4.4.8 have interpreted fiscal policy choices by individuals prior to deliberation. This section focuses on the analysis of deliberation, or collective decision-making.

Figure 4.2 illustrates that the distribution of prior personal opinions and the decision after deliberation are positively correlated. However, there are divergences from the results that would be expected had the participants taken simple majority votes; in this regard, deliberation does influence the decision. More importantly, deliberation alters the opinions of individual subjects, as indicated in Table 4.7. A change in opinion means that an individual's values, or preferences, have changed. This change in preference is a noteworthy characteristic of deliberation. Figure 4.5 shows the indifference curves of the present generation drawn on a plane with the horizontal axis as present consumption (c_1) and the vertical axis is consumption 30 years from now (c_2). For a member of the present generation, who had selected FP1 (■) before the deliberation, FP2 (▲) on the same budget line was not their choice. Fiscal Policy 2 (▲) is on the curveu_1', which is inside the curveu_1, where$u_1 > u_1'$.[21] The change of opinion to FP2 through deliberation means that the indifference curve of the present generation has been transformed into the curveu_1''. Chapter 3 (Appendix 3.1, Fig. 3.8) discussed Pareto-improving intergenerational negotiation, in which the deformation of the indifference curves did not appear. The present generation simply moved along

[21] Fiscal Policy 1 and 2 can be conceptualized as being on the same budget constraint line, as has been discussed in Sect. 4.3.1.

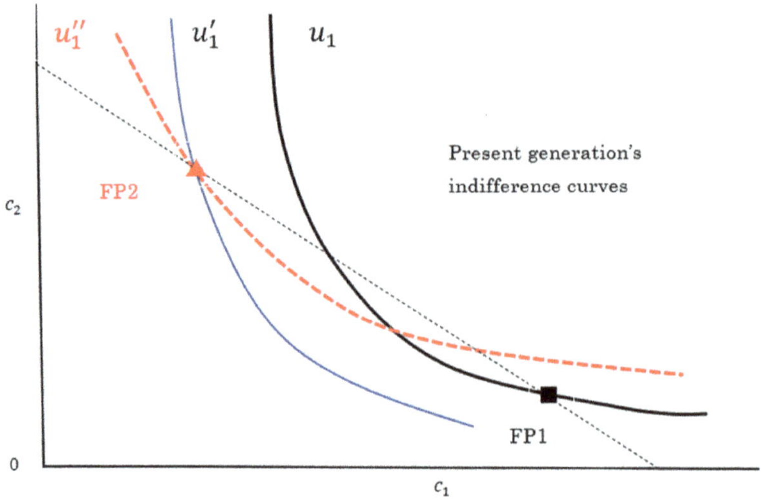

Fig. 4.5 Change of opinion as deformation of the indifference curve [FP1 (■) to FP2 (▲)]. *Note* The indifference curves of the present generation are drawn on a plane with the horizontal axis as present consumption (c_1) and the vertical axis is consumption 30 years from now (c_2). For a member of the present generation, who had selected FP1 (■) before the deliberation, FP2 (▲) on the same budget line was not their choice. Fiscal Policy 2 (▲) is on the curve u_1', which is inside the curve u_1, where $u_1 > u_1'$. The change of opinion to FP2 through deliberation means that the indifference curve of the present generation has been transformed into the curve u_1''

the indifference curves. The deformation of the indifference curves is the important feature of deliberation, and expands the possibility for intergenerational negotiation. The discussion up to the previous chapters has treated the degree of interest in the future of the present generation (the preceding generation) as an exogenous variable. Here, through the introduction of deliberation, the degree of interest of the present generation has been endogenized.

It should also be noted that the experiment results put reservations on the possibility of deliberation. Table 4.6 shows that deliberation in the present generation-only group did *not* lead to increase in the support for FP2 over the distribution of personal opinion (70% in favor of FP2). If, as Hypothesis 4 states, deliberation promotes more appropriate policy judgments through the generations, then the solid line in Fig. 4.2 must exceed not only two-thirds on the horizontal axis (122) (i.e., one supporter of FP1, and two supporters of FP2), but also one third on (112) (i.e., two supporters of FP1, and one supporter of FP2). However, the result is considerably less than one-third on (112). In other words, Hypothesis 4 is rejected. With regard to issues like fiscal policy, in which the interests of generations differ, it is naive to say that deliberation is all that is required. This is consistent with Kameda (1997), which argues that initial majority-driven decisions are more likely in decision-making where the correctness of the solution is not guaranteed.

Similar reservations need to be made in the impact of the deliberations on personal opinion. Table 4.9 shows that the change to FP2 was notably more adaptive to the majority, compared to the change to FP1. Moreover, Table 4.11 suggests that the logics in favor of FP1, i.e., the logics about optimism about the future economy and ignorance about future generations, are superior in terms of persuasiveness to the logics in favor of FP2.

Does deliberation risk steering people away from better decisions, as Sunstein cautioned? A useful survey paper to consider in this regard is one written by behavioral economists Charness and Sutter (2012) who highlight, through their literature survey, that group decisions are better self-interested decisions than individual decisions. According to them, in trust games, for example, individuals tend to make good-natured choices that are not in their own best interest, whereas when they are asked to form groups and join in the games, they tend to make self-interested choices without trusting other groups. Thereby, the gains that the individuals get from the games are lower due to less cooperation.[22] In the choice of fiscal policy, the option that serves the subjects' personal interests is FP1, whereas FP2 is the good-natured choice. Individuals who had previously selected FP2 were persuaded through deliberation that FP1 was more in their self-interest. In other words, they have come to realize that their own lives are more important than those of future generations, that the future economy may be more prosperous, or that the values of future generations may differ from their own.

What is the evaluation of the function of the IFGs? Table 4.6 shows that support for FP2 is increased in the decisions made by the group including the IFGs. The thin dashed line in Fig. 4.2 depicts the percentage of the group decision in favor of FP2, for the group that includes the IFGs, with prior individual selections on the horizontal axis. For example, in the case of a group that was classified as (12 IFG) (one for FP1, one for FP2, and one as the IFG), if the personal choice of the subject assigned to the IFG was FP1, the group is reclassified as (112) (two for FP1 and one for FP2). As the thin dashed line indicates, the introduction of the IFGs increases the overall frequency with which FP2 is chosen. Therefore, Hypothesis 5 is not rejected. As Hypothesis 5 states, through the introduction of the IFGs, more appropriate policy decisions can made through generations. When deliberating only within the present generation, the subjects' information is biased toward that of the present generation. Incorporating the voices of the future generations into the deliberation avoids biasing the decision toward the present generation. Sunstein points out that for better deliberations, it is important to incorporate opinions that participants are not normally exposed to.[23]

---

[22] The previous studies that Charness and Sutter discuss are: Kugler et al. (2007) on trust games (in which the first and second players work together and the first player's work is wasted if the second player slacks off); Bornstein et al. (2004) on centipede games (in which players choose in order, with higher gains if multiple players cooperate); and Charness et al. (2007) on the prisoner's dilemma. The study by Luhan et al. (2009), which was published after Charness and Sutter (2012) and includes Sutter as the authors, found similar results for the dictator games in which the distributor and the receiver allocate gains, and the receiver cannot refuse to accept the gains allocated by the distributor). A recent study on Future Design also points out that deliberation by only the present generation is insufficient to take future generations into consideration (Timilsina et al., 2021).

[23] Sunstein (2000, p. 115).

The IFGs increase the chances of arriving at a balanced decision, by adding the opinions of the future generations to the deliberative process.

Let us summarize the discussion of deliberation. Based on the experiment, it has been shown that deliberation can change the preferences of the present generation. However, the force of change is stronger in the direction of conformity. It does not necessarily work in the direction that encourages consideration for future generations, but encourages decisions that emphasize the interests of the present generation who participate in deliberations, which in turn reduces the consideration for future generations who cannot participate. However, many of the subjects in this experiment did not have preferences based solely on personal interests, prior to the deliberation. In many groups, the pre-passage preference was for FP2, and the deliberation generally worked in the direction of greater concern for future generations. The introduction of the IFGs into the deliberation process further encouraged decisions that take future generations into account. It also corrected the distortion that arises from the decision-making process in which issues involving intergenerational interests are decided solely by the present generation.

Here, through the mechanism of deliberation, especially deliberation with the IFGs, this chapter uncovers how to endogenize the degree of interest in the future of the present generation. Chapter 3 (Sect. 3.5.3) has pointed out the drawback of intergenerational cooperation through Kantian categorical imperative: when the preceding generation only cooperates weakly (from the viewpoint of an outside observer), the moral inspiration of the succeeding generation locks this weak cooperation. By incorporating deliberations among the present (preceding) generation (including those with the IFGs), a pathway to endogenize the preferences of the present generation, which were previously only exogenous, has been found.

4.5 Seven Keys to Solving Long-Term Fiscal Problems

Based on the findings so far, it is useful to present seven keys that should be considered in order to solve long-term fiscal problems.

4.5.1 Importance of Basing the Discussion on the Trade-Off Between Benefits and Burdens

First, it is key to set up discussion frameworks with built-in tradeoffs: as has been seen in Sect. 4.4.2, this experiment presented a package of benefits and burdens now and 30 years from now, which eliminated the enjoyment of both, high C_1^A and high C_1^B in Eq. 5.3. It is important to present choices within the framework of a tradeoff between present and future benefits and burdens. However, in the real world it is often difficult to set up the framework with the tradeoff. Fiscal rules such as the pay-as-you-go principle and no-loan policy can be viewed as attempts to set up approximate trade-offs.[24]

4.5.2 *Necessity of a System that Leads to a Greater Role of Public Judgments, Particularly that Represents Voices of Future Generations Which Are not Heard in Conventional Deliberation*

Second is the need to devise measures in light of the coexistence of personal interests and decisions distinct from personal interests within individuals, as revealed through Sects. 4.4.3.3 and 4.4.5 (Fig. 4.3). A positive finding of this chapter is that older people are not always preoccupied with their personal interests. It is necessary to devise mechanisms to elicit people's propensity to make decisions away from their personal interests.

While the results of the experiment in this chapter show that deliberation can change people's opinions, they also indicate that mere deliberation does not mean that judgement distinct from personal interests will prevail, when such judgment is limited. The findings that mere deliberation does not make judgments distinct from personal interests is consistent with the view of Charness and Sutter (2012) that group decisions are more self-interested than individual decisions. The interests of future generations are not represented in the deliberative process. As such, the participation of the IFGs in deliberations increases the diversity of opinions in the deliberative process and enhances the quality of deliberations. As the interests of present and future generations differ, future generations need to be represented.

The age-old debate about the nature of social decision-making has swung between deliberation and tallying. Proponents of representative democracy, such as J. S. Mill, have argued that deliberation is more important than simply counting votes. Delegative democracy hopes for a chance to move away from the mere aggregation of voters' interests through deliberation among representatives. However, Jean-Jacques Rousseau is a proponent of tallying. Rousseau is known for presenting the idea of *general will* that aims at the common interests of society, distinguished from *particular will* and its aggregation, *total will*. Rousseau is unique in his assertion that the general will can be derived through the counting of votes. "When a law is proposed to the assembled people, what they are being asked is not (1) Do you approve or reject this proposal? but rather (2) Is this proposal in conformity with the general will?—the general will being their will. Each man's vote gives his opinion on that point, i.e., his answer to question (2); and the general will is found by counting votes." (Rousseau, 1762, p. 56). Rousseau did not see voting as a mere tally of individual preferences, but as a process of discovering truth.

---

[24] According to the pay-as-you-go principle, expenditure in the budget should be financed by expenditure cuts or revenue increases. The no-loan policy is a principle of fiscal management that does not allow issuing of bonds.

Rousseau was not discussing intergenerational issues, but in principle, the concept of general will should not be the individual will of the present generation, but the common good of society, which includes the future. If it is believed that such general will, which includes the future, is difficult to achieve through voting among the present generation itself, then the idea of inviting future generations to vote arises, just as the IFGs have been invited in the deliberation in this chapter. Based on such understandings, new voting systems have been proposed, such as the Age-based Voting System (Ihori & Doi, 1998), Life Expectancy Voting System (Takeuchi, 2011), and Demeny Voting System (Demeny, 1986), which gives an additional vote to voters with children.

While this book does not provide comprehensive evaluations of these voting systems, it does point out some of the problems they face. In the Age-based Voting System, the problem of whether elected representatives from divided electoral groups can agree on coherent sets of policies arises. While the Life Expectancy Voting System and Demeny Voting System do not have the problem of splits in the electoral groups, their disadvantage is that the system predetermines the meaning to be attached to each vote cast. The Life Expectancy Voting System assumes that votes are cast taking into account the social conditions during the remainder of life. The Demeny Voting System assumes, in advance, that the first votes are cast based on people's own interest and the second votes based on the interests of their children. Yoshio Kamijo and his colleagues conducted an experiment that mimics the Demeny Voting System, noting that when the system is introduced, those who previously voted for the generation of their children now vote for themselves, and that the system does not promote decisions in favor of the children as much as one might expect (Kamijo et al., 2015). This result is also expected from the experiments on fiscal policy reported in this chapter. Electoral reforms that give future generations a vote, risk alienating older generations from decisions distinct from personal interests, in which they could have exerted influence from the beginning.

4.5.3 Effectiveness of Persuading to Support Sustainable Policies Based on Personal Interests

A third point is that it is also useful to skillfully persuade people on personal interests (while at the same time encouraging the judgement distinct from personal interests). As has already been shown in Sect. 4.4.3, a significant number of those who selected FP2 also did so with long-term personal interests in mind. When considering time horizons of a few decades or so, there is an opportunity to discourage the deferral of burdens, especially by alerting the younger generation to their long-term personal interests.

Figure 4.3 offers some insight with regard to building support for policies. A policy that avoids increasing the burden for the time being (e.g., for a period of 10 years) but then raises it could gain support through collusion between the elderly and the younger generation. If it is true that support for FP2 among the elderly ceases to decline, as shown in Line E, then employing tactics to take advantage of this collusion is even more promising. A sober observer will notice that the gradualist fiscal consolidations are entirely dependent on this collusion between the elderly and the younger generation.

4.5.4 Concern that the Younger Does not Necessarily Respect the Voices of Future Generations

The fourth point to keep in mind when considering long-term fiscal problems is that, as discussed in Sect. 4.4.5, even the younger generation may not fully represent the position of future generations.

Using generational accounting, Shimasawa (2017) points out that the reality in Japan is that all present generations, including the younger ones, are exploiting the unborn future generations.

4.5.5 The "Privatization" of Policies as a Dilemma and Its Countermeasures

Fifth, providing information on the personal burden makes the issue a private matter and strengthens the attachment to personal interests. In this regard, as seen in the regression analysis presented in Table 4.3, the provision of information on the amount of burden on an individual basis considerably reduced support for FP2.

In democracy, it is a principle that policy information should be disclosed to voters. However, it is unfair to allow the present generation to decide on issues privately, without the involvement of future generations, when the issues concern not only the interests of the present generation but also those of future generations. First of all, it is necessary to grasp this privatization of policy as a dilemma.

One way to address this dilemma is to limit the opportunities for policymaking while not narrowing the information provided. The idea is to include long-standing policies in the law and automate their enforcement. The law would be fully informed during its deliberation as a draft. However, once the law goes into effect, the system automatically enforces the policy, according to the predetermined program (unless the law is amended). A measure similar to this solution is the macroeconomic indexing system introduced in the 2004 pension reform in Japan. The indexing includes automatic (capped) increases in premium and automatic adjustment of benefit according to demographic trends. Although it does not go so far as to automate policy enforcement, so-called programmatic laws may be enacted to bind the actions of government agencies. In the area of social security, an example is the Program-Law for Social Security Reform enacted in 2013.

4.5.6 Importance of Problems Which the Disadvantaged Face

Sixth, the disadvantaged among the present generation, that is, those who cannot afford to live now and are not blessed with good future prospects, may tend to put their personal interests first, and policies need to be devised bearing this in mind. In particular, this chapter finds only low support for FP2 among those engaged in non-regular employment; however, it is easy to see how pressing life needs can crowd out decisions based on longer-term needs.

One way to address the problems is to increase support for the policy by making the burden on the revenue side more progressive and by including measures to improve the conditions of disadvantaged groups on the expenditure side.

4.5.7 Necessity of Sharing Appropriate Economic Views and Understanding Fiscal Policies as Problems of Resources not of Values

The seventh and final point is the importance of reaching a reasonable consensus on the long-term economic outlook among the parties involved. As has been discussed in Sect. 4.4.7 on the optimism bias, even if the setting with built-in tradeoffs between benefits and burdens is provided, if some have different optimistic views of the economy—with regard to, e.g., the prospects for future economic growth, population, and technological innovation—they may be inclined to revise the setting itself.

Qualitatively speaking, a reasonable economic outlook is defined as accepting the impossibility of gaining both, high C_1^A and high C_1^B in Eq. 4.3, and of obtaining both, high utility of generation 1 (U_1^A, U_1^B) and high utility of generation 2 (U_2). However, reaching a consensus on a quantitative outlook is not easy. One possible solution is to provide an opportunity for deliberation on the long-term outlook itself. If deliberation does not result in consensus on the outlook, the second-best strategy is to adopt a conservative (pessimistic) outlook rather than an optimistic one. This is because if the optimistic outlook is followed by profligate fiscal policy and the economy does not do well eventually, an excessive burden will be left for the future generation.

Recognizing that the fiscal policy is the problem of resource is an important countermeasure to the ignorance about future generations seen in Sect. 4.4.8. The basic facts need to be reaffirmed. That is, in the foreseeable future, future generations will need clean air, water, food, safe housing, and social interaction just as much as the present generation does, and the more abundant the resources to secure these needs, the better. The argument that we do not know what future generations will want may be a head-scratcher in cases where we recreate human beings into other creatures through genetic engineering, which would make our values changed. However, when such an argument appears in fiscal policy, it is merely an excuse for failing to consider future generations.

4.6 Generalization of the Keys in Policies Involving Multiple Generations, Such as Climate Change

Finally, this section generalizes the considerations that we have discussed for fiscal policy to policy decisions involving multiple generations in general. While separate experiments can be conducted to derive considerations for other policy issues, such as climate change, this chapter attempts to generalize, to the extent that logic dictates.

First has been the importance of setting tradeoffs between benefits and burdens. The fact that tradeoffs are not fully respected, despite their existence, is what makes intergenerational issues so problematic. Setting up a forum to discuss with built-in tradeoffs is extremely important for policymaking involving multiple generations. Taking the issue of climate change, greenhouse gases emitted into the atmosphere remain there for a long time. The total amount of gases that can be emitted without causing climate change is constant throughout generations, and present benefits are traded off against future burdens. Regarding the second point, that people do not necessarily make decisions based solely on personal interests and that deliberation can change people's opinions, there is no reason to limit its relevance to fiscal policy. Whether there are differences across policy issues in the degree to which people are free from personal interests and the degree to which deliberation is effective in encouraging judgments distinct from personal interests is an issue that needs to be examined through experiments. The political scientists, Kaat Smets and Pierangelo Isernia, report the results of a deliberative experiment in Europe. They show that attitudes toward climate change are more sensitive to deliberation than those towards immigration, which are more sensitive to ideology (Smets & Isernia, 2014). In light of this study, there is no particular reason to be pessimistic about the function of deliberation on climate change, which is a representative intergenerational issue.

Third, we consider the effectiveness of the persuasion on personal interests. Logically, the more adverse effects will become apparent in the near future, the more effective personal interest-based persuasion should be. If the adverse effects of global environmental problems will only become apparent in the distant future, then personal interest-based persuasion will not be very effective. However, according to the Intergovernmental Panel on Climate Change (IPCC), global warming has already been implicated in the occurrence of extreme weather events since the 1950s, and this trend will only intensify in the future.[25] If global warming is such a pressing issue, then personal interest-based persuasion on the issue of climate change becomes more effective. A speech by Greta Thunberg (2019) from Sweden, then 16 years old, at the U.N. Climate Action Summit in September 2019, echoed her sense of urgency on climate change. In Europe, a collusion is emerging between young people and political leadership on climate action. The fourth point, that the younger generation cannot always speak for future generations, is more valid when the adverse effects are policy issues that will manifest themselves in the more distant future. As has been

[25] IPCC (2021, pp. 8–9).

seen, the younger generation can better represent the interests of future generations if the adverse effects of climate change are already beginning to manifest themselves.

Fifth is the dilemma of the privatization of public policies. Compared to fiscal policy, which is easily converted into monetary gains or losses, there is less danger of privatization in global environmental issues. However, when climate change measures take the form of the carbon tax, they carry tangible burdens that are easy to recognize. Distributional issues, including the negative impact on the fossil fuel industry, are also inevitable. The visibility of the burden of the measures and their distributional effects, while important in democratic decision-making, raises the dilemma of privatization. The sixth point, related to the disadvantaged groups, should be taken into account in other policy issues as well. The more people are dependent on cheap fossil fuels for their livelihoods, the more economically disadvantaged they are. The Ministry of the Environment of Japan states that "carbon pricing is a measure that raises the relative price of fossil fuels, so regressive issue can be pointed out, whereby the relative burden is heavier on lower income households whose expenditures on utilities and fuel costs account for a higher proportion of their total expenditures" (Ministry of the Environment, 2018, p. 45). Coal is inexpensive but emits large amounts of greenhouse gases. According to the International Energy Agency (IEA), coal still accounted for 27% of the energy used worldwide in 2017, and for 38% of energy for power sources. In its forecast of future demand, the IEA also states that this demand is stable in China, and predicts an increase in India and Southeast Asia.[26] The Dasgupta Review, which considers biodiversity issues, finds that food production is the most significant factor in the loss of biodiversity on land (Independent Review on the Economics of Biodiversity, 2021a, 2021b). The review also warns that producing enough food in a sustainable manner will become increasingly difficult as the world population, including in emerging economies, grows.[27]

The seventh and final point is the need for consensus on future prospects, which is also important in addressing policy decisions in general involving multiple generations. Future events inevitably involve uncertainty. It is natural to be skeptical about the probability of an event as historically unprecedented as climate change. Since its establishment in 1988, the IPCC has paved the way in building scientific knowledge and consensus on a global scale. The publication of the Dasgupta Review on biodiversity, commissioned by the UK Treasury, is one effort to build the necessary body of knowledge. The good consensus on future prospects will also determine the success or failure of the introduction of the IFGs. When there is no good consensus, it is difficult to determine what the IFGs should insist on. If climate change does not occur, then the futurists have nothing to claim. If climate change is certain, then the futurist has a serious case to make.

The second part of the seventh item refers to the danger of replacing the issue of resources with the issue of value. The future generation, like the present one,

[26] IEA (2018).

[27] Independent Review on the Economics of Biodiversity (2021a, p. 3).

will need clean air and companionship, and the more abundant the natural and man-made resources to secure these things, the better. However, it is important to bear in mind that global environmental issues are more attached to the issue of value than to fiscal policy. As noted at the beginning of Chap. 1, John Locke, while arguing that everything one takes out of the state of nature becomes one's property, made a reservation that there must be enough good left for those who come after (Locke, 1689). The acceptance or rejection of this Lockean proviso is not irrelevant to the question of value. Philosophers have noted the tension between private property rights and taxes, even in fiscal matters. In their work entitled "the Myth of Ownership," Liam Murphy and Thomas Nagel take issue with the persistence in the United States of an absolute view of private ownership, and argue that private ownership is just in part a legal convention defined by the tax system.[28] With regard to the power to collect taxes, in the U.S., the 16th Amendment to the U.S. Constitution (ratified in 1913) recognizes the power of Congress to impose income taxes. In Japan, Article 30 of the Constitution stipulates that tax payment is a duty of the people. Private property rights are subject to the power of tax collection. However, in the new area of global environmental issues, the mediation of tensions between private property rights and required environmental measures is ongoing. As a result, the promotion of environmental measures is even more vulnerable to attacks from those who value private ownership, than in the case of public finance.

As discussed in Chap. 2 (Sect. 2.3), it is not easy to make intergenerational ethics a reality. How can a society be assembled to ensure the implementation of policy that is favorable through the generations but unpopular with the present generation? Under a dictatorship, this problem could easily be solved; however, the quest is to find ways to solve the problem under democratic systems. Reconstructing democracy from the perspective of intergenerational ethics is the fundamental problem addressed in this chapter, and the discussion thus far provides the answer to this question.

4.7 Conclusions and Remaining Issues

Taking long-term fiscal policy as an example, this chapter has examined the relationship between individuals' policy preferences and attributes such as age. It has also engaged in examinations of deliberation, one of the avenues for making intergenerational ethics a reality. As participants age, their support for sustainable policy is weakened; however, the older generation make their choices, based more on judgement distinct from personal interests. The simple pessimistic hypothesis of silver democracy appears to be exaggerated. As people age, they make decisions based on the interests of society as a whole, and those of their immediate descendants. Deliberations solely by the present generation do not necessarily encourage decisions that take future generations into account. However, the introduction of the IFGs into deliberations encourages decisions that take the future generation into

[28] Murphy and Nagel (2002, p. 8).

consideration. Through the process of deliberation with the IFGs, the preferences of the subjects change to those that take future generations into consideration. The IFGs are significant additions to the input into the deliberative process, increasing the chances of obtaining balanced decisions. The latter sections presented keys for solving long-term fiscal problems and generalize them to policy decisions involving multiple generations.

Finally, I will touch on a few remaining issues. The first is to further work toward social implementation of the IFGs. To this end, it is necessary to gain a more concrete understanding of the functions of the IFGs in deliberations. In the experiment in this chapter, the kind of opinions expressed by the subjects in the role of the IFGs were not recorded, and the effects of the IFGs were evaluated based on the policy decisions that emerged as a result of the deliberations. This point will be clarified in Appendix 4.1, which reports the results of another experiment. Furthermore, this chapter has focused on the preferences of the participants, especially those of the present generation, which tend to be biased toward their own interests. In order to obtain good collective decision-making, it is also important to give participants good information. In promoting the social implementation of IFGs, it is necessary to design a system that is attentive not only to preferences, but also to information.

Second, with respect to collective decision-making, this chapter examined the avenues for obtaining decisions through deliberation. It only briefly touches on decision-making through voting. While much research has already been done on voting, there is still room to focus on specific policy issues (e.g., fiscal policy, climate change) as done in this chapter. Third, this chapter included an experiment on fiscal policy that was conducted to gain insights into what should be considered in policy decisions involving multiple generations. The findings from the fiscal experiment are generalized in Sect. 4.6, but a series of experiments taking other issues, such as climate change, as examples would be useful to understand both, the specific issues involved, and how to address intergenerational issues in general.

Attachment 3: Methods for evaluating the discussions that led to the final policy decisions by groups

Types of logic	Main questionnaire items (Converted as equivalent to the logic shown on the left)
(1) My own interests should come first	(1) Interests of us (present generation) should come before those of future generations
(2) Not only my own interests but also interests of society as a whole, including those of future generations, should be considered	(2) Both our (present generation) interests and the interests of the future generation should be fairly considered
(3) The state and communities are semi-permanent beings, which have values beyond individuals, and the survival of the state and communities should come before my own interests	(3) Interests of future generations should come before ours (present generation). (Note 1)

(continued)

(continued)

Types of logic	Main questionnaire items (Converted as equivalent to the logic shown on the left)
(4) Considering my own life, the policy of immediate burden increase is too harsh	
(5) Considering my own life, a significant increase of burden after 30 years would be a major blow	
(6) Considering the lives of my children and grandchildren, a significant increase of burden after 30 years would be a major blow	
(7) Depending on future population, economy, and science and technology, the future would be better than what is expected now	(4) Because the future (2046) is uncertain, present interests should be given priority
(8) Depending on future population, economy, and science and technology, the future would be worse than what is expected now	
(9) The actual fiscal situation may not be very bad and an increase of burden may not be necessary	
(10) Considering future generations is not productive, because it is not knowable what future generations will value nor what they will really want	(5) We do not know what future generations will value, or what they will want
(11) It is doubtful whether the funds will be properly used, even if we accept an increased burden	
(12) I would like to leave as rich and healthy a society as possible to future generations	(3) Interests of future generations should come before ours (present generation). (Note 1)
(13) Discussion by IFG. (Note 2)	

[Explanation]

1. The logic used by the winner (whose selection of policy becomes a final decision as a group) is classified in the list of "types of logic" from the reason survey questionnaire
   (1) In the case of the respondents to the reason survey questionnaire, add one point directly to the relevant reasons
   (2) In the case of the respondents to the main questionnaire, add one point to similar logic in the list
   (3) If there are free comments, add one point to the relevant logic (even one point has been added in procedure (1), (2), add one more for taking seriously the fact that the winners make comments on the logic
2. Add one point to the relevant logic if the loser left a free comment that they were persuaded by the logic

(Note 1) Item (3) in the main questionnaire has meaning across the types of logic (3) and (12) by the reason survey questionnaire. Therefore, if there is a response (3) from the main questionnaire, 0.5 points will be added to (3) and (12)

(Note 2) One point is added, if there is a IFG in the group

Appendix 4.1: What Do People Say When They Become "Future People"?

The main part of this chapter has seen that collective decisions become more sensitive to future generations through deliberations with the IFGs. However, the experiment in the main part does not provide information about what and how the IFGs were talking about at the deliberation sessions.

In the joint study with my colleagues (Hiromitsu et al., 2021), I have analyzed transcripts of statements made in deliberations in a town in Japan to determine what people talk about when they are instructed to become future generation.

The deliberation was held on May 28, 2018 in Yahaba Town, which has a population of about 27,000 (2015, Census report). It is located in Iwate Prefecture, in the northeastern region of Japan. It is an old village with paddy fields, and a commuter town situated on the outskirts of Morioka City, the capital of the Prefecture. In line with Japan's nationwide trend, the population in the town is also aging. The aging rate of the population (the percentage of the population aged 65 years and over) was 23.6% in 2015 and will continue to rise. The National Institute for Population and Social Security Research has projected that the population will decline to around 24,000 in 2045. It is big event for the town that the Iwate Medical Collage Hospital was set to move from Morioka City in the fall of 2019. Along with this, facilities were developed to accommodate hospitals, including the construction of an interchange that can climb up and down the expressway, extending from Morioka City.

A total of 30 people participated in the deliberations, including 22 publicly invited residents, 4 town hall officials, and 4 officials from the national government (Ministry of Finance). Approximately 45% of subjects are female. The percentage of subjects younger than 40 and older than 60 are around 45% and 35%, respectively.[29] In the beginning, the Yahaba Town Office explained the town's ideas for formulating a comprehensive administration plan, which is the issue to be discussed among the people. As background information, the national government briefed them on Yahaba Town's financial situation as well as the national and global issues including population aging and climate change. After that, five or six inhabitants, one town hall staff member, and one national staff member were formed as a unit to form four groups, separated into different rooms. The subjects discussed twice with the same members for issues to be raised in the comprehensive plan. In the first session (Part 1), everyone was treated as part of the present generation and discussions were held for about 60 min. In the second session (Part 2), all subjects were instructed to become IFGs from 2048, and views were exchanged for about 60 min. In Part 2, the subjects received the following instructions: "As a resident of the same age, gender, and other social statuses in 2048, imagine what policies you would like the town to work on. From the perspective of humans in 2048, think about what the comprehensive administrative plan should look like." We asked town and government officials to participate in the deliberations with the same perspective as that of the residents.

[29] Of the 30 participants who attended the deliberation, 28 responded to the survey because of time constraints.

It is necessary to focus on the characteristics of deliberations. Here, these characteristics are understood using two methods. The first aimed to understand the overall characteristics through text mining techniques of the transcripts. The transcripts are divided into Parts 1 and 2, and each group (ABCD) and its characteristics are grasped. Another approach toward characterizing the deliberations is to have independent coders read the transcripts and make judgments on the characteristics of each subject's speech.

In the first method, KH Coder (Higuchi, 2014) was used to create coding rules for verbatim transcripts and to analyze the contents of the deliberations. The coding rules are as seen in Table 4.12. "Future" is a code that expresses deliberations on the future, of which "30 years later" and "2048" are words used in the instructions in Part 2. "30 years ago" contains words that are expected to be used in retrospective assessment. "Traffic" comprises words related to traffic and words representing specific modes of transportation. "Facility" comprises words related to facilities and words representing specific facilities. "New and old residents" pertain to the relationship between new and old residents. "Culture" comprises words related to culture and artistic activities. "Landscape/environment" comprises words related to landscape and environment. The landscape includes concrete scenery such as Nanchang Mountain, and the environment excludes elements related to the living environment such as the child-raising environment. "Disaster prevention" includes words pertaining to disaster prevention and safety, and safety excludes traffic safety. "Agriculture" is related to agriculture and includes specific crops. "Generation exchange/festival" comprises words related to exchanges and connections between generations and festivals in which residents gather. When words related to the elderly/youth/child coexist in the same utterance (paragraph), it is counted as corresponding to the code. The term "new technology" comprises words related to new technologies, and includes words related to technologies that have become more popular, such as the Internet, considering that discussions are conducted by local residents. "Foreign" comprises words related to foreign countries. The term "elderly/depopulated" includes words on the elderly and depopulated, as well as words on related issues such as lonely death. "Child/Childcare" comprises words that represent children up to junior high school and words pertaining to childcare. "Youth" refers to young people who are older than the high school age. "Medical College transfer" comprises words pertaining to transfer of Iwate Medical College Hospital. "Tourism" comprises words pertaining to tourism.

The results of the analysis of the characteristics of the deliberations in Part 1 (present generation) and Part 2 (future generation) by the coding rule, looking at Groups A through D as a whole, are shown in Fig. 4.6.

Here, the sizes of the squares indicate the proportion (percentage) of the paragraphs corresponding to each code in Parts 1 and 2. As a corollary, "Future" is more common in Part 2. The code "30 years ago," which represents retrospective assessment, has been significantly observed in Part 2. The codes that characterize the present generation's deliberations (Part 1) are "Traffic," "Facility," "New and old residents," and "Culture." The codes that characterize the deliberation of future

Table 4.12 Coding rules

Codes	Rules (examples)
Future	The future, 30 years later, 2048
30 years ago	30 years ago, now 2048, at that time
Traffic	Traffic, undercarriage, car, bus, taxi
Facility	Facilities, construction, playgrounds, shops, roads, pools
New and old residents	New residents, old residents, unfamiliar
Culture	Culture, art, music, traditional performing arts, dance
Landscape/environment	Landscape, Nanchang Mountain, townscape, environment (excluding "living environment"), forest, green
Disaster prevention	Disaster prevention, disaster, typhoon, Nankai Trough, safety (excluding "traffic safety")
Agriculture	Agriculture, farms, paddy fields, rice, vegetables, strawberries, zucchini
Generation Exchange/festival	Generation exchange/connection, appearance of the elderly/ youth/child in the same paragraph, festival
New technology	Electric vehicle, automatic driving, automatic translation, Internet
Foreign	Foreign, US, North Korea, overseas aid, refugees
Elderly/depopulated	Elderly people, depopulation, lonely death, social worker, unoccupied houses
Child/hildcare	Child, preschooler, nursery school, elementary school, junior high school, childcare, education
Youth	Youth, high school, university
Medical College transfer	Medical College, smart inter, hospital, medical, pharmacy
Tourism	Tourism, guide, public relations, sunflower

generations (Part 2) are "Landscape/environment," "Disaster prevention," "Agriculture," "Generation exchange/Festival," "New technology," and "Foreign." "Elderly/depopulated," "Child/childcare," "Youth," "Medical College transfer," and "Tourism" have been addressed across the deliberations. There was no difference between Parts 1 and 2.

The second method for characterizing the deliberations is to have independent coders read the transcripts and make judgments on the characteristics of each subject's speech. We hired three college students, all unrelated to this study. The coders were asked to determine whether the following three features were found in the statement of each subject in each Part.

Feature 1 (statements from the current state)

Speaking from the current state/Speaking from unmet needs.

Feature 2 (relationship with the future)

Make statements with at least two of the following four characteristics.

- Statements jumping back and forth to shake off present concerns.
- Statements treating the imagined world as real.
- Statements recognizing the present generation's actions as a prerequisite for the happiness of the future.

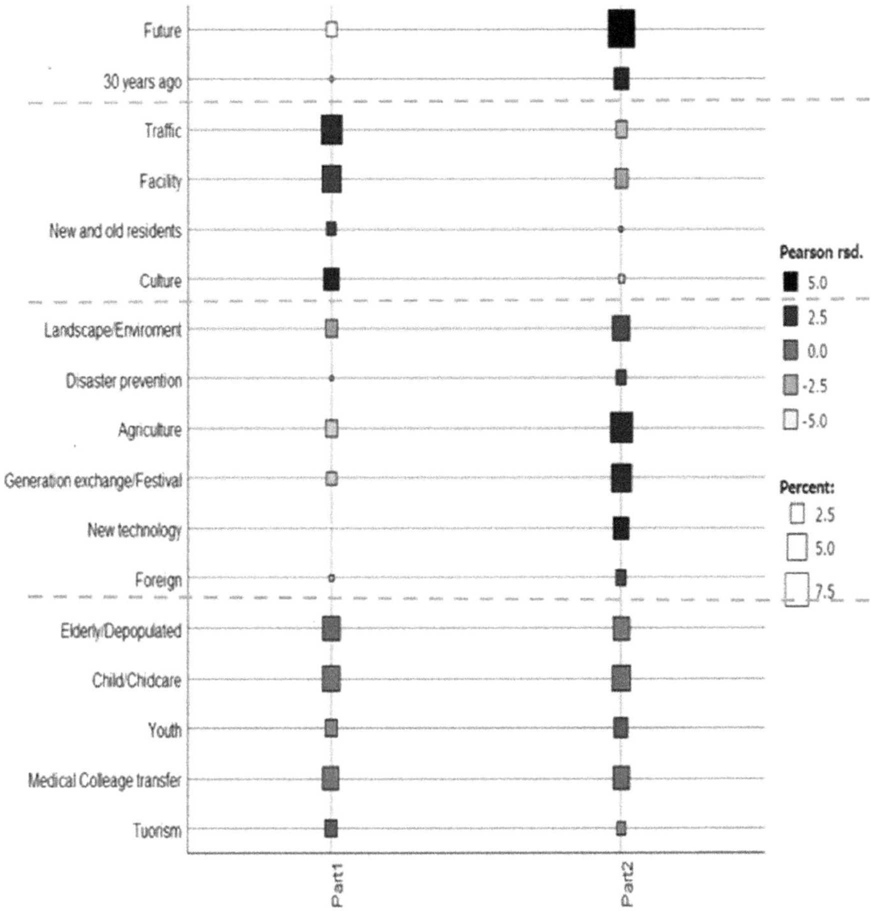

Fig. 4.6 Contents of deliberations in Parts 1 and 2 (Groups A to D). *Note* (1) The chi-square values and significance levels are as follows. Future (58.7**), 30 years ago (22.4**), Traffic (18.5**), Facility (8.5**), New and old residents (7.2**), Culture (22.0**), Landscape/Environment (6.7**), Disaster prevention (7.9**), Agriculture (21.7**), Generation exchange/Festival (20.3**), New Technology (26.0**), Foreign (6.0*), Elderly/Depopulated (0.3), Child/Childcare (0.0), Youth (0.1), Medical College transfer (0.0), Tourism (1.0). *Note* (2) **$p < 0.001$, *$p < 0.005$

- Statements perceiving the coexistence of two conflicting identities of the present and the future.

Feature 3 (retrospective assessment)

Making statements that assess the present from the future, such as "I'm glad I did XX 30 years ago (i.e., the present)/I regret having decided XX."

Keishiro Hara, Osaka University, together with Saijo, identified Feature 1 as a feature of deliberations in the present generation (Hara et al., 2019). Feature 2 can be called as a "relationship with the future." It was taken from Nakagawa et al. (2017), which analyzed the characteristics of statements obtained by interviewing those who made remarkable statements as part of the future generation. Feature 2 has four properties, however considering the limited time for discussion, it was requested to judge positive if not all four properties but two or more of the four were observed in each subject's speech. A judgment of retrospective assessment was necessary for Feature 3 based on the presence or absence of typical statements. The sums of the number of coders who made positive judgement for each Feature is set as a score (3, 2, 1, 0 points) of each subject.

Table 4.13 summarizes the judgment by the coders. In Part 1 (present generation), Feature 1 (statement from the current state) appeared in most subjects. Remarks from the current state or from unmet needs are dominant. Features 2 (relationship with the future) and 3 (retrospective assessment) are (almost) not seen. It seems that the subjects requested the town for policies based on their immediate awareness of the problem, and their request was not spread over time. On the other hand, in Part 2 (future generation), although Feature 1 (statement from the current state) was continuously observed, its presence was declining. Instead, Feature 2 (relationship with the future) is seen in each group. Although Feature 3 (retrospective assessment) was also observed, it was intensively observed in specific groups (especially Group C, then Group D). When the difference between the averages of the scores of Features 1, 2, and 3 was tested between Parts 1 and 2, the difference was significant.

These results are consistent with the overall tendency as seen in Fig. 4.6. In Part 2, it was already pointed out that the frequency of the code of the "future" had increased, and that the time horizon of the discussion had been broadened. The code "30 years ago" appeared in Groups C and D, and this is consistent with the findings by the coders of subjects with Feature 3 (retrospective assessment) in Groups C and D. Feature 1 (statement from the current state) maintained a certain presence although it is attenuated in Part 2. This fact matches the fact that codes such as "traffic" and "facility" were retreated in Part 2 in Fig. 4.6, however, issues such as "Elderly/Depopulated," "Child/Child care," "Youth," and "Medical College transfer" were kept to be discussed in Part 2. In particular, while Feature 3 (retrospective assessment) is prominently observed in Part 2 of Group C, a follow-up to the minutes reveals that a certain turning point triggered a series of statements analogous to Feature 3. The turning point is specifically as follows.

(Subject 23) "... If 30 years later, when I am here, if college students and townsmen are separated, I will feel a bit sad, so I hope to make warm relationship now. If you do something more and more to promote communications, it will make the town better for newcomers, and it is good for those who are originally there too."

(Secretary) "Everybody, it is now 2048, so now is 30 years from now."

(Facilitator) "I should have done it 30 years ago."

(Secretary) "Yeah, yeah, if I had been doing it for 30 years, it would be growing now!"

Table 4.13 Judgment by coders for the features of each subject

Subjects	Judgment by coders					
	Part 1 (present generation)			Part 2 (future generation)		
	Feature 1	Feature 2	Feature 3	Feature 1	Feature 2	Feature 3
Group A						
1	**3**	0	0	0	1	1
2	**3**	0	0	**2**	1	0
3	**3**	0	0	**2**	**2**	1
4	**3**	1	0	0	**2**	0
5	**3**	0	0	**3**	0	0
6	**3**	0	0	1	1	0
7	**3**	0	0	1	0	0
8	**2**	1	0	1	1	1
Group B						
9	**2**	0	0	**2**	**2**	0
10	**3**	0	0	**3**	**2**	0
11	**2**	0	0	0	**2**	0
12	**2**	0	0	1	0	0
13	**3**	1	0	**3**	1	0
14	**3**	0	0	0	1	1
15	**3**	0	0	**2**	**2**	0
16	1	0	0	**2**	1	1
Group C						
17	**3**	0	0	**3**	0	**3**
18	**3**	0	0	**3**	0	**3**
19	**3**	0	0	**2**	1	**3**
20	**3**	0	0	**2**	1	**2**
21	**3**	0	0	**2**	1	**2**
22	1	0	0	0	0	**3**
23	1	0	0	**3**	**2**	**3**
Group D						
24	**3**	0	0	**2**	1	0
25	**3**	0	0	1	1	0
26	**3**	0	0	**3**	**2**	0
27	**3**	0	0	**2**	**3**	**2**
28	1	0	0	**3**	0	**2**
29	**3**	0	0	1	0	0

(continued)

Table 4.13 (continued)

	Judgment by coders					
Subjects	Part 1 (present generation)			Part 2 (future generation)		
	Feature 1	Feature 2	Feature 3	Feature 1	Feature 2	Feature 3
30	**2**	0	0	1	1	0
Average	2.57/3	0.1/3	0/3	1.70**/3	1.07**/3	1.16**/3

Note (1) The number of coders (3 to 0) judged to have the relevant feature is described. In the average column, the difference between the averages of Parts 1 and 2 is tested (** 1%, * 5%, † 10% significant). (2) Feature 1: "statements from the current state," Feature 2: "relationship with the future," Feature 3: "retrospective assessment"

(Subject 18) "Thirty years ago, I did not build tall buildings, I did not touch it, so the mountain remains!"

(Facilitator) "You are talking well now."

With this exchange, remarks of the type "I am glad I did XX 30 years ago (i.e., the present)/I regret having decided XX" continued. The remarks that came out were: (1) The mountain remained because we did not build buildings 30 years ago, (2) We built a transportation facility that can be used easily, so we can go to the town center and the hospital, (3) As we had provided a place to talk beyond generations, there were no lonely deaths, (4) We left behind some ground from a former junior high school as a festival venue, so there is still some space left for events, (5) We created workplaces for young people 30 years ago, so there are young people in town, (6) Thanks to the construction of a sports ground for the elderly 30 years ago, they can still exercise well, (7) We made a child-raising facility 30 years ago, so the town did not just get old, and (8) It was good that disaster prevention and building reinforcement measures were taken 30 years ago.

Now, it is useful to characterize the statements of the future generation by integrating two methods: text mining and judgments by coders. Instructing the subjects to discuss as future generations has expanded their temporal perspective. It is easy to understand that attention to new technologies has gained strength. Increased references to foreign countries suggest that expanding the temporal perspective is accompanied by expanding the geographic perspective. Retrospectives assessment did not always occur in discussions among the future generations. The progress of deliberations in Group C suggests that in the appearance of retrospective assessment, there was a turning point in which the subjects learned the type of utterance.

Whereas there are topics that are characteristic of deliberations as the present generation, there are also those that are characteristic of deliberations as future generations. Some topics were consistently taken up by both the present and future generations. The present generation discussed complaints on public transport such as community buses, which will be abolished soon, and familiar requests for the development of specific facilities such as playgrounds, shops, roads, and pools. The future generations deliberated on topics such as landscape/environment, disaster prevention, agriculture, generational exchange/festival, which can be summarized as issues pertaining to common basic needs across generations. Landscape and environment constitute the basic living environment that the townspeople of the present and the future enjoy in common. Disaster prevention is the basis of survival for all generations. Agriculture concerns the basic human need for food, and also the basis of life for Yahaba, a rural area. Generational exchange is a joint effort to address the challenges of each generation, and festivals are opportunities for various members of the community to meet face-to-face and share time and place. Finally, there are topics that were consistently mentioned in the discussions of the present and future generations, such as the elderly, depopulation, and childcare. These issues were already clearly recognized as issues, and are expected to continue to remain issues in the future.

By being instructed to become future generations, subjects will come to think of these issues from perspectives that are detached from the here and now, and from "me." They move away from the immediate interests of community buses and facilities, and think about things from the perspective of time, place, and inhabitants that will continue from the present to the future. Since the importance of continuous issues such as aging will not change for future generations, Feature 1 (statements from the current state) will not disappear among future generations. On the other hand, there is a growing interest in common basic needs across generations, which were not paid attention to in the present generation, such as landscape, disaster prevention, and agriculture. In deliberations of future generations, Feature 1 (statement from the current state) and Features 2 and 3 coexist in the same subject's speech.

Finally, we will work on positioning IFGs in general rules for good decision making. Becoming IFGs means detachment from the here and now, and "me," and seems to have something in common with the veil of ignorance as articulated by Rawls (1971):

> The idea of the original position is to set up a fair procedure so that any *principles* agreed to will be just. The aim is to use the notion of pure procedural justice as a basis of theory. Somehow, we must nullify the effects of specific contingencies which put men at odds and tempt them to exploit social and natural circumstances to their own advantage. Now in order to do this I assume that the parties are situated behind a veil of ignorance. They do not know how the various alternatives will affect their own particular case and *they are obliged to evaluate principles solely on the basis of general considerations.* (omitted) It is assumed, then, that the parties do not know certain kinds of particular facts. First of all, no one knows his place in society, his class position or social status; nor does he know his fortune in the distribution of natural assets and abilities, his intelligence and strength, and the like. Nor, again, does anyone know his conception of the good, the particulars of his rational plan of life, or even the special features of his psychology such as his aversion to risk or liability to optimism or pessimism. (omitted) The persons in the original position have no information as to which generation they belong. (omitted) *They must choose principles the consequences of which they are prepared to live with whatever generation they turn out to belong to* (Rawls, 1971, pp. 118–119; italic by quoters).

According to Rawls, the veil of ignorance separates us from the information of who we are and makes us choose the principle of justice in the original position.

The important point here is that problem-setting after detachment becomes a matter of choosing principles. The path for choosing principles from points detached from individuality is part of the general rules to follow while making good decisions. In the context of the constitutional process, at the position detached from individual circumstances (personal, regional, and sectarian interests), deliberations and decisions on highly abstract principles (basic human rights and basic principles of governance) are taken. The reconciliation of interests on a case-by-case basis takes place after the end of the constitutional process. Taking fiscal policy as an example, most must agree with the importance of sound fiscal management while choosing principles. However, if individual circumstances come into view, various means of achieving the same goal of sound finance, such as whether to reduce expenditures or increase taxes, will be separated. If a majority vote is held in this situation, the sound fiscal policy, which is originally the majority, may be defeated by a loose-minded one because of the cracking of votes. To avoid such problems, it is conceivable to return to the constitutional process and incorporate the basic principles of sound finance into the constitution.[30]

The motif of discussion at the level of the principles is shared by the IFGs. As discussed earlier, factors that are absent in the deliberations as the current generation and present in the deliberations as the future generations are discussions on topics such as landscape, disaster prevention, agriculture, and generational exchange, as well as issues related to common basic needs. By being asked to be future generations, people focus on issues that are common to all generations. To discuss common issues is to consider them from the standpoint of principles that are appropriate and commonly applied to all generations. Working on landscape and disaster prevention is choosing principles of allocating resources to the basic needs of humans, and being involved in agriculture (for many Yahaba residents) is a return to basics as humans. Intergenerational exchange is to work together on issues that are common to all generations.

What kind of principles are actually present in the deliberations by future generations? Here, the Sufficientarianism plays an important role. It was proposed by Frankfurt (1987) as an alternative to egalitarianism, in which the moral significance is that everyone has enough income and wealth (not that everyone has the same income and wealth). Page (2007) studied Sufficientarianism in intergenerational problems and found that each generation has to ensure that the life of the future generations does not fall below the level of basic needs (universal and objective across generations). Determining the specifics of "basic needs" is a task that still remains to be addressed. However, under Sufficientarianism, basic needs should be protected, and thus it is prohibited to make choices that have the potential to devastate the future generations. The attitudes of the people who sought to be future generations in Yahaba seem to

[30] Ishida and Oguro (2017) pointed out that in such policies as fiscal consolidation, there are a lot of means to achieve a goal and that there is a possibility that votes will be broken by a majority vote. As a countermeasure, they recommended considering a voting system that is strongly set against vote splitting such as Borda voting. In contrast to their findings, our argument is that while facing similar challenges, we should separate choices of objectives from those of instruments (rather than introducing a new voting system that is immune to vote splitting).

share the principle and logic of Sufficientarianism, especially in the discussion on the issues of landscape and disaster prevention. They believe that the future townsfolk should also enjoy the beauty of Nanchang Mountain. They give up the construction of tall buildings, which affect the view. They believe that future townsmen should be protected from the Nankai Trough earthquake and that their public facilities should be reinforced.

Another principle that plays an important role is Communitarianism (e.g., Maclntyre, 1981). Awareness of the fundamental needs of generations is supported by a sense of community that encompasses multiple generations. The reference to the view of Nanchang Mountain is based on the consciousness of the town, which extends beyond a single generation, symbolized by the mountain. Agriculture and festivals, which are rooted in tradition, are closely related with community. Scheffler (2013) sought to place trans-individual values based on intergenerational ethics. He presented an "infertility scenario," in which no one will die prematurely, but no children will be born in the future. Here, people cannot be indifferent to the fact of infertility merely because they do not die early. Scheffler (2013) argued that apathy must be pervasive in society. The value we find is indeed really valuable only in the presence of life after death. We need to pay attention to future generations. This paper handles the policies of Town Yahaba, and although the focus is on the small community, the subjects are arguing that the town is a carrier of continuous value beyond its own.

Appendix 4.2: The Structure of Long-Term Fiscal Policy as an Intergenerational Issue

When considering fiscal policy as intergenerational issue, it is necessary to understand how it is structured. The starting point is that the ascending reciprocity (overlapping generations model; e.g., Samuelson, 1958) discussed in Chap. 2 (Sect. 2. 4) is socially implemented in fiscal policy. Samuelson's (1958) study has already mentioned that an example of social implementation of ascending reciprocity is the pay-as-you-go pension. However, it is not always fully recognized that not just pensions, but the entire fiscal revenue and expenditure system has characteristics of the pay-as-you-go system. This is not to say that there are no fiscal schemes with an economic characteristic of reserve funds, such social infrastructure developments. However, especially in the case of social welfare finances including medical and long-term care in many of advanced countries like Japan, the elderly generation is supported by taxes and social insurance contributions collected from the working population. When the working population grows old, the costs are borne by another generation of young people. The mechanism of intergenerational cooperation through ascending reciprocity is placed at the very center of fiscal management.

This system is an excellent mechanism to protect the elderly who have no productive capacity from poverty, and to improve the welfare of all generations in the chain.

In Japan's social welfare financing system, a substantial portion of elderly benefits are financed not entirely by taxes and social insurance premiums, but by public debt. If this portion of the public debt can be passed on from one generation to the next without redemption, then the chain of intergenerational cooperation envisioned by the pay-as-you-go system will be realized. There is some truth in the suggestion that public debt can continue to be refinanced without redemption. If, as the overlapping generations model suggests, there is a chain of cooperation and the bonds are passed down from generation to generation, then all generations can increase their welfare.[31]

Generation t − 1, as the old generation, has n_{t-1} people and Generation t, as the prime age generation has n_t people. The old generation has no productive capacity, while the prime-age generation produces per capita y goods, and society as a whole produces Y_t, according to the following production function.

$$Y_t = n_t y. \tag{4.4}$$

Here, since goods disappear after one period, the older generation has no choice but to share in the goods Y_t created by the prime-age generation. Assume that the population of the elderly and the prime age generations are equal in period t ($n_{t-1} = n_t$), and the social security system guarantees per capita consumption $y/2$ of Generation t − 1. In this period, the per capita consumption of Generation t is also $y/2$.

Now, assume that when Generation t becomes the elderly generation, the population of Generation t + 1 is decreasing ($n_t > n_{t+1}$). At this time, instead of reducing the level of social security, it is assumed that the social security system guarantees per capita consumption y/2 of Generation t when they become elderly. The output of society as a whole, Y_{t+1} is smaller than Y_t. The per capita consumption of Generation t + 1 is now $\frac{(n_{t+1} - \frac{n_t}{2})y}{n_{t+1}}$, the product of the headcount of the output of the society as a whole Y_{t+1} minus$n_t y/2$. This is smaller than$y/2$, however, to get the consent from Generation t + 1, an equivalent certificate to the reduced consumption, $\frac{y}{2} - \frac{(n_{t+1} - \frac{n_t}{2})y}{n_{t+1}} (= (\frac{n_t}{n_{t+1}} - 1) \cdot \frac{y}{2})$ shall be delivered to Generation t + 1. When Generation t + 1 ages, it is convinced that it can receive goods equivalent to the certificate if it transfers the certificate to Generation t + 2. The certificates can be thought of as convertible banknotes (government bonds) with a fixed exchange rate for the goods. For each generation, consumption in prime and old age is assumed to be indifferent, however there is a non-negative constraint on the amount of consumption in each period.

If Generation t + 1, who received the certificate, can ensure that Generation t + 2 receives the certificate when they are old.

If Generation t + 1, who received the certificate, can ensure that Generation t + 2 receives the certificate when Generation t + 1 becomes old, then the per capita lifetime consumption of Generation t + 1 is y. Generation t + 1 has a smaller population, and

[31] The discussion below in Appendix 4 is focused on elucidating the implications of the pay-as-you-go scheme in intergenerational issues. Regarding fiscal sustainability in general through the refinancing of public debt, it is important to examine the validity of Domar's (1944) proposition, and the possibility of ponzi schemes (Blanchard and Weil 1992).

with its smaller population, it supported the aging of the more populous Generation t, but it is able to maintain its lifetime consumption y. The same can continue even if the population continues to decline after Generation t + 1, as long as subsequent generations receive the certificates. Even without social security reform, high lifetime consumption can be maintained in a declining population. From the perspective of this state of the world, government bonds can be refinanced and do not need to be redeemed. Indeed, there is no need to repay the debt, and yet, high lifetime consumption can be maintained.

However, if at some point subsequent generations refuse to accept the certificate, the story changes. Generation t + i is required to receive the certificates of per capita $\left(\frac{n_t}{n_{t+i}} - 1\right) \cdot \frac{y}{2}$. The certificate amount will be larger, the smaller the population n_{t+i} is. Because Generation t + i's consumption in its prime age is non-negative,

$$n_{t+i}y - \frac{n_t}{2}y \geq 0 \rightarrow n_{t+i} \geq \frac{n_t}{2}. \tag{4.5}$$

If it is not satisfied, Generation t + i will not receive all of the certificates. The first term on the left side of the left equation indicates the total product of society. The total consumption of Generation t + i, which is that first term minus the total amount of certificates that Generation t + i should receive, must be non-negative. As the equation on the right reveals, this implies that the population of Generation t + i is more than half of that of Generation t. When this condition is not met, the preceding Generation t + i − 1 will not receive the promised goods of the certificate.

The problem does not end there. As pointed out in Chap. 2 (Sect. 2.4.2), cooperation in ascending reciprocity depends on a chain of intergenerational cooperation. In ascending reciprocity, the current cooperation depends on the inheritance of rules through the intergenerational chain, which raises the problem that cooperation cannot start when it is difficult to inherit rules. If Generation t + i − 1 anticipates its own loss, it will refuse to accept the certificate from Generation t + i − 2 from the beginning. This logic continues back up the generational chain, and eventually the pay-as-you-go social security system collapses.

The current situation in many of advanced countries is that pay-as-you-go social security systems have already been introduced, and there are a large number of certificates (public debt) to be handed over to subsequent generations. In this situation, it is in the interest of the preceding generation to continue their lives under this system, convincing subsequent generations that future generations will also receive certificates. It should be noted that in the debate over fiscal consolidation, the argument that the public debt should not be redeemed, and should continue to be refinanced, is made under these circumstances. The preceding generation may persuade its successor by providing the prospect that the population will eventually recover. However, if that prospect is off, cooperation will cease at some point in the future, at the latest until the Eq. 4.5 can no longer be met. The generation that is old at the point of failure will starve. The prime age generation at the point of bankruptcy will also lose the social security system on which it was to rely on in its old age and has no choice but to starve in its old age as well.[32] By stating the above, the structure of the problem should be clear. What the present generation is doing is similar to passing on to future generations a time bomb that will eventually explode, in exchange for the benefits they will receive from the continuation of the current system. This structure is identical to the pure intergenerational problem described by Gardiner (2009) in Chap. 2 (Sect. 2.4.2). The long-term fiscal problem is a pure intergenerational issue created by the misuse of cooperation through ascending reciprocity.

In order to successfully address this problem, it is necessary to create a situation where debt is not divergent and sustainable. This requires distancing oneself from understanding intergenerational relations as merely indirect and ascending in reciprocity. Fortunately, as indicated in the main part of Chap. 4, the older generation is not necessarily captive to personal interests. They are capable of taking into consideration the interests of the society as a whole, and those of their immediate descendants, beyond their personal interests. When each generation takes these considerations into account, they are participating in the common enterprise of providing for the survival of the nation and community; at this point, public reciprocity is established between the different generations.

Fiscal sustainability is the cornerstone of national and communal survival. It is necessary to begin by sharing the rule of doing one's share for the survival of the nation and community among the currently overlapping generations. To this end, it is important to be concerned about the interests of different generations and to acknowledge that they have a common interest in the survival of the nation and community, rather than to unnecessarily inflame the differences between them. The basis for such recognition is respect for future generations as the same people who can be the rule bearers. Deliberations with imaginary future generations can be an opportunity to recognize future people as being worthy of respect.

References

Adji, A., Alm, J., & Ferraro, P. J. (2009). Experimental tests of Ricardian equivalence with distortionary versus nondistortionary taxes. *Economic Bulletin, 29*(4), 2556–2572.

Barro, R. J. (1974). Are government bonds net wealth? *Journal of Political Economy, 82*(6), 1095–1117.

Blanchard, O., & Weil, P. (1992). Dynamic efficiency, the riskless rate, and Debt Ponzi games under uncertainty. *NBER Working Paper No. 3992.*

Blekesaune, M., & Quadagno, J. (2003). Public attitudes toward welfare state policies: A comparative analysis of 24 nations. *European Sociological Review, 19*(5), 415–427.

Bornstein, G., Kugler, T., & Ziegelmeyer, A. (2004). Individual and group decision in the centipede game: Are groups more 'rational' players? *Journal of Experimental Social Psychology, 40*(5), 599–605.

Cadsby, C. B., & Frank, M. (1991). Experimental tests of Ricardian equivalence. *Economic Inquiry, 29*(4), 645–664.

[32] If fiscal collapse means the destruction of networks of trust in society, the negative effects are even more far-reaching.

Chao, L.-W., Szrek, H., Pereira, N. S., & Pauly, M. V. (2009). Time preference and its relationship with age, health and survival probability. *Judgment and Decision Making, 4*(1), 1–19.

Charness, G., Rigotti, L., & Rustichini, A. (2007). Individual behavior and group membership. *American Economic Review, 97*(4), 1340–1352.

Charness, G., & Sutter, M. (2012). Groups make better self-interested decisions. *Journal of Economic Perspectives, 26*(3), 157–176.

Demeny, P. (1986). Pronatalist policies in low-fertility countries: Pattern, performance, and prospects. In *Population and development review, 12, supplement: Below-replacement fertility in industrial societies: causes, consequences, policies* (pp. 335–358).

Disney, R. (2007). Population ageing and the size of the welfare state: Is there a puzzle to explain? *European Journal of Political Economy, 23*(2), 542–553.

Domar, E. D. (1944). The 'Burden of the Debt' and the National Income. *American Economic Review, 34*(4), 798–827.

European Commission. (2006). "The long-term sustainability of public finance in the European Union. In *European economy* (no. 4/2006), Belgium.

Fiscal System Subcommittee Drafting and Review Committee, Fiscal System Council. (2015). *Long-term Projection for Japan's public finances.* Document 1 (in Japanese).

Fishkin, J. S. (2011). *When the people speak: Deliberative democracy and public consultation.* Oxford University Press.

Frankfurt, H. (1987). Equality as a moral ideal. *Ethics, 98*(1), 21–43.

Gardiner, S. (2009). A contract on future generations? In A. Gosseries & L. H. Meyer (Eds.), *Intergenerational justice* (pp. 77–118). Oxford University Press.

Glover, J. (1984). *What sort of people should there be? Genetic engineering.* Penguin Books.

Gotoh, R. (2018). The non-identity problem and the philosophical foundation of intergenerational equity. In *The 14th social choice and welfare conference.*

Hara, K., Yoshioka, R., Kuroda, M., Kurimoto, S., & Saijo, T. (2019). Reconciling intergenerational conflicts with imaginary future generations: Evidence from a participatory deliberation practice in a municipality in Japan. *Sustainability Science, 14*(6), 1605–1619.

Higuchi, K. (2014): *Quantitative text analysis for social research.* Nakanishiya-Publishing (in Japanese).

Hiromitsu, T., Kitakaji, Y., Hara, K., & Saijo, T. (2021). What do people say when they become 'future people'?—Positioning imaginary future generations (IFGs) in general rules for good decision-making, *Sustainability, 13*(12), 6631(article number).

Hoyos, D., & Mariel, P. (2010). Contingent valuation: Past, present and future. *Prague Economic Papers, 19*(4), 329–343.

Ihori, T., & Doi, T. (1998). *Economic analysis of japanese politics.* Bokutakusha (in Japanese).

Independent Review on the Economics of Biodiversity. (2021a). *Final report—The economics of biodiversity: The Dasgupta review, headline messages.* HM Treasury.

Independent Review on the Economics *of* Biodiversity. (2021b). *Final report—The economics of biodiversity: The Dasgupta review.* HM Treasury.

Intergovernmental Panel on Climate Change (IPCC). (2021). *Climate change 2021: The physical science basis, summary for policymakers, working group I contribution to the sixth assessment report of the intergovernmental panel on climate change.*

International Energy Agency. (2018). Coal 2018: Analysis and Forecasts to 2023. https://www.iea.org/coal2018. Accessed 21 Feb 2021

Ishida, R., & Oguro, K. (2017). Borda count method for fiscal policy: A political economic analysis. *PRI Discussion Paper Series* (17A-07).

Kameda, T. (1997). *Seeking for the wisdom of crowd: Group decision making.* Kyoritsu-Shuppan (in Japanese)

Kamijo, Y., Hizen Y., & Saijo, T. (2015). Hearing the voice of future generations: A laboratory experiment of 'Demeny voting'. SDES-2015-8, Kochitec.

Kamijo, Y., Komiya, A., Mifune, N., & Saijo, T. (2017). Negotiating with the future: Incorporating imaginary future generations into negotiations. *Suitability Science, 12*(3), 409–420.

Kato, N. (1996). "Commentary" Jonathan Glover (Author), trans. Naotake K., and Takashi. I. *Ethics in the future world: Genetic engineering and brain control* (pp. 313–332). Sangyo-Shobo (in Japanese).

Kotlikoff, L. J., Persson, T., Svensson, L. E., Samuelson, W., & Johnson, S. (1988). Consumption, computation mistakes and fiscal policy. *American Economic Review, 78*(2), 408–412.

Kugler, T., Bornstein, G., Kocher, M., & Sutter, M. (2007). Trust between individual and groups: Groups are less trusting than individuals but just as trustworthy. *Journal of Economic Psychology, 28*(6), 646–657.

Kume, K., Tsuru, K., Sano, S., & Yasui, K. (2018). What factors determine choices for social security benefit and burden: The role of individual attitudes. *Behavioral Economics, 11*, 54–74. (in Japanese).

Locke, J. (1689). *Two treatises of government, archive for the history of economic thought*. McMaster University. https://historyofeconomicthought.mcmaster.ca/locke/government.pdf. Accessed 8 Aug 2020

Luhan, W. J., Kocher, M. G., & Sutter, M. (2009). Group polarization in the team director game reconsidered. *Experimental Economics, 12*(1), 26–41.

MacKenzie, M. (2021). *Future publics: Democracy, deliberation, and the future regarding collective action*. Oxford University Press.

Maclntyre, A. (1981). *After virtue: A study in moral theory*, 2nd, edn. University of Notre Dame Press (1984)

Mill, J. S. (1861). *Considerations on representative government, electronic classics series*. The Pennsylvania State University. https://library.um.edu.mo/ebooks/b11778106.pdf. Accessed 11 Jan 2021.

Ministry of the Environment, Japan. (2018). 'Study group on carbon pricing' conclusions—Toward a smooth transition to decarbonized society and simultaneous resolution of economic and social issues (in Japanese)

Murphy, L., & Nagel, T. (2002). *The myth of ownership: Taxes and justice*. Oxford Scholarship Online.

Nakagawa, Y., Hara, K., & Saijo, T. (2017). Becoming sympathetic to the needs of future generations: A phenomenological study of participation in future design workshops. *Kochi University of Technology, Social Design Engineering Series* (SDES-2017-4).

Office of the Director of Policy Evaluation, Ministry of Health, Labor and Welfare. (2015). Report on the 2015 survey on attitudes toward public and private services in social security.

Ohtake, F., & Tsutsui, Y. (2012). Clarifying the characteristics of risk aversion by economic experiments. *Behavioral Economics, 5*, 26–44. (in Japanese).

Page, E. (2007). Justice between generations: Investigating a sifficientarian approach. *Journal of Global Ethics, 3*(1), 3–20.

Rawls, J. (1971a, 1999). *A theory* of *justice, revised edition*. Harvard University Press.

Ricciuti, R., & Di Laurea, D. (2003). An experimental analysis of two departures from Ricardian equivalence. *Economic Bulletin, 8*(11), 1–11.

Rousseau, J.-J. (1762). *The social contract,* (trans. Bennett, Jonathan, 2017). https://www.earlymoderntexts.com/assets/pdfs/rousseau1762book1.pdf. Accessed 29 Nov 2018.

Saijo, T. (2020a). Future design: An introduction. In *Future design: Incorporating preferences of future generations for sustainability*. Springer.

Saijo, T. (2020b). Future design: Bequeathing sustainable natural environments and sustainable societies to future generations. *Sustainability, 12*(16), 1–21.

Samuelson, P. (1958). An exact consumption: A loan model of interest with or without the social contrivance of money. *Journal of Political Economy, 66*(6), 467–482.

Scheffler, S. (2013). *Death and the afterlife*. Oxford University Press.

Scheffler, S. (2018). *Why worry about future generations?* Oxford University Press.

Scheier, M. F., Carver, C. S., & Bridges, M. W. (1994). Distinguishing optimism from neuroticism (and trait anxiety, self-mastery, and self-esteem): A reevaluation of the life orientation test. *Journal of Personality and Social Psychology, 67*(6), 1063–1078.

Sen, A. K. (1977). Rational fools: A critique of the behavioral foundation of economic theory. *Philosophy and Public Affairs, 6*(4), 317–344.

Shimasawa, M., Oguro, K., & Toyoda, N. (2014). Does Japan have a gray democracy? An empirical analysis of prefectural data an empirical analysis of prefectural data. *CIS Discussion Paper Series*, No. 615. Center for Intergenerational Studies, Institute of Economic Research, Hitotsubashi University.

Shimasawa, M. (2017). *The political economy of silver democracy: Strategies for overcoming intergenerational conflicts*. Nikkei-Publishing (in Japanese).

Slate, S., McKee, M., Beck, W., & Alm, J. (1995). Testing Ricardian equivalence under uncertainty. *Public Choice, 85*(1/2), 11–29.

Smets, K., & Isernia, P. (2014). The role of deliberation in attitude change: An empirical assessment of three theoretical mechanisms. *European Union Politics, 15*(3), 389–409.

Smith, V. L. (1976). Experimental economics: Induced value theory. *American Economic Review, 66*(2), 274–279.

Smith, V. L. (1982). Microeconomic systems as experimental science. *American Economic Review, 72*(5), 923–955.

Sunstein, C. R. (2000). Deliberative trouble? Why groups go to extremes. *The Yale Law Journal, 110*(1), 71–119.

Surowiecki, J. (2004). *The wisdom of crowds: Why the many are smarter than the few and how collective wisdom shapes business, economics, societies, and nations, anchor*.

Suzumura, K., & Tadenuma, K. (2007). Normative approaches to the issues of global warning: Responsibility and compensation. In J. Roemer & K. Suzumura (Eds.), *Intergenerational equity and sustainability* (pp. 320–336). Palgrave MacMillan.

Takeuchi, K. (2011). Non-parametric test of time consistency: Present bias and future bias. *Games and Economic Behavior, 71*(2), 456–478.

Thunberg, G. (2019). Speech at the UN climate action summit. https://www.nbcnews.com/news/world/read-greta-thunberg-s-full-speech-united-nations-climate-action-n1057861. Accessed 21 Feb 2021

Timilsina, R., Kotani, K., Nakagawa, Y., & Saijo, T. (2021). Intragenerational deliberation and intergenerational sustainability dilemma. *European Journal of Political Economy* (in press).

Van Lange, P. A. M., De Bruin, E. M. N., Otten, W., & Joireman, J. A. (1997). Development of prosocial, individualistic, and competitive orientations: Theory and preliminary evidence. *Journal of Personality and Social Psychology, 73*(4), 733–746.

Chapter 5
The Meaning of Equal Treatment of Present and Future Events—Time Discounting

Abstract The discussion up to this chapter has assumed that equal treatment of present and future events is desirable. This chapter considers whether equal treatment is indeed possible and worthy of support. It is necessary to resolve the problem of equal treatment rendering acts of present happiness as immoral (conflict of basic moral principles). There are two methodologies for resolving the conflict: divestment from utilitarianism and the introduction of time discounting. This chapter mainly discusses the introduction of time discounting. The rationale for the various discounts is described, and it is pointed out that there exists the idea of discounting associated with the loss of controllability over events, as the discounting intrinsic to time and consistent with the principle of equal treatment of the present and the future. This discounting is of two types: one due to the intervention of subsequent decision makers, and the other due to natural hazards. This chapter explains the function of each.

5.1 Kenneth Arrow's Conflict of Basic Moral Principles

How much should one consider future events? How much weight should one place on future events, and events that will happen to future generations? Is there any reason to give different weight to future events that are separated in time from present events? In the discussion of intergenerational issues in this book, it has been assumed that giving consideration to future events is desirable, with the important exception of the Sect. 5.2.2 that discusses Parfit's non-identity problem. In most of this book, the problem was the difficulty of paying sufficient consideration to the future, and this book has focused on finding ways to resolve this difficulty. In this chapter, it examines, once again, whether it is possible and desirable to treat present and future events equally.

This chapter also discusses the issue by assuming the existence of a social planner and examining the choices and actions taken by them. The social planner controls the state of society at each point in time, from the present to the future. The social planner evaluates the stream of social states ((s_t) from the present ($t = 0$). Equation 1.1, which

T. Hiromitsu, *Resolving Intergenerational Conflicts*, Advances in Japanese Business and Economics 33, https://doi.org/10.1007/978-981-97-0614-3_5

was explained in Chap. 1, is restated here as Eq. 5.1 as the evaluation function.

$$W_0 = W(s_0, s_1, s_2, \ldots, s_t, s_{t+1}, \ldots). \tag{5.1}$$

When the social planner has a utilitarian evaluation function, Eq. 5.1 can be rewritten as Eq. 5.2.

$$\begin{aligned} W_0 &= U_0(s_0) + \delta_1 U_1(s_1) + \delta_2 U_2(s_2) \\ &\quad + \cdots + \delta_t U_t(s_t) + \delta_{t+1} U_{t+1}(s_{t+1}) + \cdots . \end{aligned} \tag{5.2}$$

where U_t is the utility at time t, and δ_t is the discount factor at time t. $\delta_0 = 1$, and $\delta_t \geq 0$.

In general, there is the practice of discounting future events to the extent that they are future events. The philosopher Derek Parfit, who raised the non-identity problem discussed in Chap. 2, states the following:

> (M)any economists apply an SDR (Social Discount Rates) to benefits and losses, measured at the size that they will have when they occur. My example in the text is not imagined. It has been seriously suggested that, in assessing the risks of the disposal of nuclear wastes, we should apply an SDR to future deaths. More generally, Social Discount Rates have been applied, not to monetary gains and losses, but to what economists call the actual utility that will be enjoyed by future people. (Parfit, 1984, p. 480).

Under this social discount rate practice, δ_t is a decreasing function of t. especially when the social discount rate takes a constant r, $\delta_t = 1/(1+r)^t$.

However, there is a position that there is no reason to differ in one's assessment of an event, depending on whether that event occurs now or befalls people in the distant future. According to Parfit's example, using a discount rate of 5% per year, the statistical death of one person next year would be more significant than the death of one billion people 400 years from now.[1] Thus, discounting justifies a conclusion that is significantly unfavorable to future generations. Frank Ramsey, who died prematurely following an illustrious career at Cambridge University in England, noted the following: "One point should perhaps be emphasised more particularly; it is assumed that we do not discount later enjoyments in comparison with earlier ones, a practice which is ethically indefensible and arises merely from the weakness of the imagination" (Ramsey, 1928, p. 543). To treat one billion people in 400 years less than one in the next year, simply because of their different positions on the time is not in keeping with the principle that people should be treated equally.

However, if the same weight is given to what happens in the future as that of the present, the latter may be required to make great sacrifices for the future. Kenneth Arrow (1999a) addresses this issue in a multi-generational chain setting. According to him, the present generation is only one generation, whereas future generations will continue indefinitely, making any act in favor of one's own well-being condemnable. Investing for the future at the expense of the present generation can be compensated by the gains of an infinite number of generations. In his analysis of Ramsey's

[1] Parfit (1984, pp. 481–482).

pioneering optimal growth models, Koopmans also argued that once the discount falls below a certain level, postponing consumption is always considered an improvement in the infinite consumption stream, and is always recommended. He called this postponement "the paradox of the indefinitely postponed splurge" (Koopmans, 1967).[2]

Strictly speaking, if the marginal utility of the present generation becomes infinity before its consumption is reduced to zero, then the consumption of the current generation will not be reduced to zero. If future generations are as investable as the present, the present generation's degree of sacrifice can be further moderated. Arrow provides a concise explanation of this point. Assume an intertemporally additive utility function and a form of utility function called CIES (constant intertemporal elasticity of substitution). This is a functional form in which the intertemporal elasticity of substitution of consumption is constant, and is often assumed in economic models because of its mathematical tractability.[3]

$$U(c_t) = c_t^{1-\theta}/(1-\theta), \theta > 1. \tag{5.3}$$

where θ is the inverse of the intertemporal elasticity of substitution and is a constant under Eq. 5.3.

Since each generation is treated equally, the discount factor defined in Eq. 5.2 is, $\delta_t = 1$. The (generational) utilities at any point in time have equal weight. The following Eq. 5.4 is maximized.

$$W = \int U_t(c_t). \tag{5.4}$$

Furthermore, when $\theta > 1$, U is capped, and the existence of an optimal solution is allowed. Because each generation has the opportunity to invest,

$$K_{t+1} = \beta(K_t - c_t). \tag{5.5}$$

where K_t is the capital (accumulated savings) in period t, and K_0 is given. β is the productivity of capital and is greater than 1.

Arrow pointed out that this problem had been solved by Ramsey, and that the optimal savings rate for each generation is the same $1/\theta$, regardless of the value of productivity (β).[4]

Arrow mentions that there are indications that the value of θ is empirically 1.5 or less.[5] This implies a savings rate of two-thirds or more, and Arrow points out that such a savings rate is "an incredible and unacceptable strain on the present generation"

---

[2] Koopmans (1967, p.8).

[3] For example, the intertemporal elasticity of substitution is $1/\theta$ and the relative risk aversion is θ, the inverse of the elasticity.

[4] Ramsey (1928 p. 548).

[5] Arrow et al. (1996, p. 132).

(p. 16). The present generation appears to be reduced to a tool to promote the utility of future generations.

Here we are faced with a moral dilemma. Arrow points out that in this situation, the moral imperative to treat all generations equally clashes with the intuition that imposing unusually high savings rates is morally unacceptable. He states the conflict between basic principles of morality, equal treatment, and another moral law, according to which human beings should not be treated only as tools.[6] These moral principles, which Kant considered identical in their fundamental principle that human beings should be respected as people, were supposed to be merely different formulations of the moral principle.[7]

In my view, the problem posed by the conflict of these moral principles are serious. This is because the principle of equal treatment should be the guiding principle to find solutions to the intergenerational issues. In fact, the assumption made in Chap. 3 (Sect. 3.3.3) in obtaining the *optimal* solution, which should be contrasted with the subgame perfect equilibrium solution, was the procedure of summing the utilities of Generations 1 and 2 with equal weighting, and maximizing the sum. However, no principle can be upheld if the contradiction remains untouched.

In my view, there are two possible methodologies to resolve this conflict.

Methodology 1: Divestment from utilitarianism

One is to divest from Eq. 5.4. It is to depart from the utilitarian approach, which takes the utility of each generation as an additive and seeks to maximize the sum of the utilities. The origin of why the present generation is treated like a tool is found in Eq. 5.4. Indeed, as Eq. 5.5 indicates, each generation does not exist independently of the other, so some kind of principle governing the generations is necessary. However, this does not mean that the principle cannot be one that is separate from utilitarianism, such as that subsequent generations must not be harmed (harm principle) (Mill, 1859).

Methodology 2: Introduction of time discounting

Another methodology is to loosen the tight intergenerational relationship represented by Eq. 5.5, specifically, by introducing time discounting. The key is to introduce time discounting that is compatible with the principle of equal treatment of each generation. If such a compatible discount can be incorporated, it will ease the demands of the future on the present, even under the utilitarian evaluation function.

The "introduction of time discounting" might be interpreted to mean that Eq. 5.4 is transformed by way of multiplying the utility $U_t(c_t)$ byδ_t, as in Eq. 5.2. However, the discussion in this chapter will show that discounting of future events can be introduced even under the equal treatment principle, through a path where the value of provision for the future from the perspective of the present is reduced by the intervention of subsequent decision makers and the succession of natural hazards. Methodology 2, relaxing Eq. 5.5 without transforming Eq. 5.4, which implies the equal treatment principle, leads to the introduction of time discounting.

[6] Arrow (1999a, p. 16).

[7] Dasgupta (2005) also points to similar ethical tensions.

In the following, Methodology 2 will be discussed first, and the bulk of the discussion in this chapter is devoted to it. However, by returning to the discussion of Methodology 1 at the end, a deeper understanding of time discounting will be shown.

As a framework for the discussion in this chapter, it is important to specify and confirm two points.

First is to address the resolution of the conflict while taking the principle of equal treatment of the present and future as a given. In fact, there can be two sides to the question of whether to treat the present and the future equally, or evaluate them differently. With the passage of time, the members of a society are replaced. In the immediate future, there is virtually no change in society's identity. However, society gradually loses its identity and changes to what could be described as a different generation. One way of thinking is that, depending on the degree of identity, the near future should be valued as having more weight because it is closer, and the distant future should be valued lightly because it is more estranged. However, considering the principle of equal treatment discussed in this chapter, it is assumed that it is desirable to treat these events equally when there is only one difference in events, whether they occur in the present or in the future. To emphasize the near future and disregard the distant future based solely on differences in position on the time scale is considered as partiality to the near future. The cautionary consequence of this argument is that the principle of equal treatment requires not only treating the events of today and tomorrow equally, but also the future generations' events that will occur in the distant future. Although tomorrow's society and that of 60 years from now will differ greatly in terms of their members' identities, the lack of identity will not change the weight of the evaluation of social states between tomorrow and 60 years from now. In view of this consideration, in the following discussion, the concept of *generation*—which is extremely important for this book—will not appear, but will be represented by the terms the *point* in time or the *agent* at a point in time. Methodologies 1 and 2 also need to be re-presented without using the term generation, respectively (they are not explicitly re-presented here).

The second point is to consider evaluations from the perspective of social planners. Evaluations by social planners are discussed, because this chapter is not interested in how bystanders evaluate society. Rather, it is concerned with what social planners, who have the power to control present and future social states, choose from streams of multiple possible social states. Social planners can control social states, but their controllability is not necessarily unlimited. The social planner does not evaluate social states that are never realized, but chooses the best from the possible social states.

The remainder of this chapter is as follows: Sect. 5.2 arrives at the idea of discounting accompanying loss of controllability of future events, through considering the discounting compatible with the principle of the equal treatment. Section 5.3 discusses one source of such discounting, that is, the intervention of subsequent decision makers, and Sect. 5.4 considers the succession of natural hazards as another source. Building on the discussions in the previous sections, Sect. 5.5 discusses the relationship between the ethical standards of social planners and time discounting under Methodology 1. The final Sect. 5.6, provides a summary of the chapter.

5.2 Time Discounting Compatible with the Principle of Equal Treatment

5.2.1 *Various Concepts of Discounting*

It is important to note that the term time discounting includes a variety of concepts. Parfit's (1984) study is known to have organized the concept of discounting. Tyler Cowen, an economist at George Mason University, and Parfit collaborated on a study that deepened the discussion, by incorporating an economic perspective (Cowen & Parfit, 1992). The behavioral economist Shane Frederick, drawing on Cowen and Parfit (1992), proposed a framework to organize polysemous concepts of discounting (Frederick, 1999, 2006). Frederick's proposal is to dichotomize the concept of time discounting into one that 1) is derived from a reduction in the weight given to future utility and 2) is derived from a reduction in the amount of expected utility of future events.[8] This dichotomy is addressed later in the section.

This section begins the discussion by relying on Cowen and Parfit (1992), which examines the moral characters of various notions of discounting. Cowen and Parfit (1992) thoroughly examine the reasons given to explain discounting and conclude that none of them are morally permissible. The reasons discussed are: (i) the argument from democracy, (ii) argument from probability, (iii) argument from opportunity costs, (iv) argument that our successors will be better off, (v) argument from excessive sacrifice, (vi) argument from special relations, and (vii) argument from time preference. In addition to these reasons, a study by Graciela Chichilnisky et al. (2020) proposes the idea of (viii) extinction discounting.

The argument from democracy (i) is that if voters do not care much about the distant future, then democratic governments should. However, Cowen and Parfit (1992) criticize this stating that even if voters do not care about the future and believe it is morally justifiable, this does not make discounting morally acceptable.

The argument from probability (ii) is also rejected by Cowen and Parfit (1992). It is true that the weight of uncertain future events must be discounted. However, they state, "the two kinds of discount rate, temporal and probabilistic, roughly correlate. But they are quite different. It is therefore a mistake to discount lor time rather than for probability."[9] They argue that discounting must be for this reason alone, that it is a future event, even if the event is certain. As long as discussion of Cowen and Parfit (1992) is right, the argument from probability does not deserve to be called time discounting in the first place.

In the argument from opportunity costs (iii), it is true that if losses occur in the future rather than in the present, one can prepare for these losses by investing now. In this case, the nominal cost of countermeasures can be reduced by the yield compared to the case where losses occur in the present. However, Cowen and Parfit (1992)

[8] Frederick (1999, pp. 1–24, 2006, p. 669). The actual order of Frederick's explanation is (2) to (1), but in this book the order is reversed.

[9] Cowen and Parfit (1992, p. 147).

points out that this reduction does not allow one to morally view future losses as lower than current losses.

As for the argument that our successors will be better off (iv), Cowen and Parfit (1992) points out that this merely argues for the interests of the rich to be taken lightly.[10] This argument, too, is not worthy of being called time discounting.

The argument from excessive sacrifice (v) precisely corresponds to the issue raised by Arrow (1999a). Without discounting, the argument is that the slight increase in gains that continue into the future require excessive sacrifice in the present. Cowen and Parfit (1992) maintains that this excessive sacrifice is not a reason to adopt discounting, and points out that no generation can be morally required to sacrifice more than it has to. Cowen and Parfit's (1992) point is in line with Methodology 1 (divestment from utilitarianism) for resolving the conflict of moral principles described in Sect. 5.1. Methodology 1 will be touched upon later (Sect. 5.5).

The argument from special relations (vi) is that the interests of those who have a "special relationship" with us, such as our children, should be more important than those of strangers. According to Cowen and Parfit (1992), this argument from special relationships only leads to the discounting based on the degree of proximity. This, too, is not worthy of the name of time discounting.

The argument from time preference (vii) is that one may choose today's low gain even though one knows that one can get higher gains if one waits a month. This is also called impatience. As far as this goes, no doubt future events are taken lightly. However, Cowen and Parfit (1992) argues that social time preference across individuals cannot be derived from individual impatience. Cowen and Parfit (1992) points out that even if one may discount one's own pain of tomorrow, one cannot discount the pain of future generations that will not even be born.

The last is extinction discounting (viii). Gregory Ponthière (2003) has proposed that if there is a possibility that humanity will eventually die out, it is acceptable to discount future interests accordingly. Chcihilnisky has proposed extinction

---

[10] The argument that if offspring are better off, the discount rate will be higher is given representation in the Ramsey rule (1928). A study by Arrow et al. (1996) presents the following equation, as a criterion for ordering consumption streams from the present to the infinite future, which is the sum of utility at different points in time discounted by ρ.

$$Z = \int_{t=0}^{\infty} U(c_t)e^{-\rho}dt. \ (*)$$

Where ρ is the pure time preference ($\rho > 0$). As maximizing Eq. *, the following equation is obtained as the discount rate that leads to the optimal consumption path (see Arrow 1966; Dasgupta et al., 1999).

$$i_t = i(c_t) = \rho + \frac{\theta(c_t)[dc_t/dt]}{c_t}. \ (**)$$

Here, if ρ is due to Ramsey's "the weakness of the imagination," it is appropriate to set it to zero. $\theta(c_t)$ is the elasticity of marginal utility, as θ in Eq. 5.3. Letting the utility function in Eq. 5.3, θ is a constant. $[dc_t/dt]/c_t$ represents the growth rate of consumption. Equation ** shows that the discount rate is the sum of the pure time preference plus the product of marginal elasticity of utility, which is the Ramsey rule.

$\theta[dc_t/dt]/c_t$ implies the discount on future consumption if the offspring will be better off. Indeed, the existence of this discount mitigates the degree of sacrifice of the present generation. However, this only means that the optimal saving can be held down to $1/\theta$. In this chapter, the problem is that even the optimal savings may impose an excessive burden on the present generation.

discounting in the same sense, and points out that its introduction is useful in resolving the very problem raised by Arrow (conflict of moral principles) that is the issue of this chapter.

Now, in the following, I would like to present my own thoughts based on the previous studies. Cowen and Parfit (1992) points out that (i), (ii), (iv), (v), and (vi), except for the argument from opportunity costs (iii) and the argument from time preference (vii), cannot even be considered time discounting in the first place. I reserve my conclusion on the argument from probability (ii), but agree with Cowen and Parfit (1992) on the other arguments. Of these, the argument from democracy (i) does not fit the principle of equal treatment either. As for the argument from special relations (vi), as has already been seen in Sect. 5.1, this is merely partiality toward one's own, and is in direct conflict with the principle of equal treatment.

I agree with Cowen and Parfit (1992) that the argument from opportunity cost (iii), while indeed related to time, does not make discounting morally acceptable.[11] Although the argument from time preference (vii) also appears to have a relationship to time, Cowen and Parfit's (1992) point, that even if impatience makes sense within the same individual, it does not make sense between different people, is true. A similar point is made by Thomas Schelling (1995), Cowen's advisor at Harvard. To go one step further, even time preference within the same individual can be seen merely a variation of the argument from special relations (vi), which has been rejected earlier. One feels that one's today and tomorrow selves are somewhat different personalities. It is not the here-and-now self that is in pain, but the separate personality of tomorrow's self. This difference, which is not noticeable between today and tomorrow, is significant when it comes to the difference between today and 20 years from now. Time preference is the decreasing degree of interest in the future self as it ceases to be itself, as its special relationship to the present-self diminishes. The idea of personality as a discrete subject at each point in time is found in Parfit's (1984), philosophy, and in Ainslie (2001), psychiatry. In economics, Richard Thaler has discussed the issue as a matter of self-restraint, which was also discussed in Chap. 3 (Sect. 3.5.4) (Thaler & Shefrin, 1981). Another approach to time preference explains it as rational choice in the face of uncertainty, and this will be discussed later.[12] However, as long as time preference is interpreted as a variation of the argument from special relations, even within the same individual, it is neither related to time nor compatible with equal treatment.

Regarding the extinction discounting (viii), those of us living in the twentieth century and beyond are aware that human extinction is a real possibility. However, in my opinion, this argument has a fundamental weakness in light of the purpose of this chapter, which is to find discounting intrinsic to time. Since those who do not exist in the first place have no interest, there is no need to take their interests into account. Extinction discounting is simply stated in this way, and does not explain time-based discounting.

---

[11] Frederick (2006) makes a similar point.

[12] See Sects. 5.4.1 and 5.4.2.

5.2.2 Discounting for Loss of Controllability of Events

Of the eight arguments that have been examined so far, the only remaining one is the argument from probability (ii), which I have reserved my conclusion for. Cowen and Parfit's (1992) point was that temporal and probabilistic discounting are different. Is it true, however, that probabilistic discounting is not temporal discounting?

The key to solving the conflict of the basic moral principles is hidden in Arrow's paper. This key suggests that the argument from probability (ii) should be taken seriously. Arrow asks the following question: "How can people be treated differently just because they are at different places in time?"[13] The question is *who* treats those people. It is not humanly possible to treat each point in the chain of time equally, as in Eq. 5.4. Only non-human beings can look at multiple infinite utility streams $(U_t(c_t), t = 0, 1, 2 \ldots \infty)$, and determine the superiority or inferiority between them. Humans are bound to a specific point in time, are offered specific choices, and are only allowed to choose one. Human are held responsible for the consequences of their acts, since it is possible for humans to control the events that immediately result from their choices, to some extent. However, over time, events are increasingly influenced by other events. The effects of a particular choice become uncertain and finally seem to disappear, and responsibility is accordingly discharged. In making choices toward the future, humans take responsibility for the degree to which their choices affect the future and consider future events, according to their degree of responsibility. This is the reason why time-bound humans discount future interests, a time discount that accompanies the loss of controllability over events due to the sequentiality of events, which is the essence of time.

The difference between my argument and that of Cowen and Parfit's (1992) is that mine raises the issue of responsibility based on the probability of the consequences of one's choices, from the standpoint of a moral chooser bound to a particular point in time. Cowen and Parfit's (1992) argument lacks the perspective of the responsibility imposed on the chooser. Their objection to the argument from probability is that it falls into the absurdity of not needing to discount future events insofar as it is based on the probability argument, since "Predictions about the further future do not decrease in certainty at some constant rate of n percent per year" (p. 148). What they mean by "predictions" here is that some certain policy will change or a certain resource will be exhausted. This kind of prediction is meaningless. The question for the choosers is the future effects of changing some policy, and whether the change under consideration is better than the alternatives.

Rather than worrying about 1000 years from now, priority will be given to dealing with the difficulties of the same period. Note, however, that while equal treatment is abandoned, the principle of equal treatment is by no means abandoned as a fallacy in itself. Under the discounting associated with the loss of event controllability, social planners are responsible for their choices insofar as they affect the future even if the interests are in the distant future. The social planner simply cannot treat the interests at each point in time strictly equally; they are responsible for treating the interests of

---

[13] Arrow (1999a, pp. 13–14).

people in the future equally with those of people in the present, who are affected by the social planner's choices, depending on the degree to which those choices affect the future.

An important distinction to understand the discounting associated with the loss of controllability of events is Frederick's dichotomy between (1) time discounting derived from a reduction in the *weight* given to future utility and (2) time discounting derived from a reduction in the *amount* of expected utility of a future event (Frederick, 1999, 2006). The first, time discounting derived from a reduction in the *weight* given to future utility, corresponds to the discount factor δ_t in Eq. 5.2, which is the weight given to utility.[14]

However, the second type of time discounting, which derives from a reduction in the amount of expected utility of a future event, is not a weighting but a discounting due to a reduction in the amount of expected utility itself. Frederick's explanation for this is compatible with cardinal utility, and he gives an example of the discounting associated with the decrease in the probability of an event as time moves away, which has also been an issue in this section.[15] Frederick gives the example of a government that may go bankrupt before the government bonds one has purchased reach maturity.[16]

The discounting associated with the loss of controllability of an event is based on the logic that the loss of controllability reduces responsibility. There are in fact many possible ways of thinking about how to understand the reduction of responsibility, as will be discussed in Sect. 5.5. This chapter (except for Sect. 5.5) does not adopt Methodology 1 (divestment from utilitarianism) to resolve the conflict of the basic moral principles, but rather, assumes utilitarianism. A view compatible with utilitarianism is to interpret the social planner as fulfilling their responsibility to the extent necessary by achieving maximum happiness to the extent that they can choose. In particular, in situations of choice involving uncertainty, social planners fulfill their responsibility to the extent necessary, by making choices that maximize expected utility in accordance with the probability of events. From this understanding, the discounting associated with the loss of controllability of events is consistent with Frederick's second kind of discounting, which is based on probability.

A straightforward example illustrates this point. Let us assume that the social planner has m available policies $a^1, a^2, \ldots, a^m$. The social state produced by policy a^i at period t = 0 is s_0^i for sure. In period t = 1, there are n possible social states, $s_{1,1}^i, s_{1,2}^i, \ldots, s_{1,n}^i$ and the probability of occurrence of social state $s_{1,j}^i$ is $p_{1,j}^i$. Now the social state $s_{1,n}^i$ is not concrete, and is completely outside the control of the policy

---

[14] The time discounting that Frederick gives as originating from the reduction in the weight given to future utility is the discounting from time preference. Note that in Sect. 5.2.1, this chapter points out that as long as time preference is viewed as a variation of the argument from special relations (vi), it does not correspond to the discounting intrinsic to time.

[15] Frederick gives six examples of time discounting derived from a decrease in the amount of expected utility, including those due to probability. These examples include objective change, such as the deterioration of wine over time, and changes in utility functions, such as changes in tastes over time.

[16] Frederick (2006, p. 669).

a^i and is completely outside of the influence of the policy, while $s^i_{1,-n}$, the social state excluding $s^i_{1,n}$, in under the influence of the policy. When $t \geq 2$, the social state is completely outside the control of the policy a^i, $\forall i$. Social planners assess policies according to their expected utility and choose one that maximizes expected utility. Specifically, the social planner solves the following Eq. 5.6.

$$\max_i W_0(a^i) = U_0(s^i_0) + \sum_{j=1}^{n} p^i_{1,j} U_1(s^i_{1,j}) + U_2(s_2) + \ldots. \tag{5.6}$$

Here, standardizing the utility from the out-of-control social state at zero $(U_1(s^i_{1,n}) = 0;\ U_t(s_t) = 0, t \geq 2)$, Eq. 5.6 becomes

$$\max_i W_0(a^i) = U_0(s^i_0) + \sum_{j=1}^{n-1} p^i_{1,j} U_1(s^i_{1,j}). \tag{5.7}$$

$U_1(s^i_{1,n})$ and $U_t(s_t)$ $(t \geq 2)$ are missing from Eq. 5.7, because the utility from the out-of-control social state is standardized at zero. The expected utility in the first period is reduced by $p^i_{1,n}$ (probability of being in an out-of-control social state). The expected utility in the second and subsequent periods is zero because the probability of the second period being in an in-control social state is zero. Unlike Eq. 5.2, where the weight given to future utility (δ_t) is reduced, the equal treatment principle is maintained. It simply does not make sense for social planners to consider social states outside of their control when choosing a policy. In this example, the policy is chosen without any consideration of social conditions after the second period.

The discounting associated with this loss of event controllability could have two possible origins.

Origin 1: Intervention of a subsequent decision-making agent

First, is discounting that originates from the intervention of a subsequent decision-making agent. A subsequent agent may be a subsequent generation. It may also be the social planner themself who follows in time, but whose decisions cannot be controlled by themself. In a situation where each agent makes decisions in a decentralized manner over time, even if the preceding agent makes preparations for the future, those preparations may be nullified by the subsequent agent. At this time, the value of future preparedness from the perspective of the preceding agent depreciates. A previous study by Phelps and Pollak (1968) analyzed the effect of intergenerational gaming strategic relationships on savings, and points out that when the preceding generation cannot control the behavior of the succeeding generation, the equilibrium may depart from the first best savings.

Origin 2: Natural hazards

Another origin of discounting is the loss of control due to the succession of natural hazards. If a social planner decides to purchase the sovereign bond of a foreign government, as in Frederick's example, they may not be able to obtain redemption if a catastrophe occurs in that country. If the occurrence of such a default is an uncontrolled event, the expected utility that would be gained from the redemption decreases with the probability of default. Prior research has taken the approach of rationality, explaining time preference in terms of the stochastic nature of the hazard (Green & Myerson, 1996; Rachlin et al., 1991; Sozou, 1998). This chapter discusses the hazards faced by social decisions with reference to this approach.

To conclude the discussion in this section, Table 5.1 summarizes the various discounting concepts. The only discounting that is intrinsic to time and consistent with the equal treatment principle is that associated with the loss of controllability of events.

5.3 Intervention of a Subsequent Decision-Making Agent

5.3.1 The Concept

It may be the will and actions of other subsequent human beings that cause the loss of control over the succeeding event.

The relationship between discounting and decentralized decisions by multiple actors was raised by Arrow (1999a, 1999b). He states, "what one generation leaves will be influenced by its expectation of what the next generation will do with its income, which is wholly or partly determined by what the first generation gives it. The second-generation allocation (as a function of the capital it receives) will determine the utility of the first generation's bequest to the latter and therefore determine (in part) the amount the first generation will leave" (Arrow, 1999a, p. 17). Arrow suggests that he believes the classical work of Phelps and Pollack has interesting implications for the discount rate setting, but does not elaborate further on this suggestion. Phelps and Pollack point out that equilibrium may deviate from the best savings rate when the preceding generation cannot control the behavior of the subsequent generation. However, they do not develop their model to consider time discounting. The problem discussed by Phelps and Pollack can be solved as the problem of time inconsistency between preceding and subsequent decisions. However, this consideration is not fully developed in line with Arrow's inspiration to derive time discounting from time inconsistency.[17]

This section interprets the model in light of Arrow's inspiration that "The second-generation allocation (as a function of the capital it receives) will determine the utility of the first generation's bequest to the latter and therefore determine (in part)

---

[17] For example, in Strotz's (1955–1956), classic study of time inconsistency, it is pointed out that time inconsistency causes waste and excessive thrift, and the discount function also appears in Strotz's discussion. However, the focus of his argument is in the direction that the problem of time inconsistency arises when the decision maker does not have exponential discounting (p. 173), not in the discussion of deriving time discounting from time inconsistency.

Table 5.1 Various concepts of discounting

Point of view concept	Logic	Is it an intrinsic discount to time?	Is it consistent with the principle of equal treatment?
Arguments from Democracy (C&P (i))	If voters do not care much about the distant future, democratic governments should not	No	No Even if voters do not care about the future and believe it is morally justifiable, that does not make the discounting morally acceptable
Discounting accompanying the loss of controllability of events (cf. Argument from Probability, C&P (ii))	**The sequentiality of events reduces responsibility for future events with the loss of controllability over events**	**Yes** **Accompanying the nature of time, which is the sequentiality of events**	**Yes** **One is responsible for the interests of distant future generations insofar as they are affected by the actions of the present generation**
Argument from opportunity cost (C&P (iii))	If losses occur in the future rather than in the present, investing now can help protect against losses	Yes If losses occur in the future rather than in the present, investing now can counter the losses	No It does not allow for future losses to be viewed as morally lower than present losses
Argument that our successors will be better off (C&P (iv))	If one's successors will be better off, one should weigh one's present interests more than those of one's successors (Ramsey Rule)	No It merely argues that the interests of the rich should be taken lightly	Yes No contradiction
Argument from excessive sacrifice (C&P (v))	Without time discounting, the slight increase in gains that continues into the future would demand excessive sacrifice in the present	No It is enough to say that no generation can be morally required to sacrifice more than it should (Methodology 1)	Yes No contradiction
Argument from special relations (C&P (vi))	The interests of those who have special relations with one, like one's children, should be more important than those of strangers	No It only leads to discounting based on the degree of proximity and does not deserve the name of time discounting	No It is nothing but favoritism to those who are close to one

(continued)

Table 5.1 (continued)

Point of view concept	Logic	Is it an intrinsic discount to time?	Is it consistent with the principle of equal treatment?
Argument from time preference (C&P (vii))	Choosing a lower gain in the present even though a higher gain can be obtained in the future (impatience)	No It is merely a variation of "argument from special relations (vi)"	No
Extinction discounting (Chichilnisky et al viii)	If there is a possibility that the human race will eventually die out, it is acceptable to discount the interests of future generations accordingly	No It simply states that since those who do not exist have no interest, there is no need to consider their interests	– No contradictions (no consideration of those who do not exist)

Note Cowen and Parfit (1992) is marked as "C&P"

the amount the first generation will leave" and clarifies the manner in which the intervention of subsequent decision makers can lead to time discounting. The model used here is the intergenerational savings succession model developed in Chap. 3 (Sect. 3.3).

5.3.2 *Emergence of Time Discounting (1)*

As has been seen in Sect. 3.3.2, the subgame perfect equilibrium is as follows.

(1) When $\alpha_2 \neq 0$ (when the Agent 2 is interested in preparing for the doomsday),

$$s_1^* = \alpha_1 y_1 + (\alpha_1 - 1) y_2, if \frac{y_2}{y_1 + y_2} < \alpha_1 \leq 1. s_1^* = 0, otherwise. \tag{5.8}$$

$$S_3^* = \alpha_1 \alpha_2 (y_1 + y_2), if \frac{y_2}{y_1 + y_2} < \alpha_1 \leq 1. S_3^* = \alpha_2 y_2, otherwise. \tag{5.9}$$

(2) When $\alpha_2 = 0$ (when Agent 2 has no interest in preparing for the doomsday), the best response of Agent 2 is $s_2 = 0$ to any s_1, therefore anticipating this response in advance, Agent 1 leaves no savings.

$$s_1^* = 0. \tag{5.10}$$

$$S_3^* = s_2^* = 0. \tag{5.11}$$

Equation 5.8 reveals that if Agent 1 has an interest in S_3 and believes that Agent 2 does as well, then Agent 1 may save. However, if Agent 1's interest in the future (α_1) is not sufficient, then savings will be zero. Equation 5.10 indicates that if Agent 2 has no interest in preparing for the doomsday, Agent 1 will not save, because saving is meaningless.

Now, the question is what to compare this subgame perfect equilibrium to. It must assume that Agent 1 controls the choices of Agent 2. One idea is that Agent 1 can impose any choice on Agent 2 to maximize their own utility.

In this setting, Agent 1 forces to Agent 2 to pass sum of all of the savings from Agent 1 and the income of generation 2 ($y_1 - c_1 + y_2$) on to the final savings. Agent 1 determines their own consumption to maximize the following equation.

$$u_1 = (1 - \alpha_1)\log c_1 + \alpha_1 \log(y_1 - c_1 + y_2). \tag{5.12}$$

The solution is as follows. This solution shall be called "solution with the control of subsequent agent".

$$s_1^{**} = \alpha_1 y_1 + (\alpha_1 - 1)y_2, if \frac{y_2}{y_1 + y_2} < \alpha_1 \leq 1. s_1^{**} = 0, otherwise. \tag{5.13}$$

$$S_3^{**} = \alpha_1(y_1 + y_2), if \frac{y_2}{y_1 + y_2} < \alpha_1 \leq 1. S_3^{**} = y_2, otherwise. \tag{5.14}$$

The solution with the control of subsequent agent is sometimes no different from the subgame perfect equilibrium, with respect to Subject 1's savings. However, the difference is that Agent 1's savings do not go to zero when $\alpha_2 = 0$, because Agent 1 can make Agent 2 save (regardless of Agent 2's intention), even if $\alpha_2 = 0$, Agent 1 saves.

This means that the value of savings in terms of present consumption (c_1) changes depending on the controllability over Agent 2. If the savings of Agent 1 is regarded as the preparation for the doomsday, the value of the preparation for the doomsday may be discounted by the loss of control over Agent 2.

The discount factor D from the solution, with the control of subsequent agent to the subgame perfect equilibrium, is defined as,

$$D = \frac{(the\ vaule\ of\ preparation\ for\ the\ doomsday,}{(the\ vaule\ of\ preparation\ for\ the\ doomsday,} \frac{in\ the\ loss\ of\ contralablity\ of\ subsequent\ agent)}{with\ the\ control\ of\ subsequent\ agent)}. \tag{5.15}$$

Based on this definition, the discount factor $D^* = s_1^*/s_1^{**}$ is shown below.

(1) When $\alpha_2 \neq 0$ (when Agent 2 is interested in preparing for the doomsday),

$$D^* = 1, if \frac{y_2}{y_1 + y_2} < \alpha_1 \leq 1. D^*\ is\ undifinable,\ otherwise. \tag{5.16}$$

(2) When $\alpha_2 = 0$ (when the Subject 2 is not interested in preparing for the doomsday),

$$D^* = 0. \tag{5.17}$$

When $s_1^{**} = 0$, the discount factor D^* in undefinable.

Of the above, the case of $\alpha_2 = 0$ corresponds to the discounting accompanying the loss of controllability of events. The subjective value of preparation for the future from the perspective of Agent 1 depreciates with the loss of control over Agent 2. The discounting due to the intervention of the subsequent decision-makers is not from uncertainty, and is therefore not identical to Frederick's second discounting: time discounting derived from the reduction in the *amount* of expected utility of future events. In subgame perfect equilibrium, Agent 1 is under the assumption of complete information that it can perfectly predict the behavior of Agent 2, and that there is no uncertainty. However, in this example, with the loss of control over Agent 2, Agent 1 is no longer able to leave savings for the survival of the community, indicating the reduction of the value of its savings in terms of present consumption (c_1). The reduction should be distinguished from a reduction in the *weight* (δ_t in Eq. 5.2) given to future utility.

5.3.3 Emergence of Time Discounting (2): Discount Under the Principle of Equal Treatment

Discounting does not appear only in the case of depreciation from the solution with the control of subsequent agent to subgame perfect equilibrium. Discounting even emerges in the setting where the preceding agent is committed to utilitarian maximization, in accordance of loss of controllability of the subsequent agent. Finding such a discount means that even social planners, who treat agents from the present and future equally, are forced to depreciate the value of the preparation for the future. This has the significance of finding the discounting consistent with the principle of equal treatment.

Agent 1 shall be able to control the choice of Agent 2. In other words, decentralized decision-making by each agent is not allowed, and the choices made by Agents 1 and 2 are determined as a whole. Agent 1 gives the same weight to the utility of Agent 2 as it does to its own (complete altruism), and controls the decisions of Agent 2. In this case, the solution is the same as the one obtained in Chap. 3 (Sect. 3.3.3). This solution is called the "utilitarian solution *with control* of subsequent agent."

$$s_1^\dagger = \frac{(\alpha_1 + 1)y_1 + (\alpha_1 - 1)y_2}{2}, \text{ if } \frac{y_2 - y_1}{y_1 + y_2} < \alpha_1 \le 1. s_1^\dagger = 0, \text{ otherwise.} \tag{5.18}$$

$$S_3^{\dagger} = \frac{(\alpha_1 + \alpha_2)(y_1 + y_2)}{2}, \text{ if } \frac{y_2 - y_1}{y_1 + y_2} < \alpha_1 \leq 1. S_3^{\dagger} = \frac{(\alpha_1 + \alpha_2)y_2}{\alpha_1 + 1}, \text{ otherwise.} \tag{5.19}$$

As decentralized decision-making is not allowed, Agent 1 may save even if $\alpha_1 = 0$, or $\alpha_2 = 0$, (the value of $S_3^{\dagger}$ is positive).

Next is the case in which Agent 1 loses control over Agent 2. Although Agent 1 continues to be completely altruistic, they have no control over the choices of Agent 2. This solution is called the "utilitarian solution *without control* of subsequent agent."

When $\alpha_2 \neq 0$, assuming the best response of Agent 2, Agent 1 maximizes $u_1 + u_2$, and the followings are solutions.

$$s_1^{\dagger\dagger} = \frac{(\alpha_1 + 1)y_1 + (\alpha_1 - 1)y_2}{2}, \text{ if } \frac{y_2 - y_1}{y_1 + y_2} < \alpha_1 \leq 1. s_1^{\dagger\dagger} = 0, \text{ otherwise.} \tag{5.20}$$

$$S_3^{\dagger\dagger} = \frac{(\alpha_1\alpha_2 + \alpha_2)(y_1 + y_2)}{2}, \text{ if } \frac{y_2 - y_1}{y_1 + y_2} < \alpha_1 \leq 1. S_3^{\dagger\dagger} = \alpha_2 y_2, \text{ otherwise.} \tag{5.21}$$

When $\alpha_2 = 0$, Agent 2's best response is $s_2 = 0$. Agent 1 allocates between c_1 and c_2 and maximizes $(1 - \alpha_1)logc_1 + logc_2$. The followings are the solutions.

$$s_1^{\dagger\dagger\dagger} = \frac{y_1 + (\alpha_1 - 1)y_2}{2 - \alpha_1}, \text{ if } \frac{y_2 - y_1}{y_2} < \alpha_1 \leq 1. s_1^{\dagger\dagger\dagger} = 0, \text{ otherwise.} \tag{5.22}$$

$$S_3^{\dagger\dagger\dagger} = 0. \tag{5.23}$$

When $\alpha_2 \neq 0$, $s_1^{\dagger} = s_1^{\dagger\dagger}$.[18] When $\alpha_2 = 0$, $s_1^{\dagger} \geq s_1^{\dagger\dagger\dagger}$. Therefore when $\alpha_2 = 0$, even in a setting in which the preceding agent treats each agent equally, they may reduce their savings if they lose control over the subsequent agent.[19,20] In other words, the value of preparing for doomsday may be discounted. In addition, as in Eq. 5.22, even though Agent 2 does not leave final savings at $\alpha_2 = 0$, Agent 1 may leave a savings

---

[18] Note that $S_3^{\dagger} \geq S_3^{\dagger\dagger}$.

[19] Phelps and Pollack argue that in a situation in which the preceding generation cannot control the behavior of subsequent generations, even under perfect altruism, (1) If marginal utility is inelastic to consumption, then the preceding generation's savings decrease; (2). If elasticity is 1, savings are invariant; (3). If elastic, savings increase. Since the elasticity is 1 in the model of this chapter, $s_1^{\dagger} = s_1^{\dagger\dagger}$ is consistent with the work of Phelps and Pollack. However, the Phelps and Pollack assume that generations share the same utility function, whereas this chapter allows for differences in the utility function of each generation, and exactly in $\alpha_2 = 0$, there is the decrease in savings.

[20] Comparing Eq. 5.8 with Eq. 5.18, and Eq. 5.9 with Eq. 5.19, $s_1^{*} \leq s_1^{\dagger}$, $S_3^{*} \leq S_3^{\dagger}$. Not only allowing for decentralized decision-making, but also removing the condition of perfect altruism reduces both Agent 1's savings and final savings. This result is consistent with the conclusions of Phelps and Pollack.

$\left(\text{at } \frac{y_2 - y_1}{y_2} < \alpha_1 \le 1\right)$, because Agent 1 values the utility of Agent 2 as much as they do their own, and so provides the resources to increase Agent 2's utility.

The discount factor from the utilitarian solution with control of subsequent agent to the utilitarian solution without control of subsequent agent is $D^{\dagger\dagger} = \frac{s_1^{\dagger\dagger}}{s_1^{\dagger}}$, $D^{\dagger\dagger\dagger} = \frac{s_1^{\dagger\dagger\dagger}}{s_1^{\dagger}}$, and they are as follows.

(1) When $\alpha_2 \neq 0$ (when Agent 2 is interested in preparing for the doomsday,

$$D^{\dagger\dagger} = 1, if \frac{y_2 - y_1}{y_1 + y_2} < \alpha_1 \le 1. D^{\dagger\dagger} \, is \, undifinable, \, otherwise. \quad (5.24)$$

(2) When $\alpha_2 = 0$ (when the Agent 2 is not interested in preparing for the doomsday),

$$D^{\dagger\dagger\dagger} = \frac{2[y_1 + y_2(\alpha_1 - 1)]}{(2 - \alpha_1)[y_1(1 + \alpha_1) + y_2(\alpha_1 - 1)]}, \text{ if } \frac{y_2 - y_1}{y_2} < \alpha_1 \le 1.$$

$$D^{\dagger\dagger\dagger} = 0, if \frac{y_2 - y_1}{y_1 + y_2} < \alpha_1 \le \frac{y_2 - y_1}{y_2}. D^{\dagger\dagger\dagger} \, is \, undifinable, \, otherwise. \quad (5.25)$$

Even in a setting where the preceding agent treats each agent equally, if the preceding agent loses control over the actions of the subsequent agent, time discounting emerges in the sense that the value of the preparation for the future is reduced. Although the social planner continues to fulfill the necessary responsibility of achieving maximum happiness to the extent that they can choose, time discounting emerges with the loss of control over the subsequent agent. If the subsequent agent wastes the preparation for the future, the preceding agent no longer sees the value in preparing for the future.

Throughout this Sect. 5.3, we have shown that, as Arrow suggested, time discounting emerges as a reduction in the value of future events themselves under circumstances in which each agent makes decentralized decisions along time. Such discounting emerges even if social planners treat the present and future equally. Under the equal treatment principle, the *weight* (δ_t in Eq. 5.2) given to future utility is never reduced from 1. Nevertheless, without control over subsequent agents, preceding agents have no choice but to discount the value of their preparation for the future.

5.4 Natural Hazards

5.4.1 Relationship Between Hazards and Time Discounting

The second type of discounting associated with loss of control over events is due to the occurrence of natural hazards. As in the case of Frederick's government bonds, a buyer of a foreign government's sovereign bonds may not be able to obtain redemption if a catastrophe occurs in that foreign country. Note that the discounting from natural hazards still presupposes the principle of equal treatment of the present and future. This subsection continues to address the issue from the social planner's point of view.

The argument that relates hazards to discounting has been studied previously in the examination of time preference. As discussed in Sect. 5.2, time preference is not a reason for discounting that is compatible with the principle of equal treatment, insofar as it is interpreted as impatience, and is a variation of the argument from special relations. Tomorrow's self is closer to me than next year's self; however, it is incompatible with the principle of equal treatment to give preferential weight to the interests of tomorrow's self. Prior studies have taken an approach that explains time preference in terms of the probabilistic nature of hazards. This approach explains time preference from the perspective of uncertainty in the acquisition of gains due to a delay. The approach treats tomorrow's and next year's interests as equal, but considers that the subjective value of delayed gains decreases because of the possibility that the reward will be lost during the delay (Myerson and Green 1995; Sozou, 1998).[21] Indeed, the relationship between uncertainty and delay is widely known. The psychologist Howard Rachlin, in a study using a questionnaire, shows that a complementary relationship exists between uncertainty and delay (Rachlin et al. 1986). The economist Yoram Halevy has shown through economic experiments that uncertainty about current rewards weakens the "present bias," which is a strong preference for immediate rewards (Halevy, 2008).

The procedure to derive the discount function from the subjective depreciation of the reward is as follows.[22] Assume that a decision is made at t = 0. The decision maker considers the future rewards to be uncertain and has a subjective probability that the value of the reward will have been lost at time t. The following relationship is defined

$$D(t) = 1-F(t), 0 \leq D(t) \leq 1,\ F(0) = 0. \tag{5.26}$$

Here time is continuous. $F(t)$ is the failure function and represents the probability that the gain is lost by period t. $D(t)$ represents the subjective probability that the value of the reward survives and can be gained until period t, and is therefore called

[21] Conversely, Rachlin et al. (1986) argue that the probability of obtaining a gain can be converted into a delay time.

[22] This procedure has been taken from Takeuchi (2011).

the survival function of the value of the reward. This corresponds to a discount function that evaluates the reward to be gained at time t from the present (t = 0).

The shape of the discount function, defined in this way, is determined by the failure function, i.e., how the value of the reward is lost over time. If the hazard rate of loss of the reward (the conditional probability that the reward is lost at time t under the condition that the reward was obtainable up to time t) is constant regardless of time, the discount function takes an exponential form, as in Eq. 5.27. The hazard function is defined as h(t) = $F'(t)/D(t)$, and is given in Eq. 5.28.

$$D(t) = e^{-rt}. \tag{5.27}$$

$$h(t) = r. \tag{5.28}$$

As Eq. 5.28 shows, the hazard function is constant according to time. The discount traditionally assumed by economics is this exponential discount.

However, through numerous experiments, reports have been accumulated that humans and animals do not discount exponentially but hyperbolically, which discounts heavily in the near future and slowly in the distant future (Myerson and Green 1995; Frederick et al. 2002). The discount function in hyperbolic discounting is represented by Eq. 5.29, and its hazard function is Eq. 5.30.

$$D(t) = 1/[1 + rt]. \tag{5.29}$$

$$h(t) = r/(1 + rt). \tag{5.30}$$

As Eq. 5.30 shows, the hazard rate is decreasing with time t. This shows the characteristics of hyperbolic discounting, which discounts heavily in the near future, and slowly in the distant future.

Figure 5.1 depicts the discount functions with exponential and hyperbolic discounting, with time (t) on the horizontal axis. In exponential discounting, the discount function decreases at a constant rate over time. In hyperbolic discounting, the discount function decreases largely in the beginning, but gradually later on. The hazard function of exponential discounting is constant, while that of hyperbolic discounting is a decreasing function of time. Since exponential and hyperbolic discounting were drawn using the same value of r (r = 0.2), the discount function is always higher for hyperbolic discounting (except when t = 0).

Here the discount function is defined as a reduction in the subjective value of rewards. In previous studies dealing with animal behaviors, such as the work of psychologists Myerson and Green (1995), the expected value of the acquisition of rewards, such as food associated with delay, is treated as the same as the subjective value of the reward. The standard in economics, however, is to use the concept of expected utility to represent the value of uncertain future rewards, when focusing on subjective value. Therefore, when considering rewards below, the subjective value of

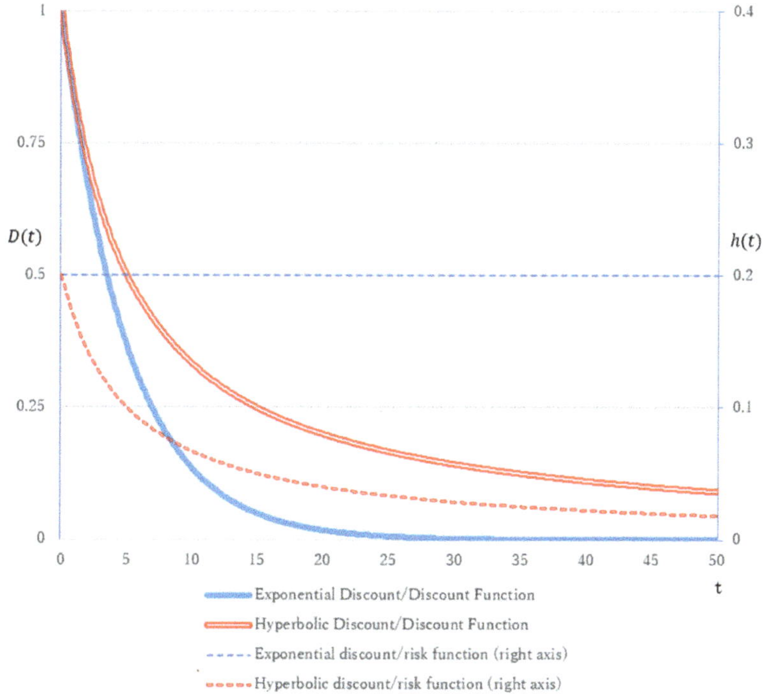

Fig. 5.1 Exponential and hyperbolic discounting (for r = 0.2). *Note* In exponential discounting, the discount function decreases at a constant rate over time. In hyperbolic discounting, the discount function decreases largely at the beginning, but gradually later on. The hazard function of exponential discounting is constant, while that of hyperbolic discounting is a decreasing function of time. Since exponential and hyperbolic discounting were drawn using the same value of r (r = 0.2), the discount function is always higher for hyperbolic discounting (except when t = 0)

reward. Particularly, since this section considers an uncertain situation, it considers Neumann-Morgenstern utility as the subjective value of the reward.[23]

5.4.2 How the Hazard Rate Can Be Reduced

It has been shown that the discounting of the value of future events depends on the nature of the succeeding natural hazards. When the hazard function is constant, exponential discounting is used. However, hyperbolic discounting, which is often observed in empirical settings, requires facing decreasing hazard rate over time.

Exponential discounting is emphasized in traditional economics because it leads to time-consistent choices. Under the discrete time setting, assume that he has

[23] In other words, the expected utility is the sum of (probability) * (the utility obtained by substitution of each reward into the utility function).

$V_0 \langle V_1, V_0 \rangle V_1/(1+r)$ (i.e., he prefers present V_0 dollar to one period late V_1 dollar). If he follows exponential discounting, he should have preferred, at T period in the past, V_0 dollar at T to V_1 dollar at T + 1 (i.e., $V_0/(1+r)^T > V_1/(1+r)^{T+1}$). His preference is consistent over time. However, under hyperbolic discounting, the choice is time inconsistent and the phenomenon of preference reversal is observed. Assuming that another person, now let us call "she", has $V_0 \langle V_1, V_0 \rangle V_1/(1+r)$ (i.e., she prefers present V_0 dollar to one period late V_1 dollar), if she follows hyperbolic discounting, she could have preferred, at T period in the past, V_1 dollar at T + 1 to V_0 dollar at T. In other words, if T is large enough, $V_0/(1+rT) < V_1/(1+rT+r)$. Even though she used to choose V_1, as time goes by, she could choose V_0 over time. To give a simple example, under exponential discounting, one who chooses 1010 dollars 101 months ahead rather than 1000 dollars 100 months ahead will also choose 1010 dollars one month ahead than 1000 dollars immediately (consistent preference). However, under hyperbolic discounting, she may choose the current 1000 dollars, and it is called preference reversal.

The lack of consistency in hyperbolic discounting is not irrational, and can be explained as rational if the hazard function of the lagged gain is a decreasing one. However, the reason for assuming a decreasing hazard rate must be explained. When left to nature, there is good reason to assume a constant hazard rate, especially when considering objective hazard rates. If a subject making a choice is in an unbiased and uniform environment, it is natural to assume that the hazards before that subject are constant. Peter Sozou's (1998) work has shown arithmetically that hyperbolic discounting can be derived from Bayesian update and other methods when the hazard rate is constant but not known a priori. However, this result is also derived based on the assumption that the prior probability distribution of the hazard rate is exponential. To that extent, the question of why the prior probability distribution is not uniform, but exponential, cannot be avoided.

To derive hazard rate that is not constant, it is necessary to change the assumption that the subject is in an unbiased environment. Another study by Green and Myerson (1996), on animal foraging, considers the hazard that other foragers in a competitive relationship will get to the food first, or that the prey will walk away.[24] A simple way to model biased environments is to consider multiple, per se constant, combinations of hazards. Among the multiple hazard rates, there are high and low rates, each of which is assumed to be constant. It does not matter whether the multiple hazard rates are real or whether the cognitive functions of the subject give the appearance of multiple hazard rates. In terms of animal foraging behavior, the former explanation is that once an animal leaves the location of food, it is more likely to attract the attention of competitive foragers while there is a large amount of food, while it is less likely to invite competition after the amount of food has decreased. The latter explanation is based on the fact that there are short-term memories that are easily lost and long-term memories that are not easily lost, and that memories of the location

[24] Green and Myerson (1996, p. 502). The discussion here treats the reduction in rewards as equivalent to the reduction in its value.

of food are rapidly lost in the near future, while those that remain until the distant future are well preserved.

By combining several hazard rates, a decreasing hazard rate can be derived. When two hazard rates are combined, they are as follows

$$D(t) = \gamma D^f(t) + (1-\gamma)D^s(t), 0 < \gamma < 1. \tag{5.31}$$

$$h^f(t) = \frac{F^{f'}(t)}{D^f(t)} = a, h^s(t) = \frac{F^{s'}(t)}{D^s(t)} = b, 0 < a < 1, 0 < b\langle 1, a\rangle b. \tag{5.32}$$

The overall discount function $D(t)$ consists of the composite of two discount functions. $D^f(t)$ is under a high hazard rate (a) and is $D^s(t)$ is under a low hazard rate (b). At $t = 0$, the proportion of $D^f(t)$ and $D^s(t)$ is fixed at $\gamma : 1 - \gamma$. Again, using the example of animal foraging behavior, this proportion is determined by the threshold to attract competitors and by the memory capacity. The respective hazard rates, a and b, are constants. The fact that the hazard rates are constants implies that each of the discount function $D^f(t)$, $D^s(t)$ is exponential.

The overall hazard function is obtained by substituting the exponential discounting formulation in Eqs. 5.27 and 5.28.

$$\begin{aligned} h(t) &= \frac{F'(t)}{D(t)} = -\frac{\gamma D^{f'}(t) + (1-\gamma)D^{s'}(t)}{\gamma D^f(t) + (1-\gamma)D^s(t)} \\ &= \frac{\gamma a * exp(-at) + (1-\gamma)b * \exp(-bt)}{\gamma * exp(-at) + (1-\gamma) * \exp(-bt)}. \end{aligned} \tag{5.33}$$

Differentiating Eq. 5.33 with respect to time t, the following is obtained.

$$h'(t) = \frac{(a-b)^2 * exp[(a+b)t] * \gamma(\gamma - 1)}{[(\gamma - 1) * \exp(at) - \gamma * \exp(bx)]^2} < 0 \tag{5.34}$$

$h'(t)$ is negative, because $(\gamma - 1)$ in the numerator is negative and the other elements of the numerator are positive. The hazard function decreases as t increases, staring from $h(0) = \gamma a + (1-\gamma)b$. That is, the hazard function is decreasing function of time.[25]

[25] When considering hyperbolic discounting, a function called the quasi-hyperbolic discount function is sometimes used. Its form is under discrete time is,

$D(t) = 1, if t = 0. D(t) = \left(\frac{1}{1+\rho}\right)\left(\frac{1}{1+r}\right)^{t-1}, if t \geq 1.$

The quasi-hyperbolic discount is the combination of a one-time discount $\left(\frac{1}{1+\rho}\right)$, and a continuous discount at a fixed rate $\left(\frac{1}{1+r}\right)$. This is essentially equivalent to the idea in this chapter, which combines multiple hazard rates to derive decreasing hazard rates. Phelps and Pollak (1968) first introduces the form of equation as the framework to consider intergenerational altruism.

By combining multiple hazard rates in this way, the discount function that discounts heavily in the near future and slowly in the distant future. Something that changes little is called stable or structural; so, the portion of the hazard rate that is kept low has a stable structure compared to the portion that is fluid and shifts easily. When this stable structure exists, some gains can be expected in the distant future. The existence of this stable structure is a reason to consider the distant future.

5.4.3 *What Hazards Social Decisions Face*

In the previous sections, it has been seen that a certain explanation of diminishing hazard rates is possible. However, the fact that an explanation is possible does not mean that actual decisions involving the future are made in the face of diminishing hazards. What are the hazards faced by social decisions is an empirical question.[26] To answer this question, it is necessary to observe the actual hazards faced by social decisions. If a social decision is intended to bring a future society to a certain state, to what extent will that intention be realized?

In theory, the necessary observations can be obtained by considering the deviations between the predictions of the consequences intended at the time of the decision and the subsequent actual results for various public decisions. Policies are adopted with the intention to produce a certain outcome, but may not produce the expected effect due to exogenous factors that were not initially anticipated. Also, the mechanism assumed to produce the effect may not function as expected. When considering whether to adopt a policy or not, social planners will not only take into account its face value, but also the probability that the effect will be realized. However, it is difficult to obtain a statistically meaningful observational sample of predicted and actual outcomes. Decisions are made in a variety of fields, and the obstacles faced by decision makers may vary from field to field. Moreover, in forecasting at public decision-making, authorities may have incentives to manipulate forecasts to their advantage. They may sprinkle in unrealistically rosy forecasts, or present only modest forecasts that are certain to be achieved.

This section approaches this issue indirectly through the method described below. The method involves taking economic forecasts made by private economists up to 19 months in advance, and observing the divergence between these forecasts and the actual statistics that eventually emerge over the course of the month. In addition, to evaluate longer-term projections, projections and actual results for life expectancy by the National Institute of Population and Social Security Research (a national affiliated research institute) were used.[27] When forecasting an indicator several periods

[26] Observing real policymakers and governments, who are similar to social planners in the real world, to see the kind of discount functions they have, is not relevant to the problems of this section.

[27] The final output of "Population Projections for Japan" is the long-term trend of the population. Life expectancy, which is part of the assumptions used in the projection, is itself a projection made by the Institute on various circumstances at the time of the projection (Kaneko and Mita, 2008).

in advance, the forecaster observes as much as possible of the economic and social picture that appears to them at the time of the forecast (including the economic and social activities planned at that time). As time progresses, events that were unobservable at the time of the original forecast are added, resulting in a discrepancy between the original forecast and the final actual statistics. Deviations also appear when the structure of the economy differs from the forecaster's understanding. From this divergence, the nature of the hazards between the forecast and actual outcomes is examined. The forecaster is not a social planner and is not given the legal or political authority or resources to control economic and social trends. Predictability is not necessarily synonymous with controllability. However, predictability is a precondition for controllability. To be predictable is to have knowledge of how the economy and society work, and this knowledge is the basis for effective economic and social intervention. Although social planners or their real-world counterparts, policymakers, may know more about the workings of the economy and society than forecasters, for simplicity's sake, it is assumed that social planners have no knowledge advantages.

In evaluating forecasts, it is useful to look at the Mean Error (ME), Mean Absolute Error (MAE), and Root Mean Squared Error (RMSE). For the n periods, from Period 1 to period n, g^i is the actual value in period i, f_j^i is the forecast value for the jth period prior to the actual value. $e_j^i = f_j^i - g^i$ represents forecast error (the difference between the forecast and the actual value). n is the total number of forecast periods (e.g., 49 periods for a total of 49 quarters in the case of GDP growth). Mean Error in Eq. 5.35, the MAE in Eq. 5.36, and the RMSE in Eq. 5.37 are statistics of the forecast error (e_j^i) for n cases of i. This section lets ME represent the prediction bias, and assume ϕ as a constant, μ_j as the error term with mean zero, estimate $e_j^i = \phi + \mu_j^i$ (using data from period 1 to period $i = n$), and test the null hypothesis that $\phi = 0$.

$$ME_j = \frac{\sum_{i=1}^{n} e_j^i}{n}. \tag{5.35}$$

$$MAE_j = \frac{\sum_{i=1}^{n} \left| e_j^i \right|}{n}. \tag{5.36}$$

$$RMSE_j = \sqrt{\frac{\sum_{i=1}^{n} (e_j^i)^2}{n}}. \tag{5.37}$$

As data for economic forecasts, this section takes the ESP Forecast (Japan Center for Economic Research, 2005–2018), which compiles economic forecasts by private-sector economists in Japan,[28] from the third quarter of 2005 to the first quarter of 2018, for quarterly real GDP growth (annualized) and consumer prices (total, excluding

[28] The analysis is based on 49 quarters in total, excluding the fourth quarter of 2008 and the first quarter of 2009, when GDP growth was in double-digit negative growth due to the Great Recession. With regard to consumer prices, there were cases where the impact of raising the consumption tax

fresh food, year-on-year rate), and the unemployment rate, average of about 40 institutions' forecasts are available for 19 months, including forecasts as of the end of the quarter in question. Preliminary figures are used for actual statistics.[29] For life expectancy, the projections of life expectancy for women, which are revised every five years, are used and compared with the actual outcomes, which become available in the years following the release of the projection. Life expectancy projections for each year have been presented since the December 1986 estimates. Data are available for seven projections for the first three years after the projection, six for the fourth to eighth years, five for the ninth to thirteenth years, and four for the fourteenth to eighteenth years after the projection. If there are multiple life expectancy scenarios presented, the medium forecast are taken.

The results are shown in Fig. 5.2. In all forecasts, it is confirmed that MAE and RMSE tend to increase as the forecast is made from a more distant point in time. However, the trends in forecast bias (ME) show the individual characteristics of each indicator. Forecasting real GDP growth is very difficult, and even the most recent forecast had an error of 1.5% in MAE. Nevertheless, it is striking that the forecast bias (ME) has remained low throughout the forecasting period: even in the 19-month forecast, the forecast bias was a negligible 0.07%, even as the MAE expanded to 2.01%. However, consumer price forecasts have contrasting results. While the last-minute forecasts are fairly accurate, the forecasting bias (ME) increases with advance forecasts. Nineteen months earlier, the forecast was over-forecast by 0.4%. In hindsight, forecasters tended to misread the ongoing deflation during this period and predicted a higher rate of price inflation. The unemployment rate forecast exhibits intermediate characteristics. Nevertheless, the forecast bias (ME) is kept low at 0.06%, despite the fact that the MAE expanded to 0.37% in the 19-month forecast. The last prediction of life expectancy is characterized by the presence of a bias that underpredicts life expectancy growth beyond that point, although as a prediction about four years ahead, the bias is low and reliable.

The first implication of this analysis is that, especially, with respect to GDP growth, the more likely it is that the forecasters have grasped something underlying the forecasts. Although, the more distant in the future the forecasts, the more likely it is that MAE and other figures increase due to errors in predicting short-term economic fluctuations. The forecasters understand the stable structure of the economy, and based on such understanding, are generally correct. Second, especially with respect to life expectancy, while accurate projections are possible as long as one understands the underlying structure that generates demographics, there comes a point where the accuracy of the projections is lost, as structural changes become more apparent.[30]

rate to 10% as planned was included in the forecast, but since the increase was not realized in the end, the forecast excluding the impact of the increase was used in the evaluation.

[29] The selection of the best forecasters by the sponsor, the Japan Center for Economic Research, is also based on preliminary figures (Kawagoe and Tsuchiya 2018). In its evaluation, the primary forecasts are used as the actual value for the GDP growth rate, and this document follows suit.

[30] In this case, the two-layer structure becomes a three-layer one.

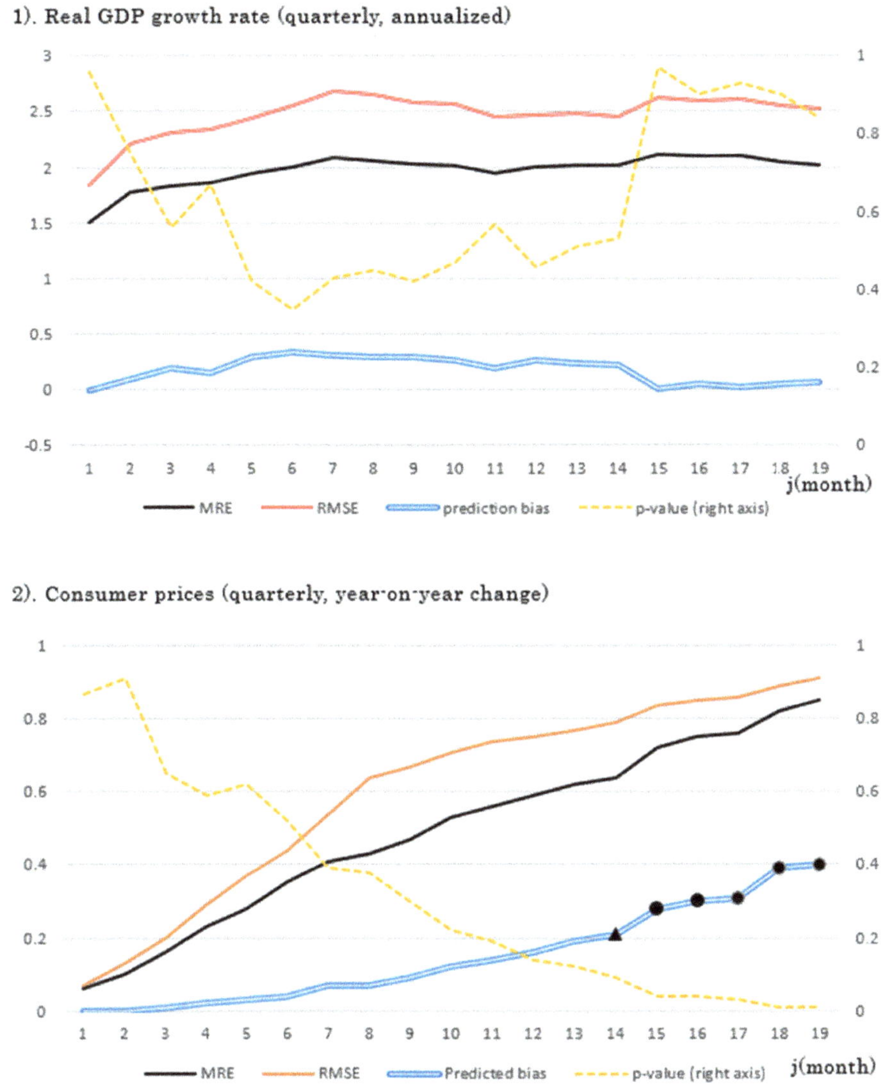

Fig. 5.2 Evaluation of predictions. *Note* The numbers on the horizontal axis indicate how long ago (in months or years) the forecast was made: in months for GDP, prices, and unemployment, and in years for life expectancy. The symbols attached to the prediction bias (ME) indicate that the null hypothesis that the forecast bias is zero is rejected along with the *p*-value, filled circle—5% significant and filled triangle—10% significant points

3). Unemployment rate (%)

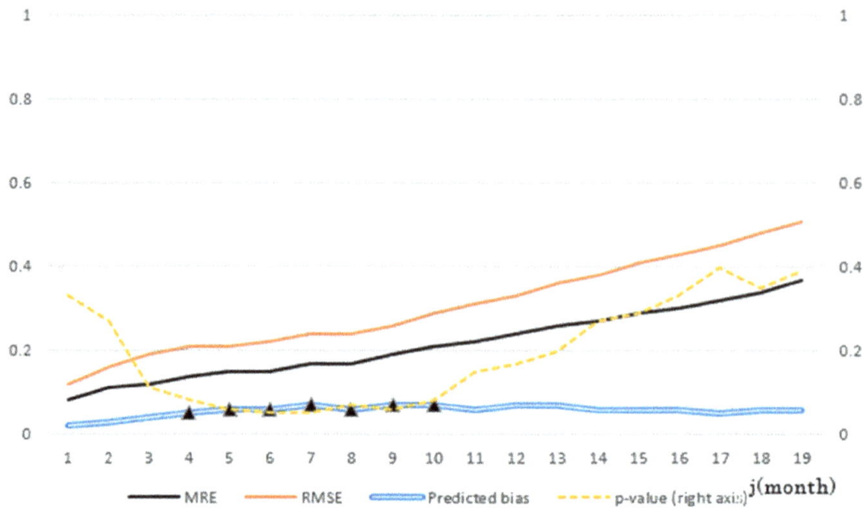

4). Average life expectancy (female, years)

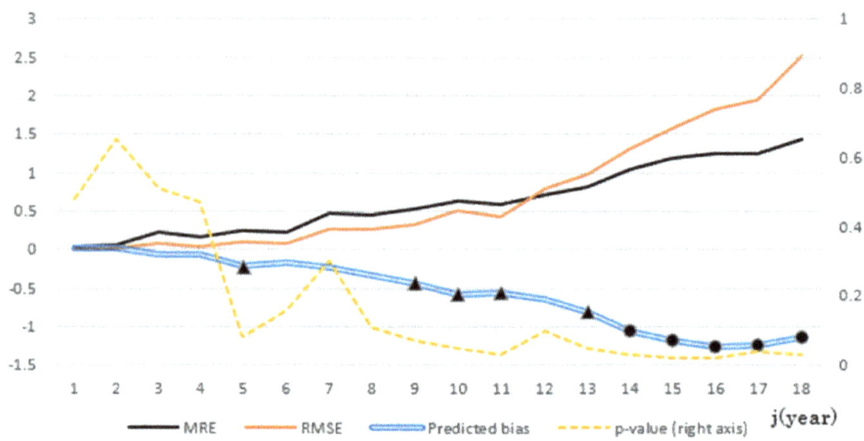

Fig. 5.2 (continued)

Structural changes in population projections include the development of new medical technologies and their uses.

Simply following short-term fluid changes is not sufficient for forecasting; it is essential to understand the stable structure of the forecast target. The societies that the forecasters observe not only change fluidly from day to day, but also have a stable structure that does not easily change. Forecasters observe the societies as having stable structures, and may succeed (e.g., GDP growth rate, unemployment rate) or fail (e.g., consumer prices) to grasp the concept of such stable structures.

On understanding the stable structure of the economic and social system, social planners can influence the present and future state of the economy and society. With knowledge of the stabile structure and the appropriate means of intervention, it is possible not only to control short-term economic and social behavior, but also the long-term shape of the economy and society through intervention in the stable structure. If the stable structures referred to here are the potential growth rate and structural unemployment rate, then the means of intervention could include a tax system to promote technological development, and labor market reforms.[31] Importantly, given such controllability, social planners are required to make policy choices that take into account not only the present, but also the long-run shape of the economy and society. Based on Eq. 5.7, and elaborating the request to the planners, if the state of the economy and society in Period 1 is controllable, then social planners are required to consider not only the state of the economy and society in Period 0 (i.e., s_0), but also the first period ($s^i_{1,-n}$).

The significance of the discussion in this section is that the interpretation of the results of the analysis suggests that social planners can control the state of the economy and society in the relatively distant future. Of course, the evidence in this section is primarily based on the analysis of economic forecasts made less than two years in advance. As has already been stated, this analysis only follows an indirect approach to the hazard rate.

However, hazard rates that are not constant are widely observable outside of the cases discussed in this section. For example, age-specific mortality rates over the human lifetime show a high mortality rate in infancy, followed by a stable period of low mortality. This mortality pattern has implications for important social decisions such as education. If parents and society are blinded by high mortality in infancy and fail to recognize the later period of stability, they may make the mistake of believing that child rearing is an unprofitable investment. A similar trend can be seen in entrepreneurship. According to the Small and Medium Enterprise Agency in Japan, the risk of bankruptcy is high for businesses immediately after opening, and then stabilizes over the years.[32] Entrepreneurship is a social decision (although not a society-wide decision). In the field of engineering, it has been noted that the hazard rate of machine failure takes a bathtub shape, with high initial and terminal stages (e.g., Dhillon, 1999; Wang et al., 2002). In other words, a bathtub-shaped hazard rate transition can be observed: (1) a period of high failure rate at the beginning of product shipment, (2) a stable period of low failure rate, and (3) a terminal period of increased failure rate again. Given the existence of this pattern of hazard rates, widely observed in organized systems in general, such as humans as living organisms, companies, and machines with complex structures, it is hardly surprising that societies under social planners are subject to a similar hazard pattern.

---

[31] Appropriate use of these means of intervention is not easy, but that is a separate issue to be discussed.

[32] Small and Medium Enterprise Agency (2006), Fig. 1.2.21; and ibid. (2011), Fig. 3.1.11.

5.4.4 Policy Implications

This section discusses natural hazards as a second origin of discounting associated with the loss of controllability over events. In concluding this section, it is useful to consider the policy implications of natural hazards, particularly diminishing hazard rates.

First, a lack of knowledge about the inherent stable structure of the economy and society can lead to shortsighted policy decisions that do not consider the long-term consequences of policy. A decreasing hazard rate can lead to social fragmentation when making policy choices. It is assumed that experts have knowledge of the stable structure of the economy and society, but that the general public may not. For example, it is difficult for the general public to understand that if they refrain from profligate spending and adopt sound fiscal policy, they will reap great rewards in the future (as interest rates and inflation are controlled). In this case, the adoption of sound fiscal policy will meet with resistance from the general public. This difference between the experts and general public is qualitatively different from the argument that the general public is impatient, and that it values immediate benefits and disregards future harms. The argument that the general public is impatient is concerned with the violation of the principle of equal treatment of the present and the future. However, when one lacks knowledge of the stable structures inherent in economy and society, the future is belittled even while the principle of equal treatment of the present and the future is followed.

Second, it is important to note that if the nature of the hazards behind the discount varies from case to case, then a different discount function will result for each case.[33] It is appropriate to discount at a high rate for short-lived choices, and use lower discount rates for decisions with lasting effects. As society progresses, social decisions will have stable effects. Furthermore, as societies develop, mechanisms are put in place to protect various rights, such as property rights, by law and to give effect to that protection in the judicial system, and once the law is amended and the allocation of resources is changed, this change will have a lasting effect. In the case of climate change, social planners shall choose between policies that either (1) increase or (2) reduce the share of greenhouse gases in the atmosphere. The social planner's current choice will affect the future climate and welfare (assuming the certainty of the scientific knowledge of the greenhouse effect, and the lack of development of technologies to capture greenhouse gases from the atmosphere, and that other additional conditions are met). In this case, the discount rate used by social planners must be low enough to take account of people in the distant future. The appropriate level of the discount rate varying from case to case is problematic because it is not easy for a society to be flexible enough to use different discount rates for different cases.

[33] In addition to the natural hazards as an explanation for time preference, this book examined one due to the argument from special relations in Sect. 5.2.1. In the case of the argument from special relations, the degree of discounting simply depends on the progression of time, since one discounts according to the degree to which one ceases to be oneself. The explanation from the occurrence of natural hazards has advantage of allowing different discount functions according to cases.

If people conventionally use discount rates from the past, when they were unaware of the climate change problem, social decisions will be made without regard to the consequences in the distant future, and negative externalities will arise from such decisions.

5.5 Divestment from Utilitarianism and Time Discounting

5.5.1 Methodology 1

The discussion so far has followed the path of resolving the conflict of the basic moral principles according to Arrow through Methodology 2 (introduction of time discounting). Specifically, introducing the discount for the loss of controllability of events has maintained the principle of equal treatment of the present and future, while avoiding the situation in which the present is exploited as an instrument of the future.

When considering the intertemporal allocation of resources, the intervention of subsequent decision makers and the occurrence of natural hazards both appear as impediments. It must be better to be able to transfer resources intertemporally than not to be able to do so. In this regard, creating conditions that ensure intertemporal resource allocation by fund establishment (constitutionalization), discussed in Chap. 3 (Sect. 3.3.3), and socially embedded stable structures could improve welfare over time. As proceeding along this line, the discount rate will decline, so the resolution of the conflicts in the moral principles through the introduction of discounting will gradually be unfulfilled. Under the uncertainty-free model of Arrow (1999a), the conflict is resolved in a way that what appears to be a "pronounced and unacceptable imposition on the present generation" (p. 16) is, in fact, a legitimate imposition. If one still takes the position that the contradiction has not been resolved (i.e., that the savings rate of two-thirds is too high), then it is more important to consider Methodology 1, noted in Sect. 5.1, which is a departure from the utilitarian formulation.

Finally, it is valuable to look at Methodology 1, which this chapter has so far skipped over. Methodology 1 is re-presented (without using the term "generation") as follows.[34]

Methodology 1: Divestment from utilitarianism

Methodology 1 is to divest from Eq. 5.4. It is to depart from the utilitarian approach, which takes the utility of each point in time as the object of addition and seeks to maximize the sum of the utilities. The origin for why the present agent is treated like a tool lies in Eq. 5.4. Indeed, as Eq. 5.5 indicates, the agents at each point in time do

[34] The reason for not using the concept of generation is the chapter's policy, as discussed in Sect. 5.1, of taking the principle of equal treatment as a given, while working to resolve the mutual contradictions in the moral code.

not exist independently of each other, and so, some kind of principle governing them is necessary. However, it does not mean that this principle cannot be one separate from utilitarianism, such as the principle that subsequent agents must not be harmed (harm principle; Mill, 1859).

There are two important parts of the re-presentation. The first is "The origin for why the present agent is treated like a tool lies in the Eq. 5.4." In the maximization of Eq. 5.4, utility at each point in time is only one element of Eq. 5.4. In order to maximize Eq. 5.4, the utility of the subject at each point in time is specified to take a certain value, and this, when viewed from the present moment, is seen as the subject at the present moment being treated as an instrument. This acting as a master of each element that utilitarianism uses for its maximization is not limited to the discussion of time discounting. Rawls, in the section discussing utilitarianism in "A Theory of Justice," states:

The latter (the classical principle of utility) is no longer the natural preference, and this suggests that *the condition of people into one is indeed at the root of the classical view*. The reason why the situation remains obscure is that love and benevolence are second-order notions: they seek to further the good of beloved individuals that is already given. If the claims of these goods clash, benevolence is at a loss as to how to proceed, as long anyway as it treats these individuals as separate people. These higher-order sentiments do not include principles of right to adjudicate these conflicts. Therefore, a love of mankind that wishes to preserve the distinction of people, to recognize the separateness of life and experience, will use the two principles of justice to determine its aims when the many goods it cherishes are in opposition (Rawls, 1971, p. 167; italic by quoters).

The sum total of the utility of "people into one" acts like the master. In addition, in discussions about the future, the degree to which the present subject is used as tool is seen as violation of the moral principle, because the future is eternally extended, and its master becomes infinitely gigantic. Reviewed from this understanding, Methodology 2 can be reinterpreted as a method to limit the master's power.

In the second part of the quotation, Rawls points to the need for an alternative principle to utilitarianism, as one to mediate conflicting demands. The second of the key passages in the restatement of Methodology 1 is "some kind of principle governing the agents is necessary." In other words, Methodology 1 is a way to resolve the moral principle conflict by rethinking the relationship with the master and replacing the master with some alternative moral idea.

This chapter has assumed the principle of equal treatment of the present and future, and has attempted to resolve the conflict of moral principles, while retaining the equal principle. In the discussion of Methodology 2, utilitarianism has been regarded as the sole principle representing the equal treatment. However, it is possible to consider principles other than utilitarianism to represent equal treatment. The harm principle of J. S. Mill, which is an example of Methodology 1, can be a representation of the principle of equal treatment, as it exerts respect for the subsequent agent as a subject with rights. As seen in Sect. 5.2.1, in response to the argument from excessive sacrifice (v), Cowen and Parfit (1992) argues that no one can be morally required to sacrifice more than they *should*. Their objection could also be a representation of the principle of equal treatment if the meaning of "should" is properly defined. Another example is that of Amartya Sen, who, in discussing environmental issues, argues that even if future generations are richer, it will be problematic if the present generation's environmental pollution violates the future generations' right to a good environment (Sen, 1982). A rights-based principle like Sen's may also be a representation of the principle of equal treatment.

5.5.2 *Methodology 2 Under Various Principles Representing the Principle of Equal Treatment*

In the discussion up to Sect. 5.4, there has been a sharp distinction between Methodology 1 and 2. Finally, we discuss the implications for Methodology 2 of allowing, through Methodology 1, something other than utilitarianism as a moral principle, to represent the equal treatment principle.

The discount for loss of controllability of events found by Methodology 2 is based on the discount for reduced responsibility with loss of controllability. Methodology 2, in the discussion up to Sect. 5.4, is on utilitarianism. The social planner is fulfilling their responsibility to the extent necessary, by achieving maximum happiness to the extent they can choose. However, once utilitarianism is replaced with the principle that no one can be morally required to sacrifice more than one should, the difficulties of the present agent, who is forced to save excessively under utilitarianism, are eased by the change of discounting future events more heavily (i.e., the value of preparation for the future is reduced in terms of the present consumption). Time discounting is not objectively determined independently of moral principles. Rather, it changes in response to newly adopted moral principles that depart from utilitarianism.

Methodology 2 has taken the position that, in a situation of choice involving uncertainty, a choice is made to maximize expected utility according to the probability of an event, thereby fulfilling the necessary limit of responsibility. However, maximizing expected utility is only one of the principles that can be chosen under that of equal treatment. In times of uncertainty, social planners may choose to adopt the safety first rule, instead of maximizing expected utility. There are various safety-first rules. For example, in the safety-fixed rule, a certain probability is taken and the policy with the highest benefit whose cumulative density is equal with that probability is highly valued.

$$\max_{x} b s.t. P\{\pi(x) \leq b\} = \zeta \tag{5.38}$$

x is the choice variable that represents the policy x. Policy x which maximizes gain b is chosen. $\pi(x)$ is the gain under policy x. P is the cumulative density function, and in particular, its cumulative density is specified to be probability ζ.

Figure 5.3 illustrates the future gain from policies on the horizontal axis and the cumulative distribution (the cumulative probability of a gain below a certain gain) of realizing a certain gain on the horizontal axis when Policies 1, 2, or 3 are taken is on the vertical axis. The probability density function of the gain from the policies are assumed to follow normal distribution, with Policy 1 having mean of 5 and standard deviation of 1, Policy 2 having mean of 5.4 and standard deviation of 2, and Policy 3 having mean of 5.2 and standard deviation of 3. When the social planner is attempting to maximize expected utility, they choose Policy 2, which has the highest expected utility. However, when they choose based on the safety-first rule, Policy 2 is not necessarily chosen. When $\zeta = 0.1$, the social planner considers the rule of maximizing gain in the rare event that only 10% of the events occur counting from the worse side, then the best policy is Policy 1. When $\zeta = 0.75$, it is the rule that maximizes the gain in 75% of the bad situations (i.e., the rule that maximizes the gain in only 25% of the good situations), and so Policy 3 is the best choice. The choice at the time of $\zeta = 0.1$ is an easily understandable as safety-first rule. Even considering the principle of treating the present and the future equally, it is supportable to choose a policy that provides better gains even in the rare case of bad luck. In the case of $\zeta = 0.75$, the safety-fixed rule looks more like a "safety is secondary" rule. However, it is possible to allow this safety-fixed rule in the equal treatment principle, as long as a reasonable explanation is given as to why higher gains must be aimed for, at the expense of safety.

To conclude this section, it is useful to discuss the precautionary principle, which is an important concept in relation to the safety-fixed rule, especially in the context of global environmental issues such as climate change. The precautionary principle is formulated in Principle 15 of the Rio Declaration on Environment and Development, which was agreed to in 1992. This principle states as follows.

> In order to protect the environment, the precautionary approach shall be widely applied by States according to their capabilities. Where there are threats of serious or irreversible damage, lack of full scientific certainty shall not be used as a reason for postponing cost-effective measures to prevent environmental degradation. (Principle 15, Rio Declaration on Environment and Development, 1992)

Although the meaning of the precautionary principle in the political declarative text is not always clear,[35] one possible interpretation is to take it as a recommendation to consider the worst-case scenarios with only a slight possibility. In this case, the precautionary principle would be the same as the safety-fixed rule, in which the value of ζ is very small. Following this interpretation, the implications of the precautionary principle for time discounting would be exhausted in Fig. 5.3.

However, noting that Principle 15 of the Rio Declaration addresses the "lack of full scientific certainty," it is necessary to understand that the precautionary principle

[35] The precautionary principle is discussed in detail by Sunstein. He points out that in this principle, the result of trying to avoid all actions that lead to significant harm with low probability is that one is forced into a state of paralysis in which one cannot choose anything, including not to act (Sunstein, 2003, 2007). The use of the precautionary principle as a guiding principle for social decision-making requires a clarification of its significance.

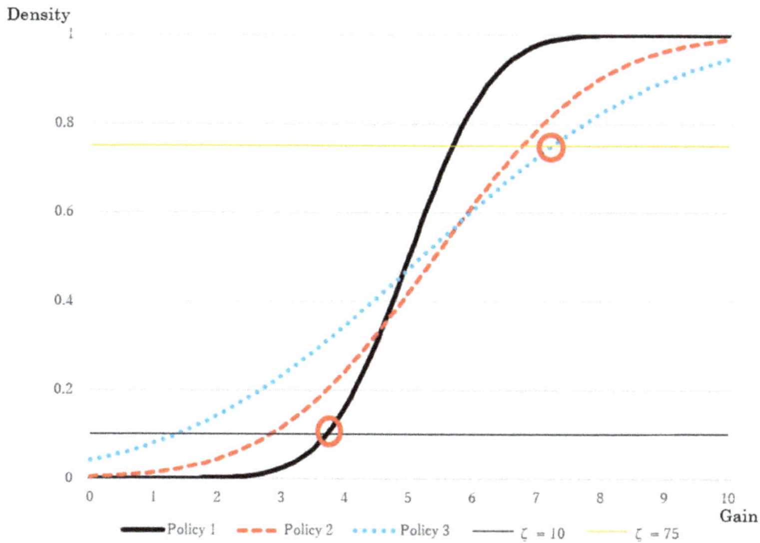

Fig. 5.3 Policy decisions based on safety-fixed rules. *Note* The probability density function of the gain from the policies are assumed to follow normal distribution, with Policy 1 having mean of 5 and standard deviation of 1, Policy 2 having mean of 5.4 and standard deviation of 2, and Policy 3 having mean of 5.2 and standard deviation of 3. When the social planner is trying to maximize expected utility, they choose policy 2. When $\zeta = 0.1$, the best policy is Policy 1. When $\zeta = 0.75$, the best is Policy 3

is concerned with situations that, with the current level knowledge, humans cannot ascertain in advance the degree of probability of their occurrence. For example, in the case of climate change, there are two uncertainties: not only (1) the environmental impacts and economic losses due to global warming, but also (2) the prospects for the development of innovative technologies to absorb and reduce greenhouse gas emissions. The future gains from the adoption (or non-adoption) of policy measures cannot be shown with the density distribution as shown in Fig. 5.3. A situation with uncertainty in this sense calls for a different solution than the case in Fig. 5.3. In a survey paper on the economic theory of the precautionary principle, the environmental economist Kenichi Akao (2010) presents the maximin approach as a solution under complete uncertainty, in addition to the criterion of choosing the one with the maximum expected utility by giving all possible states equal probability. Different solution methods lead to different behaviors, and these different behaviors represent different discount functions.

5.6 Conclusions and Remaining Issues

As long as the moral principle of equal treatment of the present and the future is followed, many of the grounds for discounting that have been raised in previous studies are unsupportable. However, this chapter has found discounting that is consistent with the principle of equal treatment, discounting that accompanies the loss of controllability over events, and has shown that through this discounting, the conflict of the moral principles as presented by Arrow can be resolved. While no principle can be upheld if it remains in contradictions, this chapter has shown that through the resolution of the conflict, equal treatment of present and future is possible and worthy of support. Furthermore, even under the principle of equal treatment, this chapter details how the two logics of the sequential appearance of decision makers and the occurrence of natural hazards discount future events.

Finally, it is necessary to raise a remaining issue. The issue concerns the empirical point of what hazard rates actual social decisions face, as discussed in Sect. 5.4.3. While this chapter has attempted to answer this question indirectly, a more direct response remains a challenge for the future. With reference to the wide range of examples of variable hazard rates like human mortality, it is desirable to obtain robust understanding, both empirical and theoretical, of the hazards that face social decision-making.

References

Ainslie, G. (2001). *Breakdown of will*. Cambridge University Press.

Akao, K. (2010), "Precautionary Principle and Economic Theory of Uncertainty," Kazuhiro Ueda and Nao Otsuka (eds.), *Environmental Risk Management and Precautionary Principle*, Yuhikaku, pp. 209–225. (in Japanese).

Arrow, K. J. (1966). Discounting and public investment criteria. In A. V. Kneese & S. C. Smith (Eds.), *Water Research* (pp. 13–32). Johns Hopkins Press.

Arrow, K. J. (1999a). Discounting, morality, and gaming. In P. R. Portney & J. P. Weyant (Eds.), *Discounting and intergenerational equity* (pp. 13–21). Resources for the Future.

Arrow, K. J (1999b). Inter-generational equity and the rate of discount in long-term social investment. In M. Sertel (Ed.). *Contemporary economic issues. International economic association series* (pp. 89–102). Palgrave Macmillan.

Arrow, K. J., Cline, W. R., Maler, K.-G., Munasinghe, M., Squitieri, R., & Stiglitz, J. E. (1996). Intertemporal equity, discounting, and economic efficiency. In J. P. Bruce, H. Lee, & E. F. Haites (Eds.), *Climate change 1995: Economic and social dimensions of climate change* (pp. 125–144). Cambridge Cambridge University Press.

Chichilnisky, G., Hammond, P. J., & Stern, N. (2020). Fundamental utilitarianism and intergenerational equity with extinction discounting. *Social Choice and Welfare, 54*, 397–427.

Cowen, T., & Parfit, D. (1992). Against the social discount rate. In L. Peter & J. S. Fishkin (Eds.), *Justice between age groups and generations* (pp. 144–168). Yale University Press.

Dasgupta, P., Mäler, K.-G., & Barrett, S. (1999). Intergenerational equity, social discount rates, and global warming. In P. R. Portney & J. P. Weyant (Eds.), *Discounting and intergenerational equity* (pp. 51–77). Resources for the Future.

Dasgupta, P. (2005). Three conceptions of intergenerational justice. In H. Lillehammer (Ed.), *Ramsey's legacy* (pp. 149–169). Clarendon Press.
Dhillon, B. S. (1999). Topics in reliability, Chap. 12. In *Engineering maintainability, how to design for reliability and easy maintenance* (pp. 224–249). Gulf Professional Publishing.
Frederick, S. (1999). *Discounting, time preference, and identity," a dissertation for the degree of Doctor of Philosophy*. Carnegie Mellon University.
Frederick, S. (2006). Valuing future life and future lives: A framework for understanding discounting. *Journal of Economic Psychology, 27*(5), 667–680.
Green, L., & Myerson, J. (1996). Exponential versus hyperbolic discounting of delayed outcomes: Risk and waiting time. *American Zoologist, 36*(4), 496–505.
Halevy, Y. (2008). Strotz meets allais: Diminishing impatience and the certainty effect. *American Economic Review, 98*(3), 1145–1162.
Japan Center for Economic Research. (2005–2018). ESP forecasting survey (monthly research reports). https://www.jcer.or.jp/esp-forecast-top. Accessed 30 Jan 2021
Kaneko, R., & Mita, F. (2008). On the basic nature and methodological framework of future population projections. *Population Studies, 64*(3), 3–27. (in Japanese).
Kawagoe, M., & Tsuchiya, Y. (2018). *Technical note on the evaluation of the 2017 ESP forecast survey*. Japan Center for Economic Research website. https://www.jcer.or.jp/jcer_download_log.php?f=eyJwb3N0X2lkIjozNjIzOSwiZmlsZV9wb3N0X2lkIjoiMzY2OTkifQ==&post_id=36239&file_post_id=36699. Accessed 30 Jan 2021.
Koopmans, T. C. (1967). Objectives, constraints, and outcomes in optimal growth models. *Econometrica, 35*(1), 1–15.
Mill, J. S. (1859). *On liberty*. Oxford University Press, Oxford.
Myerson, J., & Green, L. (1995). Discounting of delayed rewards: Models of individual choice. *Journal of the Experimental Analysis of Behavior, 64*(3), 263–276.
Parfit, D. (1984). *Reasons and people*. Oxford University Press.
Phelps, E. S., & Pollak, R. A. (1968). On second-best national saving and game-equilibrium growth. *Review of Economic Studies, 35*(2), 185–199.
Ponthière, G. (2003). Should we discount future generations' welfare? A survey on the 'pure' discount rate debate. *CREPP Working Papers* 0302, Centre de Recherche en Economie Publique et de la Population (CREPP) (Research Center on Public and Population Economics) HEC-Management School, University of Liège.
Rachlin, H., Logue, A. W., Gibbon, J., & Frankel, M. (1986). Cognition and behavior in studies of choice. *Psychological Review, 93*(1), 33–45.
Rachlin, H., Raineri, A., & Cross, D. (1991). Subjective probability and delay. *Journal of the Experimental Analysis of Behavior, 55*(2), 233–244.
Ramsey, F. P. (1928). A mathematical theory of saving. *Economic Journal, 38*(152), 543–559.
Rawls, J. (1971a, 1999). *A theory* of *justice, revised edition*, Harvard University Press
Schelling, T. C. (1995). Intergenerational discounting. *Energy Policy, 23*(4/5), 395–401.
Sen, A. K. (1982). Approaches to the choice of discount rates for social benefit-cost analysis. In R. C. Lind, K. J. Arrow, G. R. Corey, P. Dasgupta, A. K. Sen, T. Stauffer, J. E. Stiglitz, J. A. Stockfisch, & R. Wilson (Eds.), *Discounting for time and risk in energy policy* (pp. 325–353). Resources for the Future.
Small and Medium Enterprise Agency, Japan. (2006). Small and medium enterprise white paper 2006 (in Japanese).
Small and Medium Enterprise Agency, Japan. (2011). *Small and medium enterprise white paper 2011* (in Japanese).
Sozou, P. D. (1998). On hyperbolic discounting and uncertain hazard rates. *Proceeding of the Royal Society of London b: Biological Sciences, 265*(1409), 2015–2020.
Strotz, R. H. (1955–1956). Myopia and inconsistency in dynamic utility maximization. *The Review of Economic Studies, 23*(3), 165–180.
Sunstein, C. R. (2003). Beyond the precautionary principle. *The University of Pennsylvania Law Review, 151*(3), 1003–1058.

Sunstein, C. R. (2007). *Worst-case scenarios*. Harvard University Press.
Takeuchi. (2011). 'Age-based election districts' to make use of children's voices in politics: More realistic than domain voting. distribute seats according to youth. *Nikkei Business ON LINE* (in Japanese).
Thaler, R. H., & Shefrin, H. M. (1981). An economic theory of self-control. *Journal of Political Economy, 89*(2), 392–406.
United Nations Conference on Environment and Development. (1992). Rio declaration on environment and development. https://www.un.org/en/development/desa/population/migration/generalassembly/docs/globalcompact/A_CONF.151_26_Vol.I_Declaration.pdf. Accessed 14 Oct 2023.
Wang, W. S., Hsu, F. S., & Liu, P. P. (2002). Modelling the Bathtub shape hazard rate function in terms of reliability. *Reliability Engineering and System Safety, 75*(3), 397–406.

Chapter 6
Conclusion

Abstract This chapter summarizes what has been clarified in the discussion so far. Three points that are worth mentioning as prospects for further research are raised. These are: to delve into the various motivations of human beings; to promote further empirical studies including experiments; and to work on social implementation in order to solve intergenerational issues. Finally, this chapter warns against the current situation of using the future generation as one's own tool.

6.1 Main Findings

Based on the direction of appropriately conceptualizing issues through philosophy and developing them through economics, this book has addressed the intergenerational issues. In considering the issues, several experimental methods have been introduced to maintain the generality of the discussion and extend its scope beyond theoretical possibilities to what could occur in reality. The main points that have been clarified through the discussion so far are presented below.

(1) **Intergenerational issues have become problematic, due to the recent increase of human power. To resolve the new issues, it is necessary to realize the new ethics (intergenerational ethics). There are two ways to lay the foundation for intergenerational ethics: establishing duty to future generations through common understandings within the present generation and; finding reciprocity between different generations.**

Through an examination of the non-identity problem, this book has shown that intergenerational ethics can be founded on the unilateral duty from the present to future generations through common understandings within the present generation. However, there are difficulties in the realization of intergenerational ethics as duty. Whether or not the duty is implemented is left to the state of mind of the present generation, making it vulnerable to problems such as *akrasia*. Herein lies the significance of finding reciprocity between different generations, and grounding intergenerational ethics as a bilateral relationship between generations.

T. Hiromitsu, *Resolving Intergenerational Conflicts*, Advances in Japanese Business and Economics 33, https://doi.org/10.1007/978-981-97-0614-3_6

(2) **Reciprocity is found between generations as indirect reciprocity, namely, descending and ascending reciprocity, and direct reciprocity (public reciprocity), based on the sharing, among generations, of the rule to care for life after death.**

There are two types of reciprocity with a structure in which cooperation is chained between different generations: descending and ascending reciprocity. These indirect forms of reciprocity have been implemented in society in the form of education for children and pay-as-you-go pensions. However, they are dysfunctional in pure intergenerational problems (conflicts of interest among distant generations), and are fragile due to the dependence on cooperation of the chain of generations. As a new opportunity to bring about direct reciprocity between generations, this book has proposed the idea of cooperation in public reciprocity, which stems from the sharing, among generations, of the rule to care for life after death. Cooperation in public reciprocity overcomes the disadvantages of indirect reciprocity.

(3) **This book has proposed methodologies to promote intergenerational cooperation: the fund establishment (constitutionalization), Kantian categorical imperative, intergenerational negotiation, deliberation, and deliberation with imaginary future generations (IFGs). The fund establishment (constitutionalization), Kantian categorical imperative, and intergenerational negotiation are significant in promoting the cooperation, but share the weakness of fixing the preferences of the preceding generation. The deliberation with IFGs endogenize the preferences of the preceding generation.**

Public reciprocity allows for intergenerational cooperation, but does not always result in adequate cooperation. The preceding generation may anticipate betrayal by the subsequent generations, or may rely on subsequent generations and thus fail to cooperate by itself. Fund establishment (constitutionalization), which binds the choices of subsequent generations, is an effective countermeasure against the anticipation of betrayal by subsequent generations. When the preceding generation provides moral inspiration to the subsequent generation, and takes this inspiration into account, it will behave as it wants the subsequent generations to behave. This intergenerational cooperation through Kantian categorical imperative is effective as the countermeasure against both the anticipation of the subsequent generation's betrayal, and dependence on the subsequent generation. However, Kantian categorical imperative has the disadvantage that weak cooperation can be passed on through generations when the preceding generation has little interest in the future in the first place.

When there is reciprocity between generations, Pareto-improving negotiations can take place between the present and hypothetical future generations. While deliberation has the power to change people's opinions, it is clear that deliberation among the present generation alone cannot necessarily solve intergenerational issues. A mechanism is needed to represent the interests of future generations that are not represented in the usual deliberative forum. By guiding the IFGs into the deliberative forum, it is possible to change the preferences of the present generation (the preceding generation).

(4) **Through an economic experiment using long-term fiscal policy as an example, this book has presented keys to be considered in policy decisions involving multiple generations.**

Through the experiment, this book has found that the number of subjects who favor burden sharing between the present and future decreases with age. However, the decrease is slower than when the choices are based on personal interest. The so-called "silver democracy" theory is overemphasized.

In policymaking, it is important to set up a forum which has built-in tradeoffs between benefits and burdens. There is also considerable scope to persuade people to adopt policies that are more considerate about future generations, based on their personal interests, and there may be a way to broaden support for such careful policies through collusion between the elderly and younger people. It is concerning that providing information about individual burdens accompanying policies leads to the privatization of public policy and to the increase of the attachment to individual interests. Additionally, a reasonable consensus must be reached on the long-term outlook, and the conflation of resource issues with value issues must be avoided.

(5) **Equal treatment of present and future events is possible and deserves support.**

This book has also delved into the basic issue of whether it is possible and desirable to treat present and future events equally. Specifically, it set forth the task of solving Arrow's conflict of basic moral principles, and examined whether there exists time discounting that is necessary to solve this conflict; this refers to discounting that satisfies two conditions: it is intrinsic to time and consistent with equal treatment of the present and future. Through the examination, it has been shown that the discounting that is due to the sequentiality of events, which reduces responsibility for future events as a result of the loss of controllability over events, satisfies both conditions. Equal treatment of present and future events is possible and deserves support. Even under the principle of equal treatment, this book has shown how future events are discounted through two paths: the sequential appearance of decentralized decision makers and the occurrence of natural hazards.

Figure 6.1 lays out the methodologies of actualizing intergenerational ethics that have been identified thus far. To avoid duplication with what has been discussed, this section does not describe the figure in detail. However, throughout this book, I have worked on the argument to change the situation in which there are isolated generations taking decentralized decisions, to find the ties that bind different generations together, and to provide clues to encourage intergenerational cooperation. In particular, this book has focused on pioneering a methodology that has received insufficient attention in the past: an intergenerational ethics on direct reciprocity, which has been placed on the lower right-hand side of Fig. 6.1. The discovery of the possibility of intergenerational cooperation through public reciprocity, on the sharing of the rule of care for life after death, enriches the logic that encourages cooperation. Public reciprocity begins with the recognition and respect of future generations as human beings like ourselves. Recognizing different generations as beings who may share rules with us and establishing a community among generations is the basis for intergenerational cooperation.

In this book, the preferences of each generation have not necessarily been treated as fixed. The discussion here has allowed for endogenization of preferences subject to certain logics. Specifically, it has been pointed out that the preferences of subsequent generations can be influenced by the behavior of the preceding one. This book has also discussed the influence to the preferences of the preceding generation in the decision-making process, such as deliberation. These considerations take the methodology of normative economics one step further, which Kotaro Suzumura refers to as "considering institutions as selectable variables and pursuing the possibilities of their design, evaluation, selection, and implementation" (Suzumura 2016, p. 97). This book has deepened the study to consider not just institutions, but institutions that alter individual preferences in orderly fashions.

6.2 Prospects for Further Research

This book has provided a coherent discussion of intergenerational issues and has made several proposals, that have never been proposed before. In closing, this section offers three suggestions for further research.

(1) **Conduct research on various human motivations at a more fundamental level.**

First, research is needed to delve into the various human motives at a more basic level. For example, when it comes to the conformity of the successors to their predecessors, which guides the Kantian categorical imperative, the question is why people abide in the first place.[1] Engaging in such foundational considerations would be beneficial for deeper understanding of the function of Kantian categorical imperative.

Of particular importance is the basic research on reciprocity, which is the central concept of this book. People may engage in reciprocal behavior even in situations that are not in their personal interest. Why have organisms that behave this way been able to survive the evolutionary process?[2] What are the psychological and neural bases for reciprocal behavior? Although this book organizes the relationship between reciprocity and altruism based on Kolm's (2006) work, it is an interesting challenge to pin down the often-tangled relationship between reciprocity and altruism in the context of evolutionary theory and psychology/neuroscience. This book has deepened our understanding of reciprocity by using the methods of philosophy and

[1] Note 113 in Chap. 3 (Sect. 3.4.3) provides a primer on why people are sympathetic.

[2] Note 72 in Chap. 2 (Sect. 2.5.1) provides a primer on why reciprocal behavior has survived the evolutionary process.

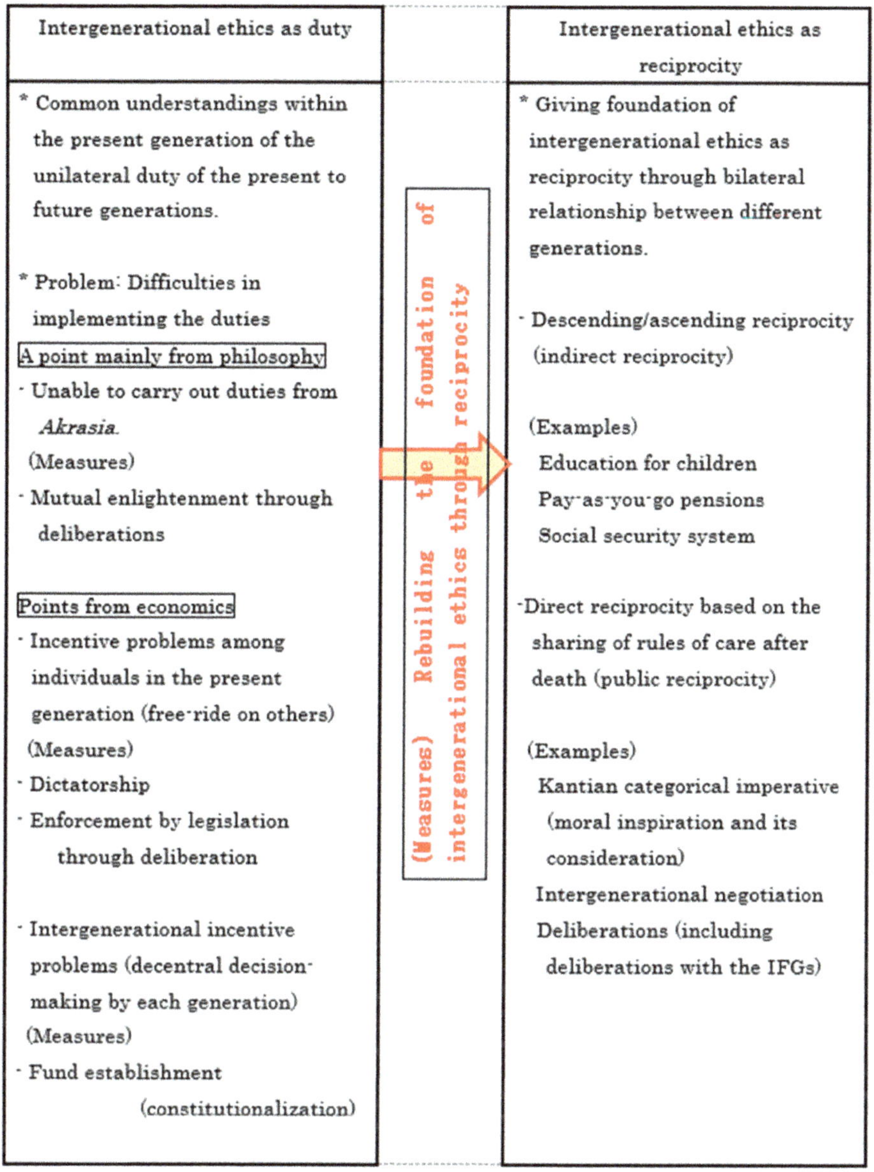

Fig. 6.1 Logics of intergenerational ethical foundations and methodologies for their actualization

economics, including experimental economics and game theory. However, further deepening our understanding of its biological foundation through psychology and neuroscience will provide clues to a new perspective on intergenerational issues, by learning what humans as organisms can and cannot do. This will provide keys to new perspectives on intergenerational issues.

In evolutionary theory, anthropologist Joseph Henrich, using the idea of group selection, wrote "The secret of our success: how culture is driving human evolution, domesticating our species, and making us smarter," and points out that culture has directed human evolution. As discussed in Chap. 1 (Sect. 1.1), it is hard to overlook the fact that the dramatic increase in human power is at the root of the problematic relationship with future generations. Moreover, if this is the case, the basic strategy to deal with intergenerational problems is to create countermeasures through the creation of new cultures, while remaining grounded in the human biological foundation. The creation of culture here refers to the creation of a new intergenerational ethics and building of new institutions for decision-making that ensure consideration for future generations. The ideas explored in this book, such as intergenerational cooperation through public reciprocity and IFGs, provide keys for the creation of such new ethics and institutions.

(2) **A accumulate empirical evidences, including those from economic experiments**

The second prospect for future research is to continue to conduct empirical research, including economic experiments. This book has provided new insights into intergenerational relations through economic experiments in Chaps. 3 and 4, but it is not possible to clarify all aspects of intergenerational relations with the limited number of experimental opportunities available. The experiment on the intergenerational savings succession model in Chap. 3 led to a methodology of intergenerational cooperation through Kantian categorical imperative; however, as has been raised (Sect. 3.6), further experiments are needed to test its function in the real world. One experiment invites new experiments. Through the examination of the divergence between economic forecasts and actual statistics (Chap. 5), this book sought to learn the extent to which social decisions have the power to control future social conditions. This question touches the very foundation of the world in which we live and decide things, and the work in this book is a first step toward understanding the same.

(3) **Work toward the social implementation of new ethics and institutions necessary to better handle intergenerational issues.**

A third and final prospect for future research is to work toward the social implementation of new ethics and institutions necessary to better handle intergenerational issues. To implement new ethics and institutions is to make social changes a reality. As noted in Chap. 2 (Sect. 2.1), philosophy's concern is to offer new interpretations of the moral obligations and values we owe, with reference to certain theoretical frameworks. Economics excels at identifying the consequences of the interaction of people acting on the basis of certain obligations and values. Combining these two disciplines with the empirically oriented methodology engaged with in this book is a powerful weapon for social change. With the creation of new rules, the prediction of the consequences of those rules with models, and their verification with the help of empirical evidence, I would like to contribute to the creation of a sustainable human society, through the repetition of this process.

6.3 Final Remarks—Do not Use the Unborn as a Tool

To the best of my ability, I have considered ways to ground and actualize intergenerational ethics. I have tried to present, in a positive way, what needs to be done, how it should be done, and the logic on which it should be based. Finally, I would like to conclude this book by presenting a *negative picture* of what the discussion so far has aimed to achieve—as a "this is not the way it should be," in order to provide a simple understanding.

> You will mock those whom you intend to destroy! No matter how much knowledge and skill you may have, you will still need the hand of your slaves in the morning to replace the world. Our life is ours, even if our bodies have been artificially remade. Life lives by the power of life. If that morning comes, we will live for that morning. We are the bird that flies over that morning again and again, spitting blood, again and again! To live is to change. Insects, slime mold, plants, trees, and humans will change. The sea of decay will live with us. But you cannot change. You just have a built-in schedule. You deny death, so…tell the truth. We don't need you." (Miyazaki, Nausicaä of the Valley of the Wind, comic version, 1996, vol. 2, p. 508)

Quoted here are words of anger. They are words of indignation directed by Nausicaä (the protagonist of Hayao Miyazaki's comic) to the Lord of the Crypt of Shuwa. The manga version of Nausicaä is not as widely known as the theatrical film (released in 1984), but it is a work of great ethical depth. The setting is a grim period environment, a time removed from the world's final war and a polluted land, in which people are constantly fighting each other for the few existing resources. While the film version provides a happy ending in which Nausicaä's surrender restores harmony between humans and the environment, in the comic version Nausicaä is confronted with a system left behind by a civilization before it was burned to the ground. It is revealed that the miasma-spewing Sea of Decay was a system created by the humans of the old world to purify toxic substances, and that Nausicaä and other humans were themselves remade beings that could survive on this contaminated land. Eventually, the world is purified and the beautiful and rich old world is restored, but Nausicaä and her friends could not live in this purified world.

The Lord, the guardian of the plan left behind by the old world, who sits in the Crypt of Shuwa, requires Nausicaä to accept the plan and perish for the sake of humanity's future. The Lord's request is plausible. The earth's environment can be purified and a beautiful and rich civilized life can be restored. Life on earth which remains polluted is short, and people are constantly fighting for little land. It is a miserable life. In order to maximize the welfare of mankind, including future generations, it is necessary to "replace the world." Nausicaä, however, responds to the Lord's request with anger.

Conflicted, she chooses to destroy the human race, plants and animals, and even the eggs of art and culture preserved by the Lord, which should be revived in the future.

It is true that for Nausicaä, it is against her self-interest to accept submission and punishment. However, as has been seen in Chap. 5, favoring the self-interests of the present generation over those of the future goes against the equal treatment of generations. Although intergenerational ethics depends on the present generation's own shared understandings of what duties it owes to future generations, it is difficult to endorse decisions that are detrimental to the survival of the human race. In "A Theory of Justice," Rawls states that "the living may, if they allow themselves to be moved by such considerations (time preference), wrong their predecessors and descendants" (Rawls 1971, p. 260). In Rawls, "civil disobedience" is permitted when a statute enacted by the majority is grossly unjust.[3] However, future generations can only unilaterally receive the consequences of injustice by the present generation, and cannot engage in civil disobedience. To ensure intergenerational ethics, one needs the support of a system like the Lord's in Miyazaki's work mentioned above, even more than in the case within the same generation. Even though the Lord may appear ruthless to Nausicaä, he cannot compromise his position. The concession is even considered a moral injustice.

How did the confrontation become such an uncompromising one? Reviewing the case again, it is clear that Nausicaä sacrifices future generations for her own benefit, but this is only half of the story. Looking at the relationship between Nausicaä's generation and the preceding generation that bequeathed the Lord of the Schuwa cemetery, it can now be understood that the preceding generation tried to control the destiny of Nausicaä's generation by turning it into a tool through the Lord's system. Nausicaä can no longer feel a sense of oneness with the preceding generation, or a sense of belonging to the same community of humankind. Intergenerational relations are at risk of instrumentalization, since the subsequent generation has no choice but to unilaterally receive the results of the actions of the preceding generation. However reasonable Nausicaä may have been, it would be demanding to ask her to sacrifice herself to save humanity.

I do not mean to imply that Nausicaä's predicament, as presented here, is the same as our present predicament. However, it is a problem that must never be erased from our minds. As long as we continue to exceed our emissions limits, and to consume beyond our means, with increasing debts, we are using the future generations as tools to improve our own lives. Treating others as tools is incompatible with the concept of reciprocity, which recognizes that different generations may share rules with us. While it is difficult to expect people to possess the high-mindedness to sacrifice themselves to save future generations, they can be expected to engage in moderation, in order to refrain from using the future generations as tools for their own personal interests. We are in contact with the future generations through atmospheric composition and debts. We must consider them as human beings, not as tools in our hands.

[3] Rawls (1971, pp. 319–323).

References

Kolm, S. C. (2006). Reciprocity: Its scope, rationales, and consequences. In S. C. Kolm & J. M. Ythier (Eds.), *Handbook of the economics of giving, altruism and reciprocity, volume 1: Foundations.*

Miyazaki, H. (1996). *Nausicaä of the valley of the wind, first volume, Nausicaä of the valley of the wind, second volume.* Tokuma-Shoten (in Japanese).

Rawls, J. (1971a, 1999). *A theory* of *justice, revised edition.* Harvard University Press.

Suzumura, K. (2016). Scope, methods, and informational bases of normative economics. *The Economic Review, 67*(2), 97–106. (in Japanese)

Postscript

Many readers may be painfully aware that our society and human existence are more fragile than we thought. Climate change is finally showing its real effects. We have heard the great societal rumblings caused by the COVID-19 pandemic. In human society, the primacy and foundations of democracy, taken for granted at the end of the Cold War, are being shaken. Academic circles are seriously debating the question of the risk to the survival of the human race. The "risk is one that threatens the premature extinction of Earth-originating intelligent life or the permanent and drastic destruction of its potential for desirable future development" (Bostrom, 2013, p. 15); it is too high to ignore, and this question may already be on our shoulders.

It is my pleasure to be able to present to the world a coherent reflection on intergenerational issues in such an age. In this book, I present a comprehensive picture of intergenerational issues, with a focus on providing new ideas rather than a summary description. In particular, we believe that it is timely to present a theoretical and empirical discussion of the function of direct reciprocity that exists between generations, prompted by Professor Samuel Scheffler's discussion of the value of human survival. It is our hope that this book will serve as a clue to handing over to the next generation the good things that our society and humanity possess.

I have been in the United States of America since May 2021. Internally, the United States is plagued by inequality and division, and externally it faces competition from undemocratic forces. I am making an effort to learn what I can here, and bring this learning to the rest of the world.

October 2023
Maryland, United States of America
Toshiaki Hiromitsu

T. Hiromitsu, *Resolving Intergenerational Conflicts*, Advances in Japanese Business and Economics 33, https://doi.org/10.1007/978-981-97-0614-3

Reference

Bostrom, N. (2013). Existential risk prevention as a global priority. *Global Policy, 4*(1), 15–31.

T. Hiromitsu, *Resolving Intergenerational Conflicts*, Advances in Japanese Business and Economics 33, https://doi.org/10.1007/978-981-97-0614-3

Index

T. Hiromitsu, *Resolving Intergenerational Conflicts*, Advances in Japanese Business and Economics 33, https://doi.org/10.1007/978-981-97-0614-3

www.ingramcontent.com/pod-product-compliance
Ingram Content Group UK Ltd.
Pitfield, Milton Keynes, MK11 3LW, UK
UKHW021410091026
15624UKWH00009B/111

* 9 7 8 9 8 1 9 7 0 6 1 3 6 *